Contents

List of illustrations		vii
Preface		ix
Acknowledgements		xiii
1	Culture and meaning in the museum	1
2	Picturing the ancestors and imag(in)ing the nation: the collections of the first decade of the National Portrait Gallery, London	23
3	Speaking for herself? Hinemihi and her discourses	49
4	Words and things: constructing narratives, constructing the self	76
5	Objects and interpretive processes	103
6	Exhibitions and interpretation: museum pedagogy and cultural change	124
7	The rebirth of the museum	151
Notes		163
Bibliography		176
Index		191

Museums and the Interpretation of Visual Culture

Eilean Hooper-Greenhill

London and New York

First published 2000 by Routledge
11 New Fetter Lane, London EC4P 4EE

Simultaneously published in the USA and Canada
by Routledge
29 West 35th Street, New York, NY 10001

Reprinted 2002

Routledge is an imprint of the Taylor & Francis Group

© 2000 Eilean Hooper-Greenhill

Typeset in Sabon by Keystroke, Jacaranda Lodge, Wolverhampton
Printed and bound in Great Britain by TJ International Ltd, Padstow, Cornwall

British Library Cataloguing in Publication Data
A catalogue record for this book is available from the British Library

Library of Congress Cataloguing in Publication Data
Hooper-Greenhill, Eilean, 1945–
Museums and the interpretation of visual culture / Eilean Hooper-Greenhill.
p. cm. — (Museum meanings ; 4)
Includes bibliographical references and index.
1. Museums—Philosophy. 2. Museums—Educational aspects. 3. Museum exhibits.
4. Visual communication. 5. Visual learning. 6. Visual perception. 7. Communication
and culture. I. Title. II. Series.
AM7 .H655 2000
069′.01—dc21
00–032182

ISBN 0–415–08632–9 (hbk)
ISBN 0–415–08633–7 (pbk)

Museums and the Interpretation of Visual Culture

THE UNIVERSITY OF
WINCHESTER

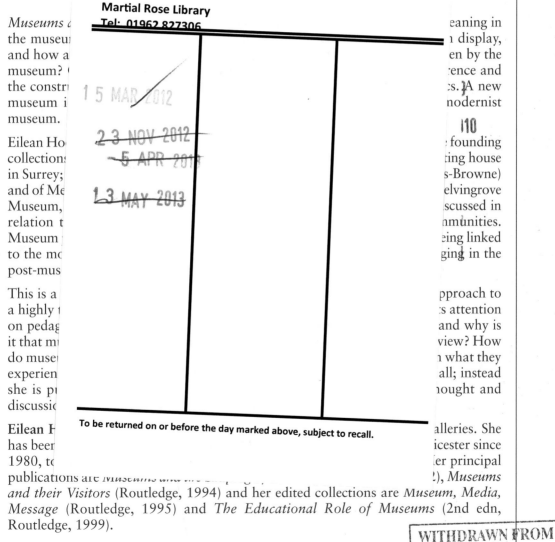

Martial Rose Library
Tel: 01962 827306

1 5 MAR 2012

2 3 NOV 2012

5 APR 201

1 3 MAY 2013

To be returned on or before the day marked above, subject to recall.

Museums ... eaning in
the museum ... display,
and how a ... en by the
museum? ... rence and
the constr ... s. A new
museum i ... nodernist
museum.

Eilean Ho ... founding
collections ... ing house
in Surrey; ... s-Browne)
and of Me ... elvingrove
Museum, ... scussed in
relation t ... mmunities.
Museum ... eing linked
to the mc ... ging in the
post-mus

This is a ... pproach to
a highly ... s attention
on pedag ... and why is
it that mu ... view? How
do muse ... n what they
experien ... all; instead
she is pu ... nought and
discussic

Eilean H ... alleries. She
has beer ... icester since
1980, to ... er principal
publications are *Museums and the* ...), *Museums
and their Visitors* (Routledge, 1994) and her edited collections are *Museum, Media,
Message* (Routledge, 1995) and *The Educational Role of Museums* (2nd edn,
Routledge, 1999).

Museum Meanings

Series editors

Eilean Hooper-Greenhill

Flora Kaplan

The museum has been constructed as a symbol in Western society since the Renaissance. This symbol is both complex and multi-layered, acting as a sign for domination and liberation, learning and leisure. As sites for exposition, through their collections, displays and buildings, museums mediate many of society's basic values. But these mediations are subject to contestation, and the museum can also be seen as a site for cultural politics. In post-colonial societies, museums have changed radically, reinventing themselves under pressure from many forces, which include new roles and functions for museums, economic rationalism and moves towards greater democratic access.

Museum Meanings analyses and explores the relationships between museums and their publics. 'Museums' are understood very broadly, to include art galleries, historic sites and historic houses. 'Relationships with publics' is also understood very broadly, including interactions with artefacts, exhibitions and architecture, which may be analysed from a range of theoretical perspectives. These include material culture studies, mass communication and media studies, and learning theories and cultural studies. The analysis of the relationship of the museum to its publics shifts the emphasis from the museum as text, to studies grounded in the relationships of bodies and sites, identities and communities.

Also in this series:

Museum, Media, Message
Edited by Eilean Hooper-Greenhill

Colonialism and the Object: *Empire, Material Culture and the Museum*
Edited by Tim Barringer and Tom Flynn

Learning in the Museum
George E. Hein

Illustrations

Figures

1.1   A walk through the galleries. A visitor to the Louvre in Paris   6

2.1   Samuel Pepys by John Hayles (NPG 211), sketched by George
      Scharf prior to recommending the purchase of the painting   45

3.1   The blessings ceremony at Hinemihi, 9 June 1995   52

3.2   A group of people in front of Hinemihi at the time of the tourist
      period before the eruption in 1886   56

3.3   The left-hand *amo*. The 1934 Reserve Bank of New Zealand
      featured the right-hand *amo* on its one-pound bank note   61

3.4   The doorway and the porch of Hinemihi   62

3.5   The carvings above the porch. Unusually, the feet are shod in
      European boots   64

3.6   Hinemihi after the eruption at Te Wairoa   71

3.7   Hinemihi at Clandon Park today   74

4.1   Makereti as a young woman, looking 'demure and submissive'
      as the label stated for 'Images of People'   78

4.2   Makereti takes control of her image as part of the tourist industry.
      She is 'on display'   84

4.3   Annie and Merton Russell-Cotes on the occasion of their Golden
      Wedding   89

6.1   One of the displays at the new exhibition at The Buried Village
      near Rotorua   143

6.2   A display panel which presents the use of archaeology to
      understand the life of the people at Te Wairoa before the eruption
      and their actions on the night of 10 June 1886   144

6.3   Louise de Kéroualle, Duchess of Portsmouth (1649–1734) and
      unnamed child, by Pierre Mignard, 1682   147

6.4   The assemblage of the harpsichord and the slave items at the
      Ignatius Sancho exhibition at the National Portrait Gallery,
      London   149

7.1   The Lakota Ghost Dance Shirt redisplayed in an old showcase
      in the main hall of Kelvingrove Museum in Glasgow   158

7.2   Marie-Not-Help-Him and Sterling Hollowhorn unfold the
      Ghost Dance Shirt on the site of the mass grave at
      Wounded Knee   161

Tables

2.1   Structures of local and national power embodied in the categories
      of the portraits at the National Portrait Gallery during the first
      decade of the nineteenth century   32
2.2   Visitor numbers for the first seven years of opening   44

Preface

This has been a complex book to put together. It has taken a long time to find a focus, and has, in the end, become a deeply personal book. There are two main concerns that unify the diverse issues that the book examines. Both of these are drawn from my background and personal predilections and passions. One is that of the teacher – the teacher's concern for the experience of the learner, the art viewer, and the museum visitor – an empathetic concern. The second is my fascination with the object. With a sculptor's response to materials, to organic matter, to form and to relationships of mass and space, objects matter to me. Thus the personal and the professional have merged in this book.

For some time I have been struggling to both map out and draw together those disparate strands of experience and analysis in which I have become involved, and which have been provoked and sustained by the study and use of museums and their collections. The strands include my experience of studying, using and producing visual culture; teaching in schools, colleges, universities, museums and galleries; and reading within sociology of education, culture and communication, learning theory, museum studies, and feminism. This book represents a provisional statement of some of the potential relationships between these areas.

It is possible that this embrace of pluralism is one feature shared by women, whose lives are frequently multiple, concerned with balancing complex and conflicting desires, and who, in my experience at least, are almost always on the edge of things, and therefore well aware of the possibilities of the beyond, and of the need to look around the edges.[1] The study of museums, however, also demands both new thinking, and interdisciplinary thinking, and I regard myself as fortunate in having been able to begin to develop the field of museum studies, which barely existed fifteen years ago.

One result of quarrying a range of disciplines is a pressing need to work out the interrelationships and to try to find some provisional working resolution between all the loose ends that call out for attention. This book is one way to try to do that. It is also a record of a journey, and a mapping exercise. It touches on a great range of areas, each with great depths that remain largely unplumbed. The aim of the book, the journey, and the map is to develop an understanding of how it is that culture shapes consciousness, and how the museum specifically relates to this process. The book is a turn to theory, to museum archives, and to object analysis, to answer an essentially empirical question – what happens when people go to museums? The two vital questions the book addresses are: how are objects and collections used by museums to construct knowledge, and how can the relationships of museum audiences to this knowledge be understood? In terms of audience research, the book remains largely at a conceptual level, and will, I hope, provide the theoretical underpinnings for future empirical audience research studies. Where it has been relevant, I have drawn on empirical studies to support my arguments, but the focus of the book is conceptual.

A polydimensional theoretical model[2] is essential in the study of museums. Museums are social and cultural institutions. Their purposes are the collection of objects and their display and elucidation. These two foci – collections and their use – are inextricably related. To begin research in one area sooner or later poses questions in the other. The questions posed are themselves integrated, and played out in the real world. In this sense, much museum research is grounded in daily professional cultural practices.

Many areas of study must be brought into play when studying museums. In analysing museums, we need to take into account: the collections and how they were collected, which involves material culture studies, art history, and other historical studies; the social and cultural role of museums today and in the past, which will involve cultural studies and sociology; the production of knowledge through exhibitions (museum studies, visual culture studies); learning in museums (education theory); and, more broadly, the experience of the visitor (psychology, sociology, and museum visitor studies). Sources from this theoretical *bricolage* inform the book.

This book is in some senses a continuation of an earlier one. In *Museums and the Shaping of Knowledge*[3] I showed how the structures of Foucault's epistemes could be used to explain different historical museum models. I showed how 'museums' were constructed according to different forms of rationality, some of which we do not recognise today. The characteristics of Foucault's Renaissance, Classical and Modern Ages explained, rather well, the selection of acquisitions, the arrangements of collections, and the range of and approach to users and visitors.

The earlier book discussed a number of museum models: the cabinet of the world, the disciplinary museum, the modernist museum. This book analyses the modernist museum in much greater depth, using several examples and case-studies of objects, collections, and museum exhibitions to examine their functions in the modern period. I retain Foucault's chronology, and understand, therefore, the modern period as emerging during the nineteenth century[4] to be still partly in place today, but subject to great challenge. In many ways, museums were the archetypical institutional form of the modern period. During the last twenty-five years, a new museum model has begun to emerge, which I am calling (at the moment) the post-museum. The book addresses the the modernist museum as the ancestor of the post-museum.

My focus of attention when analysing the museum has been that of pedagogy and visual culture, the what and the how of museum education and communication.

How and why is it that museums select and arrange artefacts, shape knowledge, and construct a view? What is this view and how does it articulate with wider social perspectives? How do museums produce values? How does this change? And how do museums' active audiences make meaning from what they experience in museums? The major themes that arise from these questions are those of narrative, difference and identity as they are articulated through individual interpretive processes and museum pedagogy.

The communication and learning theory on which nineteenth-century museums were premised positioned the visitor/learner as passive, understood knowledge to be objective and information-based, and saw authoritative linear communication as one of the main purposes of museums. Today, constructivist learning theory plays together with post-structuralist epistemologies and post-colonial cultural politics to position the visitor/learner as both active and politicised in the construction of their own relevant viewpoints. The post-museum must play the role of partner, colleague, learner (itself), and service provider in order to remain viable as an institution. This has fascinating and deep-seated professional effects.

Three major themes are woven throughout the book. The first is the shift in museum model (in theory and in actual institutional arrangements) from the modernist museum as a site of authority to the post-museum as a site of mutuality. This is analysed through case-studies of museum exhibitions, collections, and collectors. Colonialism and post-colonialism are important, as the negotiation and contestation of museum authority has been at its most evident in relation to colonial collections. The second is a discussion of the construction of meaning in the museum, which is analysed using communication and learning theory, relating both of these to modernism and post-modernism. The third is an analysis of material culture, and especially visual culture. I expand this term from its more usual use,[5] understanding museums as predominantly scopic sites. I also use 'visual culture' to problematise the relationship between museum objects and museum visitors. My focus is on the relationship between visual culture and pedagogy in the museum, and how this has changed over the last 150 years.

My approach to museum studies research may be seen by some to be contentious. I take the view that in the study of museums it is essentially not helpful to produce work which merely analyses events and which doesn't address the real pragmatic empirical worlds within which these events are constructed, and within which the events themselves construct knowledge. To hold research as separate from practice is not, to me, as useful as producing research that will begin to change or influence practice. I feel strongly that academic research, at least in this area, should be forced to confront the real world.[6]

I hold this view in part because I am involved in the education and training of museum professionals. However, I also wish to engage with a current debate in cultural studies (and one which is also now being heard within sociology). Cultural studies as an academic discipline has been reluctant to engage with a politics of culture,[7] and it is all too easy to analyse social phenomena from a lofty, academic, external stance. The real challenge, it seems to me, is to engage in research and analysis in order to influence change; to use discussions of theory and practice in order to demonstrate how museums, for example, might become more equitable; to show the meaningfulness of theory in practice such that it may enable cultural agents, including museum professionals, critically to reflect upon and review their own actions. Ultimately, I want to be able to show how those small day-to-day decisions taken by curators now and in the past have, and had, political effects. It is these small acts of the everyday that in part make up the politics of visual culture in the museum.

The book ranges widely, across a range of theories and disciplines, from past to present, from Britain to the white settler colonies, and back again. This is the product of a need to ask the broader questions. My initial impetus to write the book came after an extended lecture tour in Australia and New Zealand in 1993 – when I realised how little I knew about a major element of my own history, both national and personal. And as to how it related to museums, I knew even less. How to work out these relationships, histories and presents? This book is the product of my attempt to do so.

Eilean Hooper-Greenhill
Leicester, March 2000

Acknowledgements

This book would never have been written had it not been for circumstances that I would like to acknowledge.

The University of Leicester allowed me to take study leave in October 1993, when I was invited to Melbourne as a Visiting Fellow to speak at the MEANZ conference 'Pathways to Partnerships' in Melbourne. My interest in some of the themes of the book was stimulated at this time, and during the subsequent extended lecture tours in Australia and New Zealand. I should like to thank MEANZ (the Museum Education Association of Australia and the Museum Education Association of New Zealand) and all those involved in the lecture tours, too many to mention individually, for their invitations and generous hospitality. In Australia, the Ian Potter Foundation, and in New Zealand, the Queen Elizabeth II Arts Council, gave grants to MEANZ towards the costs of the events. I thank them both.

In April and May 1999 I was able to return to New South Wales and the North Island of New Zealand and would like to thank the Group for Education in Museums for a travel bursary, and the Education Department of the Auckland Institute and Museum for its hospitality.

Some of the ideas in the book have formed the basis of conference and seminar presentations. The conferences include: 'Cultural Management and the Nation-state', at the Ramon Selden Centre, University of Sunderland, March 1995; the Annual Symposium of CAGE (Canadian Art Gallery Educators) in Halifax, Nova Scotia, July 1998; 'Building the Image, Building the Experience – Innovative Practices in Art Museums in Europe', Fondzione Giovanni Agnelli, at Turin, October, 1998; 'Musing on Learning', Australian Museum, Sydney, April, 1999; 'Museums and Communities', the Museums Australia conference at Albury-Wodonga, New South Wales, May, 1999; and 'Museums of Modern Science', the Nobel Symposium, Stockholm, May 1999. Professional staff seminars were held at the Auckland Institute and Museum and at Te Papa Tongarewa/National Museum of New Zealand, Wellington, in April 1999.

I was granted a further four months' study leave from October 1999 to January 2000 when I was able to complete the manuscript. I thank the University of Leicester for this. I am indebted to Dr Simon Knell who took over as Head of Department during this period.

Many people have helped me in carrying out the research for this book, and in completing the manuscript. I would like to thank Gerry Conaty, Janice Frater, Alan Gallop, Renee Gillies, Sue Jeffreys, Mark O'Neill, Don Stafford, Katrina Stamp, Carolyn McLulish, Cherie Meecham, Vicky Pirie, Jim Schuster. I wish to especially thank Peter Gathercole, George Hein, and Gaby Porter, all of whom read the complete manuscript and gave me extremely helpful comments within the ridiculously short space of time that could be allowed. Shaun Garner, Simon Knell, Sam Maddra, Roger Neich, Charles Saumarez Smith, Lara Perry, and Marcia Pointon were kind enough to read and comment on specific chapters. They have saved me from many errors and inaccuracies, and for any that remain I must take responsibility. My editor at Routledge, Vicky Peters, encouraged me when I felt it was all too much and her assistants have always been unfailingly helpful.

I am grateful to all my colleagues in the Department of Museum Studies, who have sometimes listened to endless enthusiastic wafflings and whose own passions have complemented my own. I thank Jim Roberts for the figures, and for always being willing to answer silly questions about computer technology. I also wish to thank my students over the years, who have engaged robustly with many of the ideas in this book, and through their thoughtful discussions have enabled them to grow.

Finally, I want to thank my family: my husband John Eland for sharing my enthusiasms, acting as unpaid driver and research assistant in New Zealand, and for his patience as yet more weekends disappeared into this project, and my parents and children for their unfailing support.

Eilean Hooper-Greenhill
Leicester, March 2000

Culture and meaning in the museum

How is meaning produced in museums? How do the pedagogic approaches of the museum intersect with the interpretive processes of the visitor? How has this changed? In asking questions about the interpretation of visual culture in museums the themes of narrative, difference, and identity arise in relation to interpretive processes and museum pedagogy. These are complex and multi-layered matters, where meanings rooted in the past clash with contemporary interpretations that challenge their continued validity. The ways in which museums work today are based on ideas that emerged in nineteenth-century Europe – many of these ideas are no longer relevant. The idea of the museum is changing; it is being transformed and re-imagined. It is not certain yet what this new museum form, which I call the post-museum, will be and where it will come from, but its development is being driven by questions of meaning.

Issues of meaning-making in museums   *Yes + No*

The biggest challenge facing museums at the present time is the reconcep-tualisation of the museum/audience relationship. After almost a century of rather remote relationships between museums and the public, museums today are seeking ways to embrace their visitors more closely. As museums are increasingly expected to provide socially inclusive environments for life-long learning this need for closeness to audiences is rapidly becoming more pressing.

The relationship of a museum to its visitors is frequently discussed in terms which prioritise an educational relationship. The educational role of the museum is long-standing and well-established as a concept, but its focus, character and aims are the subjects of much professional debate. Part of the reason for this uncertainty about what museum and gallery education might be, and what form museum pedagogy should take, is a lack of knowledge within the museum of the profound changes that have occurred over the past century in educational processes and structures outside museums. A further issue is how far the educational role of the museum is considered in relation to broader questions about the uses of culture within society.

[handwritten margin notes: "education / good." and "Why Bad"]

In most formal institutions of education such as schools, colleges and universities, both the content and the methods used in teaching and learning have been radically changed since the turn of the century. The content of the school curriculum has been subject to debate and analysis in political and sociological fields. In addition, the professionalisation of teachers in educational institutions has become well-established. Information about the effectiveness of different teaching methods, knowledge about different approaches to learning, and experience of the use and relevance of subject-matter for specific age-groups have been the subjects of systematic research for at least the last fifty years. There has also been a considerable development of organisations that work within communities outside formal institutions, using approaches that can be described as part of a life-long learning philosophy. This work is frequently carried out within a framework that must acknowledge the political dimensions of both education and culture, as issues of resources are a daily matter. The articulation of culture, education and power is significant in this area of educational provision.

The concept of 'education' has been deepened and widened, as it has been acknowledged that teaching and learning is not limited to formal institutions but takes place throughout life, in countless informal locations. Formal educational processes are only a small, and not always very effective, part of those learning processes that are necessary throughout life, and which involve both the acquisition of new knowledge and experience, and also the use of existing skills and knowledge. A focus on enabling learning has led to an interest in the ways in which individuals make their experience of formal and informal learning personally meaningful and relevant. The focus on personal interpretation opens up issues of identity and culture.

Corresponding analyses within the museum field have come much later, and have been much less far-reaching. In many museums, knowledge about their visitors and attention to their learning processes are rudimentary. The old concept of 'education' as a formal didactic process limited to specific times and places is still in place, and thus the educational role of the museum is likely to be understood as formal provision for pre-booked groups such as schoolchildren. This work, even though it is highly skilled, is frequently relegated to junior staff, and not always prioritised within management decision-making processes. There is little understanding of the potential of museums for life-long learning, and the powerful pedagogic role of displays and exhibitions is barely acknowledged, and seldom researched. At a time when a very rapid development of a closer and more qualitative relationship to existing and new audiences is required, in many museums the necessary concepts, expertise, and staff are lacking.

During the second half of the nineteenth century museums were understood to be educational institutions with important and far-reaching social roles. However, their pedagogic approach was based both on a formal didacticism and on the conviction that placing objects on view was sufficient to ensure learning. Thus museum displays were used to transmit the universal laws of object-based disciplines (with natural history as the paradigm), which were presented in formal and authoritative ways to undifferentiated mass audiences. Today this approach is no longer appropriate. The view of education as a process that prioritises the experience and learning needs of the learner, combined with a greater recognition of the diverse social characteristics and cultural attitudes of differentiated audiences, demands now that museums develop new forms of relationships with visitor and user communities which are based on more interpersonal methods of communication, and on much broader approaches to pedagogy. The uses that visitors make of museum visits need to be considered, and this raises questions about the cultural possibilities that museums open up.

The pedagogic functions of museums can be analysed by reviewing both *what* is said, and *how* it is said. Museum pedagogy is structured firstly through the narratives constructed by museum displays and secondly through the methods used to communicate these narratives. Museum pedagogy produces a visual environment for learning where visitors deploy their own interpretive strategies and repertoires. What happens when someone enters a museum and looks at the displays and exhibitions?[1] How do they construct meaning from what they see, and how is this meaning influenced by the intentions of the producers of the exhibition? What are the conditions for the construction of meaning in museums, the conditions for the interpretation of visual culture? These complex and multi-layered matters are the questions which this book addresses.

Meaning in museums is constructed in relation to the collections which the museum holds. Questions arise about which objects have been collected and why, and what is known about them from which perspective. One critical element in the construction of meaning within museums is the presence or absence of particular objects; a second vital consideration is that of the frameworks of intelligibility into which collected objects are placed. Objects in museums are assembled to make visual statements which combine to produce visual narratives. Collections as a whole, and also individual exhibitions, are the result of purposeful activities which are informed by ideas about what is significant and what is not. Both collections and exhibitions embody ideas and values, although the degree to which these are explicitly articulated is variable.

Individual objects have shifting and ambiguous relationships to meaning. Being themselves mute, their significance is open to interpretation. They may be viewed from a number of positions, which may be diverse in history and culture. They may be drawn into a conversation through a number of different strategies, by a range of different individual subjects, who talk about them in ways that are meaningful to themselves as speakers. They may be understood through factual information, or may be invested with emotional significance. Although they all have life-histories, these may be well-known or, alternatively, unknown or forgotten. Objects are subject to multiple interpretations, some of which may be contradictory.

If individual objects are complex in relation to meaning, exhibitions – groups of objects combined with words and images – are more complex still. Here, meaning lies in the relationships between the objects and other elements; it is combinatorial and relational. The ideas that displays have been mounted to communicate are sometimes (but not always) clearly suggested in the texts of the exhibition, which may offer a preferred interpretation of the various visual elements. However, experience of the visual is not the same as experience of the text; it is more open, and at the same time more difficult to talk about. In museum exhibitions, curators, especially in art museums, frequently prefer to leave the meaning potential open and ambiguous. Even where exhibition texts may indicate intended readings of exhibitions, as in science museums, this by no means guarantees a unified way of responding to the experience of the exhibition.

Visual experience cannot always be articulated verbally, and this makes it more difficult to discuss, to share, to understand. The gut response to colour, the physical reaction to mass, the engagement with the visual that is both embodied and cerebral, remains mysterious. Within museums, the phenomenon of display (or of exhibition) is the major form of pedagogy. It is the experience of the displays that for most visitors defines the museum, and it is through displays that museums produce and communicate knowledge. However, exhibitions, as visual technologies, are problematic forms of pedagogy. Methods of producing exhibitions are well-developed, with museum professionals very clear about how objects should be brought together, considered from the point of view of physical care, and placed on public display; but the interpretation made by visitors of exhibitions are much less well understood, analysed or researched. The concept of reviewing both the interpretations of visitors and the interpretations of the curators as part of the development process of specific exhibitions is still not understood or explored in most museums. In teaching, the knowledge, attitudes and perceptions that students bring to any learning situation needs to be the starting point for the construction of learning materials; in the development of exhibitions it is still very rare to find this level of attention to the knowledge of visitors.

Exhibitions are produced to communicate meaningful visual and textual statements, but there is no guarantee that the intended meaning will be achieved. Visitors to museum exhibitions respond in diverse ways. They may or may not perceive the intended meanings, and, perceiving them, they may or may not agree with them, find them interesting, or pay attention to them. For example, where art exhibitions may be put together to show art historical schools or movements, visitors may be operating within much more personal frameworks of interpretation. A visitor to The Royal Ontario Museum, Toronto, wrote about her response to a painting in the Canadian Historical Galleries:

> My paternal Grandmother was born in Glace Bay. For my entire life I
> have wondered what her childhood was like. Until very recently, I have
> been able only to communicate with her in shouts and sign language. She
> is 92. She will die soon, but now I have seen her home. Now the words
> are not as necessary. Thank you.[2]

Displays must of course have some kind of inner coherence which should be made clear to the viewer; this is a part of the professional responsibility of the curator or exhibition development team. However, visitors will construct their own coherence none the less, which may or may not comply with that of the curator.

Meanings within exhibitions can generally be found at several levels. A collection of beehives from the Museum of Popular Arts and Traditions in Paris, for example, illustrates a range of solutions to a problem: that of housing bees. But does this illustrate how several forms (tubular, conical, spherical), using several different materials (wood, straw, bark), can be used in the same way? Does it demonstrate regional variations? Does it celebrate creativity? Does it make social statements about the French peasantry? All these interpretations are possible; the curator's text panels may indicate the intention of the display, but other meanings may also be made by viewers.

Processes of interpretation are not singular, but multiple, and they proceed from a range of starting points. According to the role being played by the visitor at the time (parent, scholar, tour guide, artist, recluse) different aspects of potential meaning will be mobilised from the materials provided by the museum. Meaning is produced by museum visitors from their own point of view, using whatever skills and knowledge they may have, according to the contingent demands of the moment, and in response to the experience offered by the museum.

The structure of museum pedagogy

The experience offered by the museum will depend on the collections held, and assumptions about what should be said using the collections. The statements that the collections make can be communicated in various ways, and different styles of display can be used; these statements and display styles embody curatorial concepts about the identities of visitors, their knowledge, and their uses of the exhibition. The pedagogy of the museum can be analysed in relation to both content and style.

Pedagogic content refers to what is said, or the subject-matter of teaching; in museums this means the statements made by the museum with its collections, the subject-matter of the permanent displays or the temporary exhibitions. Pedagogic style refers to the way in which something is said, or teaching method; in museums this refers to the style of communication in displays, which includes the way the objects are used or placed, the way the text is written, the provision within the exhibition for various forms of sensory engagement (including visual, tactile, auditory senses), the use of light and colour, the use of space, and so on.

There is of course a relationship between content and style, as the mode, or style, of communication itself communicates ideas about expected responses, or about appropriate behaviour. This 'hidden curriculum' embodies attitudes, perceptions and values, which although they are not explicitly stated seem to be recognised by visitors.

During the last part of the nineteenth century an approach to the style of museum displays evolved which was based on how objects might be known and used in the production of knowledge. Objects were seen as sources of knowledge, as parts of the real world that had fixed and finite meanings that could be both discovered, once and for all, and then taught through being put on show. The relationships expressed in the sequences of displayed objects were thought to demonstrate universal laws about the disciplines, such as what counted as the history of art,

Figure 1.1 A walk through the galleries. A visitor to the Louvre in Paris. Photo Eilean Hooper-Greenhill.

or the family relationships of birds or plants. Making this knowledge visible and available through public museums was in itself a pedagogic act; a walk through the museum galleries would result in learning (Figure 1.1.) It was thought that large numbers of people could be taught in this way at the same time, and thus a huge social gain would occur.

Today this transmission approach to education is known to be ineffective in schools and colleges, and teachers are encouraged to use pedagogic methods that accommodate individual learning styles, that offer differentiated learning experiences and that take account of the active nature of personal learning processes. Constructivist educational theory focuses on understanding how to enable individual learners to find meaning and relevance in teaching content such that learning occurs, and on providing the most effective conditions for learning. Some museums have begun to find ways to respond to contemporary educational theory in their approach to exhibitions, but many museums are still producing displays that do not acknowledge the diverse needs of individual learners.

In some museums displays have changed radically in style; the formal, authoritative appearance of museum galleries has been replaced as the methods used to communicate with visitors have become more informal, more lively, and offer more possibility for mental and physical interaction. There is an understanding that, for example, family visitors want more choice and more diverse ways of using displays. However, although many museums now produce more lively displays, some of the assumptions that lay behind the older approaches are taking longer to change. Educational theorists today recognise the fact that learners need to interact in meaningful ways with new information before it can become part of their repertoire of knowledge, and also that the negotiation of what counts as meaningful to learners is critical in the provision of helpful learning environments. It is not enough simply to provide opportunities to touch or manipulate if the concepts on which these are based are too difficult for the actual audience. Lively display styles need to be combined with audience research and clearly defined learning objectives.

Museums are struggling to find ways to incorporate audience research into their processes of exhibition development. As they do so, the interrelationships between style and content become apparent. Although audiences want to find the visual narratives of the museum both accessible and enjoyable, they are equally concerned about the content of those discourses. Within societies that are increasingly diverse in ethnicity, cultural traditions and historical experience, people within differentiated social and cultural communities respond to museums and their collections according to their own perspectives. Research among ethnic communities in England found a common perception that Black contributions to British society were ignored because a colonial view of the past still prevailed within the museum. However, museums were also felt to be places which could potentially be used by Asian and Afro-Caribbean parents to discuss their own cultural values.[3]

A visitor to the Horniman Museum in South London wrote a poem after looking at the African collections:

> Maternity figure of woman
> on Ashanti stool
> suckling child
> – wooden, still –
> milk-breathed
> and at one.
>
> Maternity figure of woman
> other situation we know full well
> no child to suckle. Child done gone.
> Sold. Mother wooden – still –
> Too drained, too whip-lashed.
> A stone; no stool.[4]

A response of this kind is not frequently heard within museums, where it is the curatorial voice and the curatorial text that prevails. If museums wish to become socially inclusive, alternative perspectives need to be recognised, acknowledged, and made both visible and audible.

In some museums, the visual and textual statements made by displays have been subject to analysis and critique, and on occasion fierce challenge. This is particularly the case in museums of ethnography, where the politics of the

7

visual culture of the museum can be seen most clearly. Many museums with 'ethnographic' collections, particularly in North America, New Zealand and Australia, have had to become sensitive to multiple histories, to competing or complementary narratives and to the subjectivities of their audiences. It is in the context of what counts as history that the constructed character of meaning is demonstrated most clearly within the museum field. The public imag(in)ing of the past is a contested area.

However, the points that are made perhaps most forcibly in the anthropological museum are of more general relevance. Displayed objects of all types are made meaningful according to the interpretive frameworks within which they are placed, and the historical or cultural position from which they are seen. Thus the interpretation of visual culture has political implications; it may be used to open or close possibilities for individuals, groups or communities.

The structure of the book

This book uses case-studies of individual objects and collections to explore some of these issues. The major theme of the book is the complexity of the production of meaning in museums, which proceeds through the articulation of publicly displayed objects and collections with individual and social processes of interpretation. I see this most clearly in relation to issues of how the past works in the present and how museums enable or prevent equitable access to the construction of useful histories. However, I know that the construction of knowledge (meaning, sense) within museums is a broader question; I try to place the position from which I approach the question within its broader framework. The main themes which cut through the case-studies are those of narrative, difference, identity, interpretive processes and museum pedagogy.

Two major tropes, or metaphorical devices, are used to enable the discussion of cultural change within museums. These tropes are two museum models: the modernist museum and the post-museum. The modernist museum is based on the nineteenth-century European institutional form that is still very familiar across the world today. The post-museum is a new idea that is not yet born, but whose shape is beginning to be seen.

This chapter introduces the main themes of the study and critically discusses ways of understanding the concept of 'culture', especially focusing on ideas developing within visual culture which seek to problematise the interpretation of cultural images. I enlarge the concepts of 'visual culture' to accommodate museum displays. Culture is shown to be generative rather than reflective and the political implications of this statement are considered.

Chapter 2 takes the form of a case-study from the 1850s, the period of the first ten years of collecting at the National Portrait Gallery in London. The collection was brought together as systematically as possible to construct a picture of the heart of the British nation. The study shows how objects can be used in a purposeful way to build a visual narrative. The narrative which is pictured, through a group of 225 portraits, shapes the way in which the character of the past and the identity of historical actors in England can be imagined. The internal structure of this imagined national community, with its social and cultural implications, has remained in place for 150 years; it is an open question as to how far it has been modified today. The ideas rooted in the 1850s about gender, ethnicity and class in relation to social action and the making of history still circulate today.

The interpretive frameworks within which objects are seen, and from which they are spoken about, act to place objects within contexts of discourse that shape meaning. Meanings may be fixed provisionally, but are susceptible to being changed as the interpretive frameworks change. Chapter 3 focuses on one object and addresses the issue of how objects and meaning work. Do objects speak for themselves as some traditional museum curators still insist, or are meanings constructed according to who is speaking within which discourse?. As Hinemihi, a complex object (a 'whare' or meeting house) from Aotearoa New Zealand, is investigated, different interpretations from a number of historical and present-day perspectives are identified.

Assemblages of words and things act to produce the self; identity is shaped, and self-image is materialised through writing and through collecting. These processes of the construction of the self operate within the framework of broader social processes of advantage and disadvantage. The imagining of possibilities for the self is materialised and made tangible through objects.

Some personal collections and museums become public spaces, others are dispersed and fragmented, but may later move into positions of public significance. Chapter 4 examines the collections and the books of two people; these can be compared and contrasted as they partly overlap in time and space. Both are records of collecting and writing in and about New Zealand during the last quarter of the nineteenth century and the first quarter of the twentieth. One writer is a woman, and Maori. Her name is Makereti, Maggie Papakura, Margaret Staples-Brown. Her many names signal her hybrid identity. The other is Merton Russell-Cotes, an Englishman who visited New Zealand with his wife Annie in 1886. Makereti lived in the place that Russell-Cotes describes in his book; she describes it in her own words. Both writers accumulated collections of Maori artefacts but for very different reasons. The Russell-Cotes Museum in Bournemouth on the south coast of England was based on the extensive collections of Annie and Merton, which included the Maori artefacts. Makereti's collections were dispersed at her death, but some are now among the treasures of Te Papatongarewa/National Museum of New Zealand.

Collections are brought together and used to make visual statements by purposeful individuals, acting on the basis of sets of ideas, attitudes and beliefs. These cognitive and emotional structures give shape and meaning to the objects. Relations of gender, ethnicity and class become embedded within the structures of collections; attitudes to the 'other' inform perceptions of the 'self'. This case-study offers some evidence of the ways in which dominant social beliefs, values and processes interact with the construction of museum collections in such a way as to be privileged and reproduced. It also indicates how histories rendered invisible at one moment may at another be retrieved if physical traces such as objects remain.

Chapter 5 addresses centrally the issue of how objects are interpreted, and examines processes of interpretation, using ideas drawn from hermeneutics,[5] learning theory, and media studies. Individuals are seen as active, creatively employing diverse interpretive strategies, some of which are the result of their involvement in specific interpretive communities. The potentially endlessly relative character of individual meanings is tempered by the authority of interpretive communities.

Chapter 6 analyses the pedagogic style and content of museums using communication and educational theory. The pedagogic approaches of museums at the end of the nineteenth century are assessed and found to be susceptible to being analysed as forms of transmission pedagogy. The shortcomings of this way of approaching communication and education are well known, and explain some of the communicative failures of museums. Today, museums are challenged to accept the findings of educational research and to invent and adopt more appropriate approaches to display content and style. Some examples are given in this chapter.

The last chapter draws together the main themes that have been discussed throughout the book, and summarises them in relation to the two museum models – the modernist museum and the post-museum. A final case-study of the life-story to date of a single object, the Lakota Ghost Dance Shirt formerly held by Glasgow Museums, shows how the meanings of objects are contingent, fluid, and polysemic, but none the less constrained by the materiality of the object. The meanings imposed upon the shirt arise from the interpretive frame within which it is placed. These frames are both material, as for example within a display, but also cognitive and affective; that is, they involve the conceptual and emotional processes of a range of individual subjects who stand in diverse historical, cultural and institutional positions. The identity of the post-museum will emerge as the cultural politics within which museums are necessarily engaged is acknowledged.

Understanding culture

During the preceding discussion, the word 'culture' has been used on several occasions. How can it be understood?

Culture is frequently thought of as having two fields of reference.[6] The first refers to the arts and higher learning – sometimes expressed as 'the best of what a society produces'. This is a tightly defined area, buttressed by a range of social institutions and practices. The second field of reference is much more holistic and inclusive. It adopts a more anthropological approach: life-ways, patterned events, and belief systems are all understood as part of culture. However, these two approaches give only the broad outlines of what has become a highly elaborated discussion, one which has occupied social and cultural theorists a great deal.[7] The 'cultural turn' in critical theory has brought cultural processes and institutions into a more focused debate, and provided a fertile climate for discussion.

One of the major theorists of culture in recent times is Raymond Williams. He suggested four contemporary uses of the concept 'culture'.[8] First, 'a general process of intellectual, spiritual and aesthetic development'; second, 'the works and practices of intellectual and especially artistic activity'; third, 'a particular way of life, whether of a people, a period or a group'; and fourth, 'the signifying system through which necessarily (although among other means) a social order is communicated, reproduced, experienced and explored'.

Culture is a concept with a history.[9] Williams explains how one of the earliest usages of 'culture' was as a noun of process – 'the culture (cultivation) of crops or (rearing and breeding) of animals, and by extension the culture (active cultivation) of the human mind'.[10] This early use underpins Williams' first definition, which assumes that 'culture' is something that can be acquired, and acquired differentially; some of us are more 'cultured' than others. 'Culture' is the pursuit of the spiritual rather than the material; it is a state of mind that may be achieved through the family, through going to the right school, through participating in the arts and higher education, and through visiting museums. In this use, culture is understood as a training in discrimination and appreciation, based on a knowledge and responsiveness to the best that a society can produce.

This approach to culture rests on another, which is encapsulated in Williams' second usage. 'Culture' is made up of specific products that may be characterised as painting, sculpture, music, literature, and drama, along with their associated practices. This is the traditional and the dominant view of culture in the West today.[11] This understanding of culture is embodied within a range of key cultural institutions, including the educational system, the media, and in those institutions that would be seen as 'cultural' within this definition, such as theatres, museums and galleries.

These two ways of understanding culture, as personal cultivation and as a body of works, are two sides of the same coin. It is the collected works of the best that a society can provide that forms the material with which the cultured person should be familiar. Both uses are based on the expectation of an absolute universal standard. Both are premised on notions of cultural value and judgements about what counts as high quality. Culture from this perspective is a way of describing supposedly universal standards of beauty, value, and judgement. In addition, the cultural sphere is understood to be separate from the economic and political sphere. Culture is raised above the everyday, the mundane, the quotidian.

This understanding of culture positions it as the positive pole in relation to less desirable opposites. Culture (of and in itself frequently characterised as 'high' or 'elite' culture) stands against its opposite 'mass culture'.[12] The cultured person is the antithesis of the uncultivated masses. Culture and education go hand-in-hand. The masses are uncultured in large part because they are uneducated. As the public museum emerged during the nineteenth century one of its priorities was the education of the public; museums as pedagogic organisations could be used to expose large groups of people to culture, to those finest works that society had produced. This reformist role for culture[13] would use it as a tool to change the gross and sensual into something altogether more refined.

11

Williams' third usage of 'culture' takes a more anthropological approach. 'Culture' is not the attribute of an individual, but describes ways of life of groups, subcultures, or ethnicities. Each society, ethnic or linguistic group, has common customs, ways of being and ways of thinking. Culture is no longer singular, but plural – 'cultures'. This approach avoids the hierarchy explicit in the previous views of culture. From this perspective, all cultures are equally interesting. A more relative approach to culture is adopted. This approach to culture signals an intention to be inclusive,[14] to view social groups in a relative rather than absolute way, to defer judgements of worth or value. However, this expanded view of culture is too inclusive for the analysis and understanding of museums and the interpretation of visual culture. The anthropological approach includes all elements of patterned life-ways, and as such is a broad but blunt analytical tool.

The anthropological approach to culture, where it is defined as a field of shared experiences, has also been criticised as being defined in Western ethnocentric terms.[15] Henry Giroux points out that in contrast to the overtly harmonious concept of 'shared experience', the notion of 'difference' has made visible how power is inscribed differently in and between what he calls 'zones of culture'. Zones, or locations of culture, focus on the centres and margins of culture, and questions arise about cultural borderlands. These concepts raise questions of relations of inequality, struggle and history, and demand knowledge of how differences are expressed in multiple and contradictory ways. In this perspective culture is seen as a site of multiple and heterogeneous borders where different histories, languages, experiences and voices intermingle amidst diverse relations of power and privilege.[16] Where many cultural theorists focus on the production of knowledge through culture, and examine the systems through which culture is produced and consumed, Giroux prioritises the conflictual elements of culture, to highlight the inequalities that different groups experience. He reminds us that culture is not merely about images, objects and aesthetics, but about representations of value and truth, and that these representations have effects on lives.

The fourth use of 'culture' suggested by Williams represents a fairly recent conceptualisation,[17] one that can be located within the intellectual field of cultural studies.[18] This approach will be the most useful for our purpose in this book. It is also capable of responding to Giroux's concerns. It understands 'culture' not as a separate domain of high-quality people and artefacts, nor as a whole way of life, but as a dimension of all institutions. 'Culture' is a set of material practices, which in their performance construct meanings, values and subjectivities. Williams defines culture as a 'realized signifying system'.[19]

In recent years, the 'cultural turn' in the human sciences, and especially in cultural studies, sociology of culture and learning theory, has emphasised the importance of the making of meanings in the understanding of culture. Culture is not a set of things, but is made up of processes, sets of practices. Culture is concerned with the production and exchange of meanings – 'the giving and taking of meaning'.[20] Signifying practices are those practices which make things mean.[21] Within this approach to 'culture' knowledge is a major constituent, with epistemological and pedagogic concerns lying at the heart of cultural analysis. Culture is 'the social production and reproduction of sense, meaning and consciousness'.[22] Processes of knowledge-production, meaning-construction and learning are deeply embedded in processes of signification. Through signification, 'reality' is accomplished. Life-worlds are constructed through what and how we come to know.[23] Culture, therefore, is deeply implicated in interpretive and learning processes and practices.[24] These interpretive practices will vary according to cultural background, experience and knowledge[25].

Hall insists that communication demands shared language and visual codes to become possible, but this leaves the argument at the point at which Giroux wishes to take it forward. Who defines the codes? Who has access to the defining processes? Culture can transmit dominant values, but can also be seen as a site of resistance[26] where dominant shared codes may be disrupted or displaced, and where alternative shared codes can be produced.

This discussion of the meanings of the term 'culture' suggests that no single definition of 'culture' is possible. Instead, a set of uses, each accompanied by a set of underpinning ideas, related concepts, beliefs and implied actions has been found. Culture has been shown to be multi-discursive – that is, it is used within a number of different discourses. We can understand discourse as sets of words and things, practices, beliefs and values that provide contexts of use for the construction of meaning.[27] The term 'culture' can be mobilised within a number of different discursive contexts.

The key to understanding 'culture' is to identify the discursive context within which it is used, which may be discourses of anthropology, communication studies, educational theory, art history, curatorship, museum visitor studies, and so on. In each case, the meaning of 'culture' will be determined relationally, according to the other terms within the context of use. It will therefore be defined negatively, rather than positively: it will not be defined by reference to any intrinsic or self-evident properties.[28] The use of the term 'culture' alerts us to the need for analysis of the character of the discourse which gives it meaning. This discourse needs to be reviewed critically, not accepted as given.

Culture is frequently conceived as *reflective*. However, this is less accurate than the idea of culture as *constitutive*. Cultural symbols have the power to shape cultural identities at both individual and social levels; to mobilise emotions, perceptions and values; to influence the way we feel and think. In this sense, culture is generative, constructivist. Reflection theory[29] is rooted in ideas about culture as a semi-autonomous zone in a realm above the practical world of everyday reality, whose mirror image is thrown back by art. We have seen how this separation of spheres is one component of the high culture theory. Culture, as a set of signifying practices, does not stand apart from and, through art objects, reflect society. It plays a more important role; it constructs society, through the images it creates of social possibilities and the stories it tells of social achievement. Museums are deeply involved in constructing knowledge in this way through those objects, peoples, narratives, and histories that they bring to visibility or keep hidden. These processes set agendas for imagination and interpretation.

The specific form of cultural practice that museums are engaged in is that of visual culture, and it is to this idea that we turn next.

Visual culture

Whereas 'culture' as an idea can be traced back to the late Middle Ages,[30] 'visual culture' is a new concept and an emerging field of study. It can be seen as an encounter between sociology and fine art, or the application of theories from social and cultural studies to those artefacts and practices that would conventionally be included within art history, such as painting, sculpture and architecture. Visual culture, however, also broadens its focus to include other visual media, such as advertisements, family photographs, television and film, which are conventionally encompassed by media studies. The concept of 'visual culture' allows the examination of all those signifying practices, representations and mediations that pertain to looking and seeing, and it allows an analysis that is not shaped in advance by the values of high culture. 'Visual culture' as a concept and a methodology refuses to accept the distinction between high and mass culture.[31] This is useful in the problematisation of culture, pedagogy, and knowledge.

Visual culture as a field of study raises theoretical questions about the social practices of looking and seeing, which are related to processes of learning and knowing. It is concerned with artefacts, but also examines the social institutions and practices that act as visual apparatuses which frame those artefacts. Vision is analysed as a social practice rather than taken as a simple given. Visual culture works towards a social theory of visuality,[32] focusing on questions of what is made visible, who sees what, how seeing, knowing and power are interrelated. It examines the act of seeing as a product of the tensions between external images or objects, and internal thought processes.[33] However, this is not to set vision apart from other senses, or visuality aside from other social and political processes;[34] rather, it is to examine the visual as one dimension of culture.

One of the prime functions of the public museum is to present material culture to be viewed. Nineteenth-century museums were intended to 'speak to the eyes'.[35] The assumption was that looking could enable the brain to absorb information more quickly than by other means. Learning through the visual was thought to be more effective than learning through words, especially for those that had not had the benefit of lengthy schooling. Thus the organising principles of displays, based on the basic structures of specific subject areas, were intended to transmit and teach those structures. At the same time museums were also charged with demonstrating and thereby transmitting the basic principles of citizenship through their clean and ordered spaces where controlled behaviour could be observed.

In the museum, objects, or artefacts[36] are put on display. They are there to be looked at. Museums are sites of spectacle, expository spaces, where exhibitionary complexes[37] are sited. Museums pride themselves on being places where 'real objects' can be seen. This notion of 'the real' is a powerful and enduring one.

However, the assumption that vision is autonomous, and that objects are unmediated, needs to be examined. Vision should be aligned with interpretation rather than perception.[38]

Looking is not commonly understood as a complex matter. Generally, vision is treated as autonomous, free and pure.[39] However, looking is not a simple matter, and seeing is related both to what is known and to what counts as available to be observed. What is seen depends on who is looking, at what, in which site. Seeing is relative rather than absolute.

> The perceived thing is not an ideal unity in the possession of an intellect . . . It is rather a totality open to a horizon of an infinite number of perspectival views, which blend with one another according to a given style which defines the object in question.
>
> Perception is thus paradoxical. The perceived thing is paradoxical; it exists only in so far as someone can perceive it.[40]

The gaze is 'caught up in an endless reciprocity.[41] It is directed at what is visible, but in order to know what to observe, elements or factors must be recognised. But to recognise something, it is necessary to have prior knowledge of it – thus observation depends on already knowing that for which one is searching. This contradictory and complex situation is at the heart of the museum experience.

Much interpretation of visual culture has in the past presupposed an essential viewer.[42] That is, a single interpretation of an object has been presented, and this has been presented as what the object means. This interpretation has generally been formed in relation to the meaning of the object within specific intellectual or disciplinary fields; for example, the history of art. The idea of varying interpretations constructed by different gazes has not been seriously accepted until fairly recently. Visual culture theory, however, enables a focus on the relationship between the seen and the seer, with a prioritisation of the seer. It problematises the acts of looking, and disturbs the conventional notion of the transparency of the visible. It insists that vision is socially constructed[43] and thereby provides some theoretical tools and analytical methods that may be used for the analysis of vision and visuality in the museum. The constructions of meaning in the museum are based on visual interpretations, which are differentiated according to the social discourses within which these interpretations are placed. Treating museums as visual discourses enables the questioning of the relationships between looking, knowledge and power.

Visual culture theory enables the problematisation of two further matters that are often taken for granted. The first is the meaning of an artefact in its setting. In much art history, and indeed some work within the visual culture paradigm, the site of display of, say, a painting, is taken for granted. It is invisible to analysis; regarded as neutral. However, the style of the setting, the display technology used, and the codes of design are all influential in the construction of meaning in museums. Things mean differently in different contextual settings.[44]

The second is the provenance of artefacts. Conventionally this is the account of the life-journey of, for example, a piece of sculpture, which is researched and recorded. The provenance is a matter of inventory rather than analysis. This naturalises processes of collection, of ownership, and museological processes of acquisition and documentation, all of which need to be subjected to scrutiny. A critical provenance asks questions about all these matters which are ultimately concerned with relationships of power, knowledge and value.

However, in the use of visual culture theories and methods in the museum, it will be necessary to make some adjustments and additions. Visual culture takes for its focus those artefacts and practices that have formed the basis of art history (paintings, sculpture, architecture), and broadens this by including visual imagery that might form the basis for media studies (advertising, film, television). In the deployment of visual culture theory in the museum, however, this focus will need to be angled in another direction to include artefacts that would normally fall outside of the parameters of visual culture, but, in this instance, must be allowed to be included by virtue of their inclusion within a museum collection.

All objects that are exhibited within museums and galleries may legitimately be regarded as visual media; all those within museum collections, whether currently on display or not, are there as potential or actual signs or symbols, or as resources for visual communication and learning. Any artefact, specimen, or object within a museum collection plays its part in the complex processes of bringing to visibility, of making visible, of constructing visual meaning, and is therefore subject to analysis as part of visual culture.

The broad range of two- and three-dimensional artefacts that can be found today in museum collections can be analysed in relation to the ways in which they are used today. However, very many of these collections were assembled many years ago; the analysis of what is seen and known today must encompass the dimension of time. Objects in museum collections may embody the ideas and values of past social formations. In analysing the interpretation of visual culture during the present day, it will be important to consider how far, and in which dimensions, past interpretations, past understandings, are still being circulated.

Mapping, materialising and imagining

The public museum emerged during the nineteenth century, during the period now known as the modern period. Modernism is a complex concept; there are many discourses of modernity, which refer to a range of economic, political, social, and cultural transformations.[45] For some social theorists, the modern period is the period that follows the 'Middle Ages' or feudalism, and thus it encompasses the last 400–500 years; others equate the modern period with the Enlightenment and the championing of reason as the source of progress in knowledge and society. Aesthetic modernity, characterised as the period from 1820–1975,[46] is linked to the avant-garde rebellion against the alienating aspects of rationalisation and those other defining elements of modernity, industrial-isation, secularisation, and urbanisation. These processes took place beside those of the exclusion of women from the public sphere, the genocide of the period of imperialist colonialisation,[47] and the introduction of disciplinary institutions.[48] Modernism is sometimes seen as an unfinished project,[49] and despite new cultural shifts today, analysed as post-colonialism and post-modernity, many of the social and cultural structures and values of the modern period remain.

The museum idea which I call the 'modernist museum' traces its intellectual roots to the Enlightenment, and its institutional form to the European public museums that emerged during the nineteenth century. I am most familiar with the British variations of the idea.

It has been suggested that three technologies of power characterise the modern age: the census, the map and the museum.[50] Although these technologies were in existence before the modern period, it was at that time that they changed radically. Anderson points out that these signs of modernity, the census, the map and the museum, all of which are ostensibly objective technologies for observation and classification, also act as technologies for value and for power.

The map has been used as a metaphor for the museum, which plots material geographies of taste and value.[51] The functions of maps are to select from the totality of the world those aspects that can serve to depict it through ordering, classifying, and constructing pictures of 'reality'. That which is marked on the map is affirmed as 'real';[52] is that which is known and significant. To be 'off the map' is to be of no significance, to be obsolete or unknown; to be 'on the map' is to be acknowledged, given a position, accorded an existence or an importance.[53] Maps depict values and picture relationships. They delineate power relations, map boundaries of influence and provide schema for imagining the world. These cartographies are never neutral; being placed on the map gives legitimation.

Maps are always put together from a point of view; they serve interests.[54] Through the apparently neutral and technical processes of mapping, specific world pictures are constructed and that constructed picture is understood as 'reality', as 'how it is'. European colonisers, for example, routinely named the features of the territories in which they settled after themselves, and in so doing they constructed a landscape in the image of the lands from which they came. The highlands of Bermuda are called Scotland; at least one of the mountains of the Rockies, Rundle Mountain, is named after a missionary; waters in Australia are named after the explorers – Murray River, Darling Harbour; pre-existing local names were ignored. The unfamiliar territory was both made familiar and claimed through the giving of names that place the land within a known schemata. The capacity to suggest both discovery, order and ownership underlies the power of the map and the key role played by cartographers working for governments and monarchies during periods of colonial expansion.[55] Things on the map become 'real' within the interpretive framework of the map.

The modernist museum shares many of the cultural and epistemological functions of maps. It unifies and rationalises, pictures and presents relationships. The modernist museum depicts 'reality' and shows 'the way things are' in an apparently neutral way. Both museums and maps work through a combination of word and image. In maps, these fix a name and a shape to a place. In the modernist museum the texts next to the objects signal how the object should be viewed. Relationships between people, nations, and ideas are produced through the objects selected, the way they are displayed and the relationships between them. Hierarchies of value are constructed, inclusions and exclusions made, the self and the other separated. Maps do this conceptually, with drawings and two-dimensional symbols. The modernist museum does this with things, which are understood as fragments of reality itself.

Maps are official, legitimating documents. They, like modernist museums, have the authority of the official, the authenticated. They, like museums, are not neutral, may be inaccurate, may bear little relationship to territory – the concrete that they supposedly accurately reflect. Maps and museums both bring the world into an apparent single, rational framework, with unified, ordered, and assigned relationships between nature, the arts, and cultures.[56] Museums, like maps, construct relationships, propose hierarchies, define territories, and present a view. Through those things that are made visible and those things that are left invisible, views and values are created. These values relate to spaces, objects and identities.

However, the relationship between museums and maps is more than merely that of metaphor. Museums which emerged during the nineteenth century, especially ethnographic and natural history museums, were formed by collections brought to the West from the rest of the world. The drawing together of these objects from disparate parts of the world was as much a form of cartography[57] as the drawing of a map – both created cultural unities from disperse experiences. The relationship between maps and museums is more than incidental; maps established the world-view that travellers leaving home discovered, objectified in their collections, and returned to the home country to be displayed in museums. Those things that would become 'collections' were 'recognised' through the foreknowledge[58] that travellers carried with them, both as mental schemata and as maps to show the way. In many ways the collections of early travellers concretised their maps, made their maps tangible.

The establishment of collections, like the drawing of a map, is a form of symbolic conquest. A major function of museums during the modernist period was the mapping of the world through the collection of artefacts. As explorers, traders, missionaries and others voyaged across the world they brought back artefacts, many of which were to be drawn together in museums in such a way as to map out the world. The extremities, the margins, the peripheries and the limits of the known world were pictured and imagined. This picture was presented as a universal and complete world-view, with the home territory acting as the centre from which the world was viewed.

The character of the evidence that museums assembled was compelling. Things, seen to have a material character, were understood as 'real', as identical to the way in which they were conceptually grasped. The materiality of the object confirmed its function as evidence. This materiality also supported the construction of abstract concepts, such that ideas could be built as part of mental structures. Seeing the concreteness of objects enabled abstract ideas to be sustained. Those abstract ideas positioned peoples, nations and territories and constructed boundaries to social and cultural processes. Thus objects played, and still play, pivotal roles in the construction of the politics of culture.

Cultural politics in the museum

Subjectivity, meaning, knowledge, truth and history are the materials of cultural politics.[59] Museums are deeply involved in all these areas, and especially in their interrelationships with power; the power to name, to represent common sense, to create official versions, to represent the social world, and to represent the past.[60] Questions of meaning are questions of power, which raise issues of the politics of representation. Questions also need to be asked about access to culture and cultural production.[61] Who has the power to create, to make visible, and to legitimate meanings and values?

Cultural politics concerns itself with issues of ethics and morality, sociological questions of exclusion and inclusion, advantage and disadvantage, and these concerns are of extreme relevance within the museum. Museums have the power to affect lives by opening up or closing down subjectivities, attitudes and feelings towards the self and others. Individual curators can make a difference according to the position they take towards issues of democracy and empowerment. Modern social theory proposes that knowledge can make a difference in our lives – the kind of lives it is possible to imagine and help to create.[62] And this is the difference between cultural politics and cultural theory – politics implies the possibility of agency, or action, rather than mere abstract theorising, as the purpose of analysis.[63]

Culture is not an autonomous realm of words, things, beliefs and values. It is not an objective body of facts to be transmitted to passive receivers. It is lived and experienced; it is about producing representations, creating versions, taking a position, and arguing a point of view. As such, emotions and feelings are involved.[64] The present is deeply influenced by the past, thus the interpretation of objects and collections in the past affects how they are deployed today. Knowledge is both cultural and historical, involving history and tradition. Reclaiming and rewriting history are central issues in cultural politics, and especially in the museum. Exhibitions can open up ideas that have long been suppressed, and can make formerly invisible histories visible.

The Australian Museum in Sydney opened a new permanent gallery, 'Indigenous Australians' in 1997. The exhibition themes, spirituality, cultural heritage, family, land, health, social justice and the future, were chosen in consultation with indigenous Australians and followed extensive market research with the museum's visitors.[65] The exhibition tackles issues that are rarely openly discussed in much of Australia. It points out, for example, the extreme differences in health statistics between indigenous and non-indigenous Australians. It is overt about both the richness and sophistication of Aboriginal heritage and culture, and about the attempts to destroy this culture. Formerly largely unknown histories are made

19

visible through images and artefacts alongside factual and statistical information. The exhibition opened at about the same time as the Australian Parliament spent only thirty minutes discussing the shocking statistics revealed by the Royal Commission into Aboriginal deaths in custody – a period that was too long for the Prime Minister who left the Chamber during the debate.

The exhibition waives the curatorial voice in order to hear the voices of the indigenous Australians themselves. The view of Des Griffin, the museum director at the time, is that: 'The time when the curatorial voice could be dominant in presenting the history of various cultures of which we are not a part is long gone.'[66]

Research into the responses of visitors to the exhibition was carried out by the museum to see what had been learnt. Learning was defined as: 'making some difference in people's lives'. Visitors reported several kinds of activity that had been stimulated by the exhibition. These included: buying a book relating to the exhibition, purchasing Aboriginal art works, using the information in school projects, recommending the exhibition to others, bringing others to see it, returning to the exhibition, thinking differently, and specifically gaining more respect for indigenous people.

People's comments included the development of new awareness. In the context of the stolen children, as those children of indigenous families who were taken from their homes and families have come to be known:

> It wasn't that long ago and you think if it happened today. You wouldn't let it happen today. I was hurt by that because I grew up in this country as a young child and it was happening around me as a child. No, definitely. You look back and you think, I was a part of it, I wasn't a part of it, but I *was* a part of it.

For some, the materiality and the visuality of the exhibition as a communicative medium brought existing knowledge into a sharper, more acute focus:

> I've been interested [in indigenous issues] for probably about six years. [When] I went to school it was Captain Cook who discovered Australia. I read *The Fatal Shore* and then I remember [my daughter] did a school project and I rang up Aboriginal Affairs and they sent me out this information which I read and then became appalled and shocked. Horrified, mortified. And then I saw the exhibition and I had the same response to the photographs, the people in chains. I must say I was aware of that but it really coalesced those images in *The Fatal Shore* – just to see those photographs. I really couldn't walk past, I read the information, but those photographs, those people in chains. And I remember trying to get the family to go through it to show them these things.[67]

As this example demonstrates, museum displays are culturally generative;[68] they construct frameworks for social understanding. The metaphors and rhetorics, the content and the style, of displays play pedagogic roles in the construction of knowledge and identities, in producing potential for learning, and in the mobilisation of desires.

Much of the work of museums in the past has involved the establishment of a canon. Canons create order by giving authority to certain texts, figures, ideas, problems, discursive strategies and historical narratives. This is a strategy of boundary maintenance through which some are enabled to speak and are empowered but others are silenced and marginalised. The process of making a display is a process of making a new series, of seriating. As objects are brought together new series are made, and statements are iterated and reiterated.[69] New statements may speak old messages, but also have the potential to construct different ones. Through display, museums can make new meanings which are produced through new equivalences. Museums thus have the power to remap cultural territories, and to reshape the geographies of knowledge. These are political issues, concerned with the opening up or closing down of democratic public life.

This is why museums are sites of contention, but also why they are potential sites for change. Cultural struggles today take place on shifting grounds; they move across borders to re-view, see again, former narratives from new perspectives; and they involve re-constructions, rearticulations, of culture. Cultural struggles are taking place within museums, but events are site- and occasion-specific. There is a more general need to re-view and re-construct the museum idea itself, to think more deeply about the character and possibilities of museums for use in a more democratic society. This involves interrogating museum histories and present-day processes and practices from the perspective of the politics of visual culture; it involves the reinvigoration of those practices which are useful, the rejection of those which are found to be discriminatory, and the development of new processes where gaps are found.

Although things are changing, much of contemporary museum practice is still premised on the practices of the past. The museum of the modernist period, the modernist museum, which emerged in the nineteenth century, developed characteristics which were shaped in relation to the ideas and values of the period. The museum was a vibrant and active social institution at this time, with clearly defined aims. Since this time, however, these ideas and values have been challenged, modified, put away. Rapid social and technological changes combined with radical changes in attitudes to objects as sources of knowledge left the purpose and the character of museums unclear. The vibrancy was lost. During much of the twentieth century, many museums became divorced from the communities they were set up to serve. Others oriented themselves towards powerful social elites. Many museums became inwardly focused and introspective institutions that turned their backs on societies that no longer fully upheld the purposes for which museums had been founded.

Today long-standing social structures are in flux; formerly strongly held values are questioned; new opportunities are being demanded and seized by those who feel their life-ways have been subject to disadvantage. Territories are fragmenting and identities are being reshaped and reasserted. The cultural sphere has become newly prioritised as the generative power of culture is recognised and exploited. In terms of theory, post-structuralist and post-colonialist writers analyse these phenomena of social and cultural change; post-modernist theorists examine their effects on many cultural practices. As societies change, the idea of the museum must be reborn. What would the post-museum look like?

The challenge for museums today is to identify the character of new forms of vibrancy that are in tune with the cultural changes that herald the twenty-first century. The idea of the museum needs to be reworked, and much of this will entail the development of an understanding of the relationship between museums and their audiences.[70] The post-museum is still embryonic; its identity is still overshadowed by the personalities and characters of its parent. But it is struggling to emerge, and some of its distinctiveness is becoming clear. In the struggle of the post-museum to develop its own identity, it will need to examine its heritage critically, and find ways to adapt long-standing family practices to the new circumstances within which it will find itself. The chapters which follow discuss some of those elements of the post-museum's inheritance which seem at the present time to be in the most pressing need of analysis and development in order to shape the character of this new museum idea.

2

Picturing the ancestors and imag(in)ing the nation
The collections of the first decade of the National Portrait Gallery, London

Museum collections have the power of representation. Groups of objects, brought together in one place to form a collection and then displayed, make visual statements. The beliefs, attitudes and values which underpin the processes of acquisition become embodied in the collections, as some objects are privileged and others are left to one side. The public display of these collections makes a visual narrative which naturalises these underpinning assumptions and which gives them the character of inevitability and common sense. The presentation of what appears to be (and is) visual evidence, materialises and thereby appears to confirm the 'reality' and the inevitability of these visual pictures. The apparent completeness and the unification of the presented image renders the work of its construction, and the selection processes that were deployed, invisible. In addition, collections may have been acquired over long periods of time, but their intended trajectory will have been established from the first. Founding structures, with their ideological underpinnings, shape the displays that we see today.

Portraits make particularly powerful visual statements. Images of people form part of the world of the everyday; in the West, images of those important to us are familiar parts of everyday domestic life. They encode our memories and emotions and thus are held dear to us. Portraits are less frequently sold by their owners than other kinds of paintings; they embody ancestral links and are passed from generation to generation to ensure continuity.[1] At the same time, we are also surrounded by images of those who govern and manage us; the carrying of symbolic portraits is one element of the display of protest or aggression. Portraits have the character of familiarity.

Presented as a display, groups of portraits illustrate relationships between people, demonstrating the importance of certain groups through their exposition and, by implication, the lack of importance of those left unseen. Portrait galleries are intended to hold up certain groups of people for admiration and emulation, of, for example, standards of beauty, achievement and social behaviour. The pedagogic role of portrait galleries is thus open to being a moral one, achieved through the assembling and bringing to meaning of certain pieces of visual culture.

Portrait galleries play a specific role in picturing significant members of societies. They are produced when a need is felt to capture and ground in concrete form an idea of general importance. A portrait gallery makes tangible the ephemeral, makes visible the imagined, and offers a powerful space for pedagogy.

The National Portrait Gallery in London was established in 1856, at a time when the boundaries of the British Empire were so extensive that they encompassed one in every five inhabitants of the globe.[2] Objects were flowing into Britain from these extremities at an ever increasing rate. As these objects found their ways into collections and began to illustrate, map and plot out corners of the Empire, so it became important to map the heart of this empire. One of the projects of the modern period has been the collecting together of a vast archive, to document, to control and to place the peoples of the world in relationships of domination and subservience. As the establishment of museums got slowly underway in nineteenth-century Britain, a collection emerged that would act as the public face of the managers of this collected world. The National Portrait Gallery enabled the achievement of that peculiarly masculine aspect of English culture, the representation of the self to the self.[3] This self was pictured as the nation.

The museum in modern culture: constructing master narratives

The museum has been called emblematic of the modern period.[4] One of the characteristics of the modern period has been the construction of master narratives,[5] grand narratives, universal stories, that were intended to stand as valid outside the context of the site from which they were spoken. These master narratives were intended to enable mastery of the messy and complicated real world. As Barthes said: 'Is it not the characteristic of reality to be unmasterable? And is it not the characteristic of system to master it?'[6]

Master narratives are created by presenting a large-scale picture, by eliminating complicating and contradictory detail, by disguising difference, by hiding those elements that don't quite fit, and by emphasising those that do. Unity rather than difference is emphasised; gaps that emerge when the story doesn't quite work are filled somehow, and those things that would have shown a different interpretation of events are excluded. The whole is naturalised through links to other supporting discourses. A homogeneous mapping is produced, the constructed character of which is not often readily apparent, partly because of the confidence with which it is usually projected, and partly because of the network of other supporting material. These master narratives are therefore naturalised as universal, true, and inevitable.

Museum narratives are constructed through bringing together onto one site diverse objects from a range of different sources. Brought together, they are then sorted, classified, and ordered through display into a visual narrative. Each individual item is given its significance by being placed within a larger group, and by the story that is told by this particular conjunction of artefacts. The master narratives that museums construct depend on a number of techniques of inclusion or exclusion. These include hierarchies of value (which relate to the intentions of the museum), authenticity (the object is both there to be observed and is presented as 'the real thing'), and verifiable knowledge (the provenance of an object demonstrated through documentation). These combinations produce apparently reliable and trustworthy material evidence.

Museums create master narratives through acting as both the constructor of a present-day 'reality' and through bringing into focus a memory of the past that (coincidentally) supports that present. Museum master narratives concern Art, Nature, Man [*sic*], and Nation. From these constructions, broad views of the world and the place of individuals and peoples within it emerge. 'The nation' is a powerful and enduring master narrative, although the modern sense of the word was not familiar before the eighteenth century.[7] The 'nation' is itself an artefact.[8] During the nineteenth century, the 'nation' was constructed, in part, through the arts and museums. Major themes for its construction were citizenship, unity and education. On all of these fronts, museums could be used as enabling technologies.

Museums are major apparatuses in the creation of national identities. They illustrate the nation as cultured, as elevated in taste, as inclusive and as paternal. Visual representations are a key element in symbolising and sustaining national communal bonds. Such representations are not just reactive, depicting an existing state of being, they are also purposefully creative and they can generate new social and political formations. Through the persistent production of certain images and the suppression of others, and through controlling the way images are viewed or artefacts are preserved, visual representations can be used to produce a view of the nation's history.[9]

The utility of culture: museums in mid-nineteenth-century-Britain

At the beginning of the nineteenth century in Britain, government had a limited scope. As the century progressed, the state enlarged its sphere of operation and its power to influence and control those who became understood as its citizens.[10] The greater involvement in political matters that the various extensions of the franchise enabled raised concerns about the ability of the electorate to act responsibly and consequently the need for education became seen as a priority.[11] By the end of the century, education for all was accepted as a state responsibility, as were health and welfare. Responsibility for state subsidies to the arts was embraced with more reluctance, and even when funding was forthcoming it was generally limited and somewhat stunted the growth of the arts and museums. However, during the century the arts increased markedly in significance, with the audience for them shifting from one limited to the aristocracy and upper classes to one that included the middle and lower classes. During this period of rapid population increase, the fear of what was conceptualised as a 'mob', or a mass, combined with the perceived need for education, would provide new roles for the arts and museums.

Perceptions of the function of the arts and museums shifted over the century. By the 1850s, a generally agreed group of purposes had emerged. The arts were understood to have a clear moral purpose. They could act in social improvement, and as a form of public education.

Henry Cole expressed the idea clearly in 1853:

> 'Indeed, a Museum presents probably the only effectual means of educating the adult, who cannot be expected to go to school like the youth, and the necessity for teaching the grown man is quite as great as that of training the child. By proper arrangements a Museum may be made in the highest degree instructional. If it be connected with lectures, and means are taken to point out its uses and applications, it becomes elevated from being a mere unintelligible lounge for idlers into an impressive schoolroom for everyone.'[12]

The arts could be open to all classes of society, and in their enjoyment the lower classes would become both more like their betters and more easily governable. Allan Cunningham, a writer on art and artists, illustrated popular responses to the National Gallery by describing 'poor mechanics there, sitting wondering and marvelling over those fine works, and having no other feeling but that of pleasure or astonishment; they have no notion of destroying them . . .' When asked to specify the class of people he was referring to, he said: 'Men who are usually called "mob"; but they cease to become mob when they get a taste.'[13]

By the end of the nineteenth century different views on the relationships of the arts to society prevailed. Ideas of using the arts to promote inclusion and unity had largely given way to a view that the arts constituted a sphere separate from the everyday, one that was only accessible to those who had a specific sensibility, who had taste 'naturally'. By the end of the century, the art museum had largely ceased to act as a pedagogic institution,[14] although some few galleries had been established with specifically philanthropic purposes.[15] However, as they emerged, museums of natural history and ethnography would continue to be seen as educational instruments.

By mid-century the British middle classes were becoming more established. A range of reforms in the first half of the century had opened the way for the wider social participation of a critical sector of the middle class, which partly enabled the consolidation of former disparate interests into a powerful unified culture.[16] The economy was growing at an extraordinary rate; it was a period of increasing parliamentary power, constitutional debate, and colonial expansion.[17] However, an emptiness in the cultural sphere had opened up: with the wars against France at an end, and with the American colonies lost, these external definers of the British nation were no longer potent. It became necessary to find new ways of defining the nation, and one of these ways would be through its depiction in material images.

During the first half of the century, Britain lagged behind continental Europe in the provision of cultural organisations. France had established a national gallery, the Louvre, in 1793, and the Swedish had followed suit a year later; the Rijksmuseum in Amsterdam was founded in 1808 and the Prado in Madrid in

1819; but Britain waited for a national gallery until 1824.[18] In Europe, former princely collections had been handed over to the state; the Louvre was based on former royal collections, the Uffizi in Florence, based on the collections of the Medici family, was handed over to the state of Tuscany in 1737, and the Albertina in Vienna opened as a national collection in Austria in 1781. In Britain the Royal collections remained intact, and, in comparison with European nations, the British nation looked weak. Britain had also fallen behind in design education, such that British products were demonstrably inferior to those of the French. Trade and industry were affected. Parliament established the Select Committee on Arts and Manufactures which sat during 1835 and 1836 to review the state of the arts in Britain, and the need for art and design education.

The review revealed a strongly held view that local museums and galleries would be useful to provide models for industrial design, and in raising the quality of British art and national taste.[19] It was thought that working people would welcome the opportunity to visit museums if the opening hours were appropriate. The evidence of contemporaries suggests that by the 1840s the more educated working classes were using museums as forms of entertainment and places of instruction.[20] In 1845, the Museums Act licensed any town with more than 10,000 people to open museums, although this was not mandatory.[21] At the same time, however, an older view of the arts as property was indicated in the Museums Bill which was entitled ' A Bill for the Protection of Property contained in Public Museums, Galleries, Cabinets, Libraries and other Public Repositories, from Malicious Injuries'. This Bill introduced particularly severe punishments for those who sought to damage works of arts in public collections: imprisonment, hard labour and whipping.

Museums and galleries were imbued with complex functions in the nineteenth century. For radicals, access to the arts and culture on the part of the working classes was a mode of self-education. Others were less philanthropic, and accorded to the arts and museums a civilising function that was closer to that of control, taming 'the mob' through the contemplation of things of beauty. Gladstone, for example, stated that the arts, as 'the highest instruments of human cultivation are also the guarantee of public order'.[22] Museums were seen as capable of solving internal problems of social unrest, and could be used to bind the lower classes into the main body of society.

However, museums and galleries could also be used on a broader stage – that of the nation itself. At the national level, museums were signs of the secular religion of nationalism, indices of a general maturity of taste and level of civilisation, as well as markers of the responsibility of the state towards those for whom it was gradually becoming more responsible. In France, the Louvre had an intentional remit to educate and elevate its citizens. In Britain, by mid-century, there were a number of state-funded art institutions that performed these functions. The British Museum, the Royal Academy, and the National Gallery had preceded the Museum of Manufactures (which would become, in turn, the Museum of Ornamental Art, the South Kensington Museum, and then the Victoria and Albert Museum) that was established following the 1851 Great Exhibition.

If the existing museums displayed art and design, no museum in Britain at this time provided a perspective on history. As the nation-state became more powerful, it became necessary both to position it historically and to picture it so that it could be identified, understood and imagined as the heart of Empire. As the peripheries of the nation were mapped in increasing detail through the collections brought back by travellers, missionaries and colonial administrators and officials, so it became necessary to materialise the centre. It became imperative to picture the nation through a pantheon of its heroes.

A new master narrative: the National Portrait Gallery in London

The British nation-state was (and is) constructed and defined through the institutions which comprise it, institutions of education, culture and governance. The National Portrait Gallery, London, is one of these institutions, whose specific task in the mid-nineteenth century was to picture the nation, to legitimate its character, and to construct its past. It achieved this, in part, through the depiction of an 'imagined community',[23] a community that drew its constituents from the past (those who were to be viewed), and from the present (those who were to be the viewers). The intersections of these imaged and corporeal bodies, juxtaposed through imagined connections between the past and the contemporary, created a new cultural nodal point, one that was constituted through perceptions of the identity of the nation which were deeply cut through with assumptions about class, gender and race. As it became more deeply embedded during the second half of the century, this picture of the nation would be underpinned by theories of social evolution which proposed, ultimately, a master class and a master race.[24] The emerging British middle class saw itself in the image of this master class and sought to construct a representation that demonstrated this position. The main themes of this representation were nationalism, unity, masculinity and history. Part of the developing middle-class public sphere, the National Portrait Gallery in London pictured a historical and individualised vision of the British nation, the heart of an immense empire.

The 'national portrait gallery' as an idea had already been introduced through certain publications, bound collections of prints, which were issued periodically. By the 1850s this weak materialisation was poised to be established as something altogether stronger and more significant, a fully fledged institution which would act to define the nation-state through the promotion of the middle-class values of capitalism, individualism and freedom.

One of the methods used was the adaption of the strategies and tactics of power employed by the traditional leaders of society. Since the seventeenth century, the aristocracy (and the gentry to a lesser degree) had owned collections of paintings, with among them collections of family portraits. Family portraits, hanging in the family home, acted as visible and tangible witnesses to the family claim to rule, and demonstrated the permanence of their lineage. By the late 1830s, industrialists, financiers, and commercial magnates were replacing these noble connoisseurs as the country's major art collectors, and the middle classes were beginning to develop their own preferences and tastes in art.[25] By the last quarter of the nineteenth century and the first quarter of the twentieth, a range of government-funded art galleries and museums would be established across the country which would attest to the wealth, power, taste and social responsibility of the state. But more important than this was the need to picture the face of the state, to display the ancestors and the history of the nation.

The emergence of the National Portrait Gallery was a particularly specific articulation of the right to power: it enabled the 'family' and antecedents of the nation-state to be hung up for public inspection, tangible testimonials to the right to rule. Where aristocratic portraits had been viewed only by close family and social associates, the picturing of the nation was open to all, to an imagined community of visitors that in itself also represented the nation.

Pointon[26] has chronicled in detail the foundation of the National Portrait Gallery. I want here to draw attention to some of the statements made about the functions and intentions of the new institution which reveal the strategies and tactics that it would deploy to achieve its objectives. Earl Stanhope addressed the House of Lords on 4 March 1856, and a resolution was duly passed asking if the Queen would be graciously pleased to consider the 'expediency of forming a Gallery of the Portraits of the most eminent Persons in British history'.[27] During the debate, Stanhope quoted from a letter of support he had received from Sir Charles Eastlake, president of the Royal Academy and Director of the National Gallery and who went on to become a founding trustee of the NPG:

> 'Whenever I hear of portraits for sale of historical interest I cannot help wishing that a gallery could be formed exclusively for authentic likenesses of celebrated individuals, not necessarily with reference to the merit of the works of art. I believe that an extensive gallery of portraits with catalogues containing good and short biographical notices would be useful in many ways and especially as a not unimportant element of education.'[28]

These sentences indicate some of the elements that would come together to form the gallery as a site of representation. The portraits were to be of people who were 'celebrated individuals' in the history of Britain; the parliamentary resolution had referred to people who were 'eminent' in British history. One of the main aims of the new institution was to represent a national past through its important individuals, its heroes. But how was this history of the nation to be structured? What was deemed appropriate for inclusion, and what would be left out? What categories of eminence were to be constructed and how?

During the debate in the House of Lords, it was suggested that heroes and discoverers should be represented. But should the representation be broader than this, to include those whose names stood for the maintenance and development of the whole national tradition? The distinction is an interesting one and the decision would clearly be crucial for the way that the new collection would develop: 'Heroes and discoverers' was a narrow grouping; the individuals who had formed 'the whole national tradition' could include more broadly those involved in religion, governance, the arts and other appropriate areas. The decision to take the broader view reveals the essentially middle-class nature of the enterprise; the adoption of broader and vaguer categories allowed for a freer and less restricted hand in deciding who could be admitted to the national pantheon, and allowed for flexibility in the categories for inclusion as circumstances changed. The portraits collected during the first ten years of the Gallery reveal how 'the national tradition' was invented, imagined and represented through images.

The establishment of the National Portrait Gallery represents an effort to select from and structure the past in order to present the mid-nineteenth-century state as the natural bearer of power. This structuring of the past had a range of excellent models on which to build. The most obvious was perhaps the aristocratic family portrait collection, some of which made reference to gendered portrait assemblages popular in Europe since the sixteenth century, collections of heroes (men) and beauties (women).[29] A second model was that of the collection of Edward Hyde, Lord Clarendon, who had written a history of the English Civil War, and as part of the same enterprise had assembled a large collection of historical portraits which has been described as an ancestor of the National Portrait Gallery.[30]

The third model is in some ways the most interesting. With the growth of publishing houses and a corresponding market for books, a proliferation of 'National Portrait Galleries' had occurred – collections of prints that were published as part-binders, sometimes with accompanying biographies or texts. These collections were of illustrious and eminent individuals, but were not, at first, described at a national level. It was not until the end of the first quarter of the nineteenth century that the national character was stressed, at a time when the need for a national identity became more pronounced. These collections operated both locally and nationally, bringing together their own imagined communities. At the local level we find collections of local gentry, justices of the peace, bishops and landowners.[31] At the national level, the collection consisted of portraits of kings, queens, rulers and political heroes.[32]

These print collections illustrate the central and local distribution of power that was to be found in mid-nineteenth-century Britain, where national rulers and local hierarchies of power combined in structures of control.[33] Both the local and national collections celebrate the power and status of the individual, and give expression to what could well be called 'the national tradition'. In addition, these collections construct both the wealthy middle-class subject and those of more limited means as connoisseurs:[34] instead of collecting full-scale paintings which were expensive and required a great deal of space, the collection of prints enabled a more humble form of collection. These two-dimensional portrait galleries of national heroes and local notables and worthies opened a space of semiosis that would be more fully developed in a three-dimensional way by the National Portrait Gallery and its collections.

The social functions of the National Portrait Gallery

One of the main functions of the National Portrait Gallery, in common with other contemporary museums both in Britain and in Europe, was education. During the discussion of the financial vote on 6 June, this was clarified by Palmerston, the Prime Minister. First he robustly dismissed an objection made by one MP:

> 'Now Sir, this is a very small Vote. It must not be supposed that we are going to ransack country houses to collect pictures of gentlemen's uncles and aunts. That is not the object . . .'[35.]

He went on to outline the educational value of the proposed institution:

> 'There cannot I feel convinced, be a greater incentive to mental exertion, to noble actions, to good conduct on the part of the living than for them to see before them the features of those who have done things which are worthy of our admiration and whose example we are more induced to imitate when they are brought before us in the visible and tangible shape of portraits.'[36]

The Gallery was intended to encourage and enable 'mental exertion', 'noble actions', and 'good conduct'. Encoded within these prescriptions were contemporary social values. 'Mental exertion' – signifying intellectual work as opposed to manual labour, was highly valued in a progressive bourgeois society, where merit was deemed as important as high birth. Many Members of the House of Commons, for example, had achieved their position through effort rather than through the family name. In fact, the main characteristic of the middle class was that it was a body of persons of power and influence, independent of the power of birth and status. To belong to this class, a man had to be recognised as someone who counted *as an individual*, whether as an industrialist, a university professor, a lawyer or a doctor.[37]

'Noble actions' – here there is a moral emphasis and an appeal to a self-denying, high-minded, pure way of life, as summed up in the *noblesse oblige* attitude of the philanthropic aristocracy. This was an attitude that was still admired and that could equally, in fact, describe the activities of the benevolent state. Noble actions were those of which society as a whole might be proud, and were claimed to be those that signified national identity. Linda Colley has pointed out how the anti-slavery movement, for example, was one way in which Britons could assert a British citizen's right to freedom as a vital component of a specifically British identity. This positioned Britain as superior to both the Americans and the French. Anti-slavery became an emblem of national virtue during the last quarter of the eighteenth century, and this moral imperative remained potent for some time after Britain pulled out of the international slave trade (in 1807) and abolished slavery in the British West Indies (in 1833).[38] Assumed superior moral integrity underpinned Britain's claim to be the arbiter of both the 'civilised' and the 'uncivilised' worlds, and was one way of demonstrating that British power in the world was due to more than merely industrial and economic success.

Those who were unable to deploy either mental exertion or noble actions were exhorted to maintain 'good conduct'. This inducement to good behaviour, to a clean and proper way of living, lay at the heart of the purposes of museums at this time.[39]

The National Portrait Gallery was intended to raise the national character through the display of those 'who are worthy of our admiration'. In 1856 these people were described as celebrated individuals, eminent in British history. The 1949 catalogue describes in more precise terms the collection as it had evolved by that time. The portraits are described as those of 'kings and rulers, the heads of religious and secular foundations, chiefs of families and local worthies'.[40] These categories relate closely to those of the part-binder collections of the early nineteenth-century, indicating a continuity of idea. These are clearly powerful and dominating individuals in many spheres. The structures of areas of power suggested by these categories operate as an index of governance and control (see Table 2.1).

Within these categories of individuals are inscribed the major systems of social management; firstly, the fundamental patriarchal system with the king envisioned as the father of the nation, and the chiefs of families who hold power in local areas both over their own families and over neighbouring families of lesser social significance. Secondly, the administrative system is plotted both centrally – rulers – and locally – local worthies (local gentry and lesser members of the aristocracy). Thirdly, the systems of moral and social control are inscribed through the heads of religious and secular foundations – churches and schools. These individuals have attained celebrity both by ascription through birth (kings) and by achievement (rulers). The possibility of social mobility that had opened up with industrialisation and modernisation, where entrepreneurial and capitalist endeavours had enabled a degree of penetration of the traditional structures of power, is inscribed into the fabric of the discourse of the museum.

The description of the categories of eminence reveals a view of society that is stratified and hierarchical, but one where social mobility is a real possibility if specific individuals are possessed of sufficient moral worth and power. Society is, of course, fundamentally patriarchal (monarchs are kings, not queens). It is organised with a strong generating centre, which supports an active periphery, which is itself organised in terms of both central and peripheral power, and is

Table 2.1 Structures of local and national power embodied in the categories of the portraits at the National Portrait Gallery during the first decade of the nineteenth century

	Centre	*Local*
Fundamental patriarchal system	Kings	Chiefs of families
Administrative system	Rulers	Local worthies
Moral and social control	Heads of religious and secular foundations	

connected through many links to the centre. There is a strong underpinning notion of the organisation and administration of Britain as a unified nation, managed tightly and competently through individuals worthy of respect and emulation.

Disguised in these categories is the extent to which this well-managed and efficient nation-state was dependent on peripheries external to its own territories. In Britain in the mid-nineteenth century, although slavery had been abolished, the wealth of the trade had been the route to local power and influence for many. Much of the industrial wealth of Britain was dependent on workers and products from overseas. The wealth of the colonies would continue to pour into Britain for the next hundred years. A constant traffic existed between this compact heart and the many cultures and communities that lay outside it. The categories of the collections of the National Portrait Gallery perfectly described the centre/margin structure of both imperialism and colonialism. But how did these collections begin? On what basis were the first portraits collected and what categories of distinction emerged from the early collections?

The portraits of the first ten years

The establishment of the National Portrait Gallery was agreed in March 1856. The new gallery set itself specific criteria for collection.[41] In making purchases or receiving donations, the Trustees would look to the celebrity of the individual pictured rather than the merit of the artist who had produced the portrait. The historical character of the Gallery was secured from the beginning. Celebrity would be estimated 'without bias to any political or religious party', and faults and errors on the part of the individual under consideration would not be regarded as a problem. Portraits of living people would not be accepted, with the exception of 'the reigning sovereign and . . . his or her consort'. (Exceptions were allowed for groups of people, some living and others deceased.) No portrait was to be accepted as a donation unless three-quarters of the Trustees present agreed; and no modern copy of an original was to be admitted. An early copy of these Rules is annotated by the hand of George Scharf, the first Secretary to the Trustees, who adds some Private Rules, which decree that 'Three shall be a quorum; Purchase shall be decided by the majority; Casting vote with Chairman; Scry [*sic*] to record votes when required to do so.'

During the first year of operation only one portrait was acquired. The Chandos portrait of Shakespeare was donated by the Earl of Ellesmere as a symbolic inaugural gesture. This portrait was at the time accorded emblematic status. Shakespeare was seen as the archetypical successful individual, a man whose personal power was due to mental exertion rather than to family status. As a British hero he was unshakeable. The portrait was thought to be from life, and was therefore authentic. Given as a gift by a member of the aristocracy, this portrait of a non-aristocratic hero perfectly expressed the partnership of power that existed between the middle classes and the older ruling elite.[42]

By February 1857 collecting had begun in earnest, but the pace was slow, with about twenty-five items being added per year. By Christmas 1866, 225 portraits had been acquired. George Scharf lists them for the visitor to 29 Great George Street, Westminster, which was the temporary home of the Gallery at that time.[43] The works are listed alphabetically as they were displayed throughout the house. The early collection was embryonic,[44] but set the model for the future. What do these 225 portraits show about the way in which the British nation was being imagined? What lessons does this picture teach?

Scharf's Christmas list gives a certain amount of information about the portraits. First, the names of the sitters are given, accompanied with the dates of birth and death (where known). Sometimes, a further detail is added: for example, 'John Law, inventor of the Mississippi scheme; 1681–1729. Queen Mary II., Consort of King William III.; 1662–1694.' The names of the artists are also listed, and donations are indicated by an asterisk. The works are grouped according to where they are displayed within the building, but little information is given that indicates the category of eminence into which the sitters fall. Many of the sitters would probably have been known to the visitor (Coleridge, Dr. Parr, James Watt had all died in recent decades). Where details are supplied, they give interpretive information: 'General Sir Thomas Picton, killed at Waterloo, 1758–1815; Earl of Sandwich, after whom the Sandwich islands are named; 1718–1792.'

Of more use in identifying the categories of eminence and distinction is the *Consecutive List of Portraits* printed for the Trustees in 1909.[45] The registration number of each work is noted in order of acquisition, as is the name of the sitter. Whether the portrait was acquired through purchase or donation is specified, and the name of the person from whom it was acquired, with the date, by month of acquisition. For example, we learn that in February 1857 a portrait of William Wilberforce (NPG 3) was donated to the gallery by Sir R. H. Inglis. On 23 March 1857, a portrait of Dr Parr (NPG 9) was purchased from Messrs Colnaghi, and in February 1858, a portrait of Joseph Wright (NPG 29) was given by W. M. Rossetti.

The most recent catalogue of the collections[46] gives more information about sitters' identities and some further details about the portraits and their history. Here we learn that NPG 3 is a canvas 96.5 × 109.2 cm (38 × 43 in) painted by Sir Thomas Lawrence. William Wilberforce, the anti-slavery campaigner, is described as a 'philanthropist and reformer'. Dr Parr was a 'pedagogue and Whig pamphleteer'. Joseph Wright is described as 'Wright of Derby – painter', but as NPG 29 is labelled 'See Unknown Sitters' it may be inferred that the portrait has subsequently been proved not to have been of the painter after all. In 'Unknown Sitters' we find NPG 29 languishing sadly along with many others who remain unidentified.

The 1981 catalogue adds a gloss to the 1909 List of Portraits. Working between the two documents it is possible to compile outline data concerning the identity, dates, status and social role of the sitter, the identity of the artist, the medium of the portrait (painting, drawing, medallion, bust) and how the object was acquired. From this information a number of loosely shaped groups into which the portraits fall may be suggested, and from this the most important categories of distinction, and their significance, may be extrapolated.

Caution must be exercised in defining these groups, as there are a number of difficulties. Firstly, the main descriptors (e.g. painter, poet, philanthropist, reformer, judge, scholar) that are used in this study to compile the groups are taken from the 1981 catalogue. This is itself based on earlier catalogues, and especially one compiled in 1970.[47] The descriptors seem reasonably stable, but none the less, it is possible that the groups into which the portraits appear to fall may relate as much to late twentieth-century perceptions as to mid-nineteenth-century intentions. Secondly, although broad groups can be suggested, some sitters are defined such that they could be placed in more than one category. Sir Walter Raleigh, for example, is described as soldier, sailor and author. Although most of the sitters are described along one index of activity, several are not. In this case, the first descriptor has been used in this study. Thirdly, with a small number of the works, approximately fifteen, the original identities have been reassessed, and although nine of these can be traced and accounted for, it is beyond the scope of this analysis to account for the remainder. The original identities are used for the purposes of this analysis, as it is these that caused the work to be accepted in the first place. Finally, the identification of the artists has become more reliable as scholarship has progressed since initial purchase. The authenticity of the works is assessed from the perspective of the 1981 catalogue, but it must be remembered that earlier misattributions to some extent reflect the information available at the time. In addition some sitters are represented more than once (I have counted each image rather than each sitter), and some of the images are relatively insignificant (but all are here considered equally). Group portraits have been omitted from the analysis. The picture of the first ten years of collecting can be drawn in outline only.

Bearing in mind these caveats, how can we analyse the portraits of the first ten years? The portraits date from the earliest days of portraiture up to the period immediately before the opening of the gallery. In a first and preliminary analysis the portraits fall readily into groups concerned with the field of interest, status and gender of the sitter, the mode of acquisition, and the 'authenticity' of the portrait.

One of the most striking divisions is that between men and women. There are twenty-two portraits of women; all the others (203) are of men. The largest and most significant groups turn out to be those into which the male portraits fall, where descriptors of eminence and distinction are both more numerous and much more finely graded. Although there are a number of sub-groups, these can be put together to form a broader outline picture which consists of five major groups. The largest group of works is that of men who have occupied a range of public positions of leadership, administration or governance; this group consists of statesmen and diplomats (51), colonial administrators (5), judges (7), naval officers (10), military officers (11), one explorer, and one financier. Many of those represented occupied the highest levels; the group of statesmen and diplomats includes four Prime Ministers,[48] two Lord Chancellors[49] and a president of the United States.[50] The naval officers include eight Admirals and one First Lord of the Admiralty, and the military group contains seven at the level of General or above.

The second largest group is that of people concerned with the arts, with thirty-eight writers and poets (Burns, Dryden, Keats, Congreve, Richardson, Byron, Pepys, Blake), seventeen painters and other artists, three actors and one musician (Handel). A further group of works can be assembled concerned with the sciences to include portraits of six engineers, eight doctors and physicians, five scientists (only three sitters as there are three portraits of Joseph Priestley [1733–1804], two of which are medals). Then there are twenty churchmen (which includes archbishops, bishops, cardinals, one apostle of temperance and two coal-heavers and preachers), seven philosophers and three educationalists. There are ten portraits of male members of Royal families.

There are twenty-two portraits of women. These include fourteen of queens and princesses, two writers, one actress, one courtier (Elizabeth Hamilton, the Countess of Gramont, who is referred to as 'La Belle Hamilton'), one connoisseur, one philanthropist (Elizabeth Fry) and one woman who is given no descriptor outside her family affiliations. She is Elizabeth Talbot, Countess of Shrewsbury (1518–1608), 'Bess of Hardwick', wife of the 6th Earl of Shrewsbury. In addition, a painting of Nell Gwyn, thought to be by Peter Lely, was purchased in 1858, which was later re-identified as being of Catherine, Countess of Dorchester.

The male portraits can be divided into five broad groups of recognisable and worthy activities: public leaders (86), the arts (59), science (19), religion (20), philosophy and education (10), and royalty (10). With the female portraits there are far fewer categories and they are less clear-cut and recognisable. The largest is that of 'Royalty', and here many of the queens are consorts of kings. One of the women, Bess of Hardwick, defies identity except as herself. One, Nell Gwyn, takes her place as a King's mistress, although this role is not identified in the early references to the portrait.

Fields of social activity are pictured as much more complex, active and multi-layered for men than are the social roles for women. Men appear actively involved in leadership as military or naval commanders, as governors or politicians. They are engaged to the full in the arts of writing, painting, the theatre and, to a lesser degree, music. They are represented as educationalists, engineers, astronomers, and philosophers. They control the Church, from the level of archbishop to that of coal-heaver and preacher, and of course, many of them, as kings, are hereditary rulers.

Outside the field of 'Royalty', there are very few women represented. Where they are, many of the images themselves are not strong. Elizabeth Fry is represented by a miniature.[51] The painting of Bess of Hardwick is by an unknown artist.[52] Of the other six images of non-royal women, three are studio copies[53] and one is a small drawing.[54] Of the fourteen portraits of royal women, only four are original works by named artists, and of these one is a miniature[55] and one a very small watercolour;[56] of the others, six are from known studios and three are by unknown artists. One, of Mary Queen of Scots, is a plaster copy of a monument.[57] The representation of women is limited, both in number and the quality of the work, (although it is true that many of the male portraits are also of similar quality). Apart from the 'Royalty' category, the portraits of women are marginal to the main collection.

How were these portraits acquired? When the Gallery was first agreed in Parliament, a leader in *The Times* suggested that if the Government provided a building, it would be fair to expect a considerable number of donations: 'Ours is a country of old-established houses, great wealth and no small patriotism. Hardly a family of old standing does not possess a work that would fitly take its place in such a collection'.[58] It had also been suggested that societies might like to donate some of their portraits to this national endeavour. By Christmas 1866 just under one-third of the collection had been donated, seventy-one portraits in all,[59] and only one society had come up with the goods. This was the Mines Royal, Mineral and Battery Societies, which gave a panel portrait of Queen Elizabeth I in 1865.[60] Many of the donations came from the old aristocratic families appealed to by *The Times*, but the opportunity to memorialise relatives and consequently the family as a whole was also taken up by others. A marble bust of George Tierney (1761–1830) was given by his son in 1864,[61] for example, and the widow of Richard Cobden (1804–1865) presented a bust of her husband to the gallery in 1868, three years after a painting of him had been purchased.

The founding rules for the Trustees of the National Portrait Gallery stated that in looking to the celebrity of the person represented in any portrait they might be thinking of acquiring, they would 'attempt to estimate that celebrity without bias as to any political or religious party',[62] and it is true that men from many different parts of the political spectrum are represented. However, it was not the aim of the Gallery to promote a specific political perspective, but rather to convert a well-established aristocratic power tactic in order to promote the power of the nation-state. In constructing a public site for the display of portraits, the progressive middle class acted in partnership with the traditional elite, the aristocracy and landed gentry, and in doing so, secured both the tactics and the opportunity to be depicted and imagined as powerful, natural rulers. Parliament, the legislative and governing body of the state, had appointed a group of Trustees who were, on the whole, from the aristocracy. By being publicly displayed in the company of leaders and heroes from the past, the immediate predecessors of the national administration were given recognition as appropriate rulers; by using the social and cultural capital of the aristocratic Trustees, Parliament ensured the establishment of a worthwhile cultural institution. On both accounts, the state benefited.

The founding Trustees enabled the National Portrait Gallery to be meshed with contemporary discourses of museums, art and history. Earl Stanhope, the first Chair, had been appointed Trustee of the British Museum and President of the Society of Antiquaries in 1846. Sir Charles Eastlake was President of the Royal Academy and the first Director of the National Gallery. The Earls of Ellesmere and Wemyss both owned substantial personal collections. William Hookham Carpenter was Keeper of Prints and Drawings at the British Museum. Lord Macaulay and Sir Francis Palgrave were historians, and the latter also Keeper of the Public Records Office. On the death of the Earl of Ellesmere shortly after the opening of the Gallery, they were joined by Thomas Carlyle, whose book *On Heroes, Hero-worship and the Heroic in History*, had been published in 1841.[63]

Three other Trustees were aristocrats powerful in Parliament, Lord Robert Cecil as both Foreign Secretary and Prime Minister.[64]

The representation of the eminent and distinguished at the National Portrait Gallery demonstrated the partnership between the old and new rulers. It is difficult to distinguish all the landed gentry who are represented in the first 225 portraits without a very detailed knowledge of the families concerned, but it is possible to identify the aristocracy, who are generally conveniently labelled with a title such as earl, baron or lord. Images of non-aristocrats, most of which are by definition part of the middle classes, make up just under two-thirds of the total number of portraits. The gender split is particularly interesting: where about one-third of the male portraits are of aristocrats, four-fifths of the female portraits are from the highest levels of society. Ideas about gender united men across class divisions.[65] The construction of femininity implied dependence within a family structure, just as the construction of masculinity implied the responsibility for dependants (women, children and the lower classes) achieved through success in the public sphere.

Women were largely excluded from the new public world that was emerging at this time.[66] They had a very limited role in political, professional, or cultural fields, and so could only be represented where their power and influence was due to their family status. With men, the opposite was the case: the achievements of individual politicians, professionals, or other holders of significant positions due to the exercise of mental exertion outnumber the achievements through family status.

It is interesting to note the relationships of aristocratic and non-aristocratic portraits within the five broad groups identified above. Most of the portraits of aristocrats fall into the groups of portraits of leaders and of churchmen. In the arts and sciences, the numbers of aristocrats are very small indeed. Clearly in the field of the arts, the middle class comes into its own. The doctors, engineers and scientists are also all middle class. The portraits reveal the emergence of the professions, at least for men. They also reveal that the aristocracy is still deeply embedded within traditional modes of exercising power, through military or naval forces.

In the founding of the National Portrait Gallery the authenticity of the portrait assumed great importance. Early statements about the intentions of the Gallery stress the importance of the 'authenticity' of the portraits. The meaning of 'authentic' is close to that of 'original', and indeed Stanhope had used the expression 'original portraits' in his initial presentation of the idea to the Commons in June 1852.[67] As Paul Barlow points out, the idea of 'authenticity' was a defining concept for the Gallery at its inception.[68] Some sense of the significance of the term can be gained from Thomas Carlyle's remarks to David Laing in 1854:

> 'in . . . Historical investigations it . . . is one of the most primary wants to procure a bodily likeness of the personage inquired after; a good *Portrait* if such exists; failing that, even an indifferent if sincere one. In short, *any*

representation made by a faithful human creature, of that Face and Figure, which *he* saw with his eyes, and which I can never see with mine, is now valuable to me, and much better than none at all.'[69]

The emphasis in this statement from Carlyle is on the face-to-face encounter between the artist and the sitter. It is this direct link with the sitter that is valued. Portraits are 'authentic' if made directly from life.[70] The impression of the sitter, presented by a sincere person who has been able to produce an image gained from gazing directly at the eminent individual concerned, enables the present-day viewer of that impression to 'see through the artist's eyes', to share the space of semiosis, and thus to perceive the celebrated person unencumbered by the weight of the intervening years. The portrait itself as a material artefact once occupied the same historical space as the sitter which it represents, and it thereby acted in a metaphysical way to bring the sitter and the present-day viewer into an almost personal contact. This direct contact with the past was regarded as much more important than the quality of the work so produced – *any* representation would serve to make the connection. This tangible link with the individualised past was vital for the embryo National Portrait Gallery, which was to be understood as a museum of history. 'The claims of art', thundered *The Times*, two days after Stanhope's address to the House of Lords, would be postponed 'to the even higher purpose of collecting the authentic portraits of those who have in their several paths of eminence illustrated the history of their country.'[71]

Carlyle had emphasised how the fact that the portrait had been produced by a 'faithful human creature' who had actually looked into the face of the sitter, enabled a tangible link with the celebrated individual. But how many of the first 225 portraits were 'authentic'? If we take 'authentic' to mean 'having been produced in the presence of the sitter', then we can examine the names of the artists to see whether, and for how many works, this was the case.

Many of the portraits are by named artists, and these we might call 'original' portraits. Equally, many are 'from the studio of', 'after', or 'attributed to' specific artists; some are 'copies' or 'replicas'. These we might call 'non-original'. In order to understand this we need some insight into the political economy of the production of portraits. Some portraits were produced in a genuine face-to-face situation, although many of these will have been completed in the studio of the artist. These works are justifiably 'by' a named artist. Some artists ran large studio organisations, employing many assistants, some with particular expertise in the painting of hands, or drapery, for example. Portraits which seem close in stylistic terms to the work of a particular artist, but which lack the spark of the personal touch, or which merely resemble the overall 'look' of the work of a specific artist, are often called 'studio of . . ' 'Attributed to . . .' means that it is likely that the named artist painted the portrait, but not completely certain. 'After . . .' is a close copy, probably of an actual portrait, which has possibly been identified.

Very few, if any at all, of these 'non-original' portraits will have been painted in a face-to-face situation with the sitter. It is more likely that they will have been produced through copying an existing model, sometimes many years after the model itself was produced. Not all of these models will themselves have been produced at a face-to-face sitting.

Over one-third of the first 225 portraits are found to be 'non-original'. In some of the categories, the proportions of 'non-originals' is very high: three-quarters of the portraits of royalty, for example, are 'studio of' or 'after', or from some other 'non-original' source. Half of the portraits of churchmen are 'non-originals', and so are nearly half of the portraits of public leaders. In the field of the arts, there is a high proportion (over three-quarters) of 'originals'. The quality is better here as many self-portraits were donated by artists or their families. In the small field of the sciences, the proportion of 'originals' is also high.

How are we to understand this? Why, when there has been such an emphasis on the 'authenticity' of the portrait, of the direct link back to the past and to the sitter him/herself, are so many portraits accepted that clearly do not offer the tangibility of this immediate link? The answer must lie in what these portraits do offer. They offer the opportunity to represent, to picture, to insert a particular subject into the space of history. They enable a more detailed picture, a more complete vision of the national past and the national memory. The portraits as a whole mark out a territory, they mobilise forces – the forces of the Church, and the forces of royalty, for example. They organise a domain of perception, a domain of visible history. They create a reliable, solidly material, core of value and emulation at the centre of a vast, diverse and dispersed empire.

The bulk of the non-original portraits are in three of the categories: three-quarters of the portraits in the 'royalty' category, over half the portraits in the 'Church' category, and just under a half of the portraits in the 'leadership' category. The structures of the portraits reveal an interesting game. The traditional power-elites, royalty and the Church, are mobilised, but so too is the new holder of power, the nation-state. The nation-state establishes itself as powerful, like the Church and the royal family. The state is the inheritor of these holders of power, who are, in this depiction of history, represented as its immediate ancestors. And such is the imperative to make these statements, to construct the master narrative of the history of the nation, that any potential blockage to their emergence, such as the unavailability of authentic portraits, is side-stepped by using any rendition that comes to hand.

The pedagogic lessons of the imag(in)ed nation

Those who took their place in the historical picture entered the national pantheon by virtue of their mental exertions or their noble conduct. These categories of distinction, applied to the sitters for the portraits that were acquired in the first ten years, describe the valued attributes of both the middle classes, whose eminence was achieved through their mental efforts, and the aristocracy, whose claim to fame was through the nobility of their families. The National Portrait Gallery was intended to display the social worth and historical standing of these heroes. But it was intended to do more. For those who were unable to act intellectually or nobly, it would be enough to behave well, to be inspired to 'good conduct'. Those whose families were not noble, or who were not capable of high-minded moral actions, those whose intellect was not thought to be great – those, in fact who had no place in the picture-book of the national past – were expected to visit this space of emulation,[72] gaze on the celebrated and eminent persons there enshrined, and learn to mind their manners.

Robert Young describes how an intrinsic enabling relation between education and culture operated in the constitution of the subject in the nineteenth century.[73] The National Portrait Gallery reproduced this relationship. The definition of education proposed by Durkheim expresses the objectives of the new cultural institution; education was understood as:

> the influence exercised by adult generations on those that are not yet ready for social life. Its object is to arouse and to develop in the child a certain number of physical, intellectual and moral states which are demanded of him by both the political society as a whole and the special milieu for which he is specifically destined . . . It follows from this that education consists of the methodical socialisation of the young generation.[74]

Appropriate physical, intellectual and moral states will ensue if the museum succeeds in generating good conduct, mental exertion and noble actions. Durkheim describes society in the mid-nineteenth century as moving from 'punitive' to 'therapeutic' forms of control; Foucault refers to the 'disciplinary' society that, through establishing programmes, regimes and technologies of control, establishes individuals as their own self-regulators.[75] The National Portrait Gallery as a disciplined, therapeutic, and educational space aimed to exercise an influence through the picturing of the nation and its history on those 'that are not yet ready for social life'.

And who were they? Clearly, one category of the unready is that of young children, but in mid-nineteenth-century British society there were many categories of people who were regarded as having the characteristics of children. Evolutionary theory proposed that the European bourgeois was a member of a superior race, at a higher stage of human evolution, as distinct from the lower orders who remained in the historical and cultural equivalent of childhood or at most adolescence.[76] The bourgeois was, of course, the male bourgeois, whose assumed superiority in the political and cultural field rested to a large part on the imposed inferiority of his wife and children in the domestic field.[77] And the assumed superiority of the male bourgeois was propped up by a racist ideology that defined non-whites as 'beardless children whose life is a task and whose chief virtue consists in unquestioning obedience'.[78]

In fact, everyone except white males from the middle and upper classes, those sectors of British society which were seen as cultured, were regarded as not quite fully developed and therefore not yet ready for social life.[79] These 'others' included women, the working classes, and members of the so-called 'primitive' races. The National Portrait Gallery represented one example of the many programmes that were established to ensure that as far as possible, and for as long as possible, this was seen as 'natural'.

The National Portrait Gallery worked at several levels to invent and, through invention, to construct structures of power. These structures can be identified in relation to gender, class and race, geography and history.

In terms of gender, a very clear binary divide is made. Men and women are both represented in the history of eminence. But a clear binary divide emerges, by accident as it were. The categories for men are complex, multi-layered and active. Men occupy spaces of power, they deploy strategies of power through the processes of the law, of administration and governance, and the arts, the sciences and the Church. Women are represented as almost entirely contained within the family, and only worthy of note if that family is royal. The categories for women are fewer, much simpler, and the numbers represented are tiny. All but royal women are marginalised, and this is pictured very clearly.

In terms of class, the picture is not quite so clear. A hierarchy emerges, with the royal family at the top. But the relationship between the aristocracy and the middle class is complex and open. Power is held by both the traditional landed elite and the new progressive middle class, with the traditional rulers holding onto the repressive forces (the navy and the army), while the new rulers have appropriated the newer political, administrative and ideological structures of power. The power of inherited land is still strong, but newer economic structures are equally powerful. The lower classes are invisible, and are more marginalised than women in this representation of the national past.

In terms of geography, a centre of power and influence is established, where the fundamental patriarchal system still holds sway, in partnership with the new middle class administrative system. This London-based central power-base is supported at the local level by male landowners and chiefs of families, and by local male worthies (see Table 2.1). This is underpinned by the heads of religious and secular foundations who exert moral and social control. The complete power matrix acts to create a central nexus of power, supported within Britain at the local level and outside Britain by naval and military powers and by local colonial governors. The 200 million people ruled over by the British Empire at this time (one-quarter of the world's population)[80] are largely invisible, only occasionally glimpsed as servants and menials. They are *implied* in some of the portraits; a portrait of Captain Cook,[81] for example, was acquired in 1858. But their presence is vitally important in its absence. British identity is defined in opposition to all those other races who inhabit the empire and the colonies. They constitute the margin that defines the centre. The construction of public history in museums, of which the National Portrait Gallery is merely one example, is one of the many strategies used to create white mythologies.[82]

The analysis of the first 225 portraits has exposed a deployment of power that reveals clearly the strategies and tactics of power in mid-Victorian England. The picturing of this deployment is in itself extraordinary. However, what is even more extraordinary is that this image is constructed through a *historical* picturing. The celebrated individuals that constructed the image were not contemporary with the institution – as we have seen, the rules of the Trustees expressly disallowed the acquisition of portraits of people who were still living.[83] In the first 225 portraits a picture of the structures of the deployment of mid-nineteenth-century power was constructed through an assemblage of portraits of historical individuals whose claim to fame could be used, converted, to support and underpin the contemporary modalities of power. In expressing contemporary individual positions of power in historical terms, not only was the past inscribed into the present but the past became the present in such a way as to legitimate entirely both the way the present was organised and the way the past had been selected. The present and the past effectively naturalised each other, and in doing so naturalised the silencing of the disruptive relations of gender, class and ethnicity.

The picturing of the power-relations of the present under the rubric of 'the history of the nation' can be understood as one of the strategies of the disciplinary museum, which enmeshes its subjects in systems of visibility and normalisation.[84] The National Portrait Gallery distributed portraits of celebrated individuals in space; it made visible, normal and morally correct, deep-seated relations of advantage and disadvantage. It presented a master narrative.

Viewing the nation's ancestors

By the end of the first decade of collecting, the raw materials for the construction of that master narrative were in place. If the three criteria for being seen as a nation were history, culture and domination,[85] the National Portrait Gallery could display them all, though only the first two of these would be overtly acknowledged. And this representation of those who apparently really belonged together naturally and about whom a consensus could be assumed, would be recognised as those who felt a part of it, who are 'part of us'.[86] The public rhetoric of the museum generated a productive matrix which defined the social and which made it available as an objective of and for action.[87]

However, the presentation of the collection to the public was problematic. The collection of portraits had been slow, at a rate of about twenty-five works per year, and until 1896, for the first forty years of its existence, the collection was virtually itinerant, with a succession of temporary and inadequate homes. As a cultural institution, it barely held its own against the success of the Royal Academy and the museums complex at South Kensington.[88] As a public institution, attempting to use aristocratic techniques of display, the National Portrait Gallery was outclassed by the royal collection. In addition, there was still a strong feeling that the true place for the portrait was in the country house.[89] Although the government felt strongly about the power of art to civilise and to educate, it was reluctant to spend a great deal of money on this paternalistic aim. Subsidies for all the state-funded museums were inadequate,[90] and the National Portrait Gallery was never as generously funded as the National Gallery.[91]

Many of the portraits that were desirable were unavailable, as they were in the hands of people who were not prepared to donate them; portraits had to be picked up as they became available.[92] When portraits did come onto the market, they were frequently beyond the means of the Gallery. Many of the portraits available were not of the best aesthetic quality, and this is not surprising as the quality of the portraits was secondary to the eminence of the sitter. In an account of the Gallery and its collection in 1896, on the occasion of the opening of the new and permanent home of the building next to the National Gallery, one writer comments:

> But anyone who expects that the National Portrait Gallery contains a selection of the best portraits by the best artists will be disappointed. In the first place its object is historical and not artistic, and in the second, there are no portraits to be found of some of the most eminent and interesting men and women. Moreover, when they exist, they are often unobtainable, for, however patriotic a man may be, he hesitates to part with the most cherished of his family possessions, and when they come onto the market they often fetch prices beyond the modest income of the Gallery.[93]

By December 1857 the collections were installed at 29 Great George Street.[94] This was a domestic building with what was described as 'two apartments of very moderate size, a very small back room on the same floor, and the walls of the staircase'.[95] The Trustees agreed that George Scharf, the first Secretary to the Trustees and Keeper of the National Portrait Gallery, should live over the shop, and he was allocated some of the upstairs rooms;[96] in 1860 he moved in his 'elderlies' – his mother and his aunt.[97] George Scharf was very active in investigating portraits for purchase by the Trustees,[98] visiting auction houses and picture collections and keeping a lively sketchbook of all that he saw where he noted down details of colour, condition, location, ownership and other relevant matters. He drew John Hayles' portrait of Samuel Pepys in 1859, noted its location in 1863, and it was finally purchased in 1866[99] (see Figure 2.1).

In the list of Christmas 1866, Scharf lists the works and locations of works displayed at Great George Street: fifty-six works displayed on the staircase, seventy-three displayed in the front room, sixty-two in the boardroom and thirty-four in the back room.[100] By 1859 the museum was open to the public on Wednesdays and Saturdays to those who had obtained tickets in advance from major print-sellers.[101] The Trustees' reports of the first ten years give details of visitor numbers. These increased regularly over the period (see Table 2.2).

Table 2.2 Visitor numbers for the first seven years of opening

Year	Visitors	Year	Visitors
1859	5,305	1863	10,475
1860	6,392	1864	14,885
1861	10,907	1865	16,642
1862	17,927		

Source: *Ninth Report of the Trustees*, 1866: 3

Figure 2.1 Samuel Pepys by John Hayles (NPG 211), sketched by George Scharf prior to recommending the purchase of the painting.
Photo by courtesy of the National Portrait Gallery, London.

In addition the early reports give interesting details about some of the visitors. George Scharf states in the third Trustees report:

> I have the honour to state that our Easter holidays have passed off in the most satisfactory manner. All the visitors were very orderly, and there was not one instance to be seen of any attempt to touch the pictures. The only danger was from an accidental push of an elbow from people crowding or in turning suddenly round. All very fortunately went off well.[102]

Comments such as these appear in each of the reports of the period, in a somewhat repetitive and formulaic fashion. There is an obvious concern expressed about the behaviour of the visitors, and an underlying fear that violence will erupt. A reason is given for this fear when it is pointed out that the first three days of the Easter holidays are 'very frequently regarded as a period of holiday among the working classes'. Indeed 'many young lads and factory-boys were among the visitors', however, 'from first to last, everyone was quiet and well-behaved'.[103] 'There was a little crowd all day around the Chandos portrait,[104] but no attempt to touch it or any other objects in the gallery was either seen by myself or the constables in the gallery.'[105]

The Trustees' reports express fear of indiscipline, and relief at the 'good conduct' that is observed. The galleries were clearly policed by both the Keeper and the constables ('police constables on duty' as they are referred to in a slightly later report[106]), who were expecting and were prepared for trouble. Initially, tickets had been required in order to limit those who entered to those who were prepared to take the trouble to acquire a ticket, but very shortly after opening these were dispensed with over the Easter period.

The National Portrait Gallery was a site where good behaviour could be observed. The bodies, against expectation, were docile. But what of the minds? There are some comments on this too (although they are outweighed by the comments on behaviour). Scharf notes at Easter 1864:

> I was surprised to find that the amount of ready knowledge which many of the visitors brought to bear on reading the names affixed to the pictures [*sic*]. Many of our visitors today were working men; very many were printers.[107]

Many of the visitors this Easter were 'children, even charity children, and those belonging to the humblest classes'. In 1867:

> Our Easter Monday visitors have behaved extremely well. Nothing could exceed their decorum, and the attention which they manifested towards the pictures themselves. They studied the printed lists, which were freely circulated gratuitously as before, and in several instances I ascertained that they had brought with them the lists which they had taken away the year before. It is gratifying to see the interest which parents take in pointing out to their children the great celebrities and the best characters of past times, and I was much pleased to observe the large proportion of intelligent lads, apparently from printing and large warehousing establishments.[108]

The Trustees' reports are conscious of the roles accorded to museums at this period. They detail each year the events over the Easter period, and make clear how efficacious the Gallery is in producing good behaviour, and how the spaces act as emulative for those who might in other circumstances act in a more disruptive fashion. It is all deeply impressive, but it is the gaps in the narrative that suggest that matters might not be quite so rosy. The opening period over Easter was limited to three days. What happened during the rest of the year? It is only in a private letter that a different picture can be glimpsed. Writing to the Deputy Chairman of the Trustees on Good Friday evening, Scharf says:

> this is a dull week – between the presence of the gentry and the presence of the snobs[109] (i.e. Easter week when the public will be let in without even a snip of a ticket) . . .[110]

During most of the year, it is the gentry who visit the Gallery.[111] Their presence causes no anxieties and arouses no fears; they are those who the Trustees would expect to visit. Nothing is recorded about them other than their numbers. And of course, they vastly outnumber the working people visiting during their leisure time over Easter. In 1860, when 6,392 people visited the Gallery over the period of the year, the visitor numbers over the Easter period were: 9 April (771), 10 April (440), 11 April (426)[112] – 1,637 in all. In 1863, total visitor figures were 10,475; figures for the Easter period were 1,592. The Easter visitors make up a substantial proportion of the annual return, but their presence offers more than mere numbers; they legitimate contemporary claims concerning the power of art and museums to civilise the lower classes. By the latter years of the nineteenth century, when these claims were heard far less frequently, these comments are no longer found in the reports. The Trustees are preoccupied with the business of running a museum, and this business is focused around the acquisition and lending of portraits. The responses of the visitors, and the identities of these visitors, are no longer of interest. They are reduced to an undifferentiated mass: by 1883, visitor numbers were as high as 146,187.[113]

During the first ten years, the collections were embryonic and their location uncertain. However, the pedagogic lessons that this new institution embodied were to stabilise and become more emphatic as the decades passed. They acted as the foundations on which the future development of the Gallery would be built. The attitudes to history, people and cultures that the early collections generated became to a large extent the 'common sense' that has structured much of British society throughout the late nineteenth and twentieth centuries. In 1957 a former Director of the Gallery wrote:

> Before one comes to assess a national face, one must have a clear realisation of the distinction between national and racial faces. Any Britisher owes the shape of his head to an ancestry, the elements of which include most of the known branches of the white race; the British nations are all of vividly mongrel stock.[114]

So deeply have these attitudes permeated, that this essay, republished without alteration in 1978, was again republished in a popular large glossy format in 1992.[115]

It is only in very recent years that these long-standing lessons are being reassessed and reappraised. At a time of radical cultural change, many of the institutions established by the nineteenth-century state have found themselves subject to re-evaluation. At the National Portrait Gallery, new displays (in the Twentieth century galleries, for example) use visually exciting exhibition techniques, and innovative ways of broadening the audience.[116] Some temporary exhibitions, such as that on Ignatius Sancho, bring to visibility formerly hidden histories.[117] However, the legacies of the past remain deeply rooted.

This case-study has shown how bringing objects together to form a group or make a series also constructs a social and cultural representation. This is of course particularly clear in the case of objects such as portraits, but the point is a more general one. In making decisions about which objects form series, and of all the potential objects within that class which are the significant ones, museum collections make statements about how the world and its peoples, histories and cultures are conceptualised. Relationships of equivalence are constructed, and are then made public through display. These visual statements, these constructed pictures, generate their own discourses and act to confirm the discourses with which they are affiliated. Where the founding collections are of long standing, the discourses so generated may well be subject to challenge today.

3

Speaking for herself? Hinemihi and her discourses

Groups of objects brought together in the form of a collection generate social and cultural statements. These statements are produced through the objects combined together in such a way that each individual object confirms the statement as a whole. Visual and material statements generated by grouped objects in museums combine to produce discourses which take their place within the broader social world. But can objects be placed in more than position? Does the apparently inevitable unity and the assumed completeness of museum displays mask a more disordered state of affairs? Can objects be placed within a range of discourses where they may become part of diverse statements? How do objects become involved in the construction of identity and difference?

Seeing and knowing

It is an old but persistent museum fallacy that objects speak for themselves, and that the task of the curator is limited to presenting the object in as aesthetic, tasteful and ideologically neutral a fashion as possible for visitors to interpret the objects for themselves.[1] Objects are thought to 'communicate perfectly by being what they are'.[2] Behind this lies the idea that objects have a unified, stable, and unchanging meaning and natural positions which are self-evident within 'a universal view of man's achievement or knowledge'.[3]

Cultural theory, however, does not support this point of view, insisting rather that meanings are contingent upon the circumstances within which meanings are made. A deep connection exists between looking, seeing and knowing; perceptions are structured by knowledge – seeing and saying are limited by what can be thought. Foucault's 'gaze' – the look of the knowing subject[4] – questions the distinction between the visible and the invisible, the said and the unsaid. Foucault suggests that these distinctions are not constant, but vary across time and space. The gaze works according to the epistemology that directs it, and as this epistemology modulates, inflects or ruptures, new alliances are forged between words and things.[5] Knowledge directs the target of the gaze and makes visible aspects of things that otherwise remain invisible.[6] Foucault further demonstrates how knowledge and power are coupled together. The wide-ranging semiotic possibilities of things are reduced and controlled by power. Each society has its 'regime of truth', its discourses which are accepted as rational, and its methods for ensuring that the production and maintenance of 'truth' is policed.[7] Meaning is contingently constructed through the epistemological and social limits to rationality.

Far from 'speaking for themselves', it seems likely that objects are made meaningful according to how they are placed within relations of significance, and that these relationships depend on who is determining what counts as significant. Objects are likely, therefore, to be spoken, rather than to speak. This is not to say that all meanings are of equal value, of the same power, or of the same validity. In relation to objects, meaning is to some extent constrained by material character, but the material character of an object can be given many different interpretations. In addition, meanings are frequently attributed from positions of ignorance. Myths are recycled uncritically, unknown histories are ignored, and 'common sense'[8] which supports rather than subverts the present state of things is generally accepted rather than interrogated.

Meanings are always constructed within social relationships, and social relationships are always enmeshed in power networks. The meanings that are most likely to be publicly upheld are likely to be approved by those who hold the most power. But this does not mean that dominant meanings are always accepted. Running alongside dominant meanings alternative meanings are always found. The struggle over meaning is ongoing.

Meanings have social effects. Although meanings, beliefs and values may be misinformed, factually incorrect, historically ignorant, they may well form the basis for social action. Individual agents act because of convictions, which then have consequences which influence the deployment of resources, the emphasis of one image over another, the privileging of some texts rather than others.

As far as ideas are concerned, once an idea becomes dominant it is sometimes extremely difficult to recover older ones, or to propose alternative ideas. With objects, it is different. The meaning of an object is dependent on the framework of ideas and objects within which it is placed, but the concrete material presence of an object has two specific effects on meaning. Firstly, the material character constrains the meaning that it is possible to construct, and, secondly, if the meaning so constructed is a secondary or later meaning earlier meanings still remain as traces. Earlier meanings are not entirely effaced as long as the material matter is still in existence. Earlier meanings or events may even be marked on the object itself in the form of erosions, surface patina, or evidence of damage. Earlier signification may, therefore, still be dug up, evoked, made visible.

Small remaining traces of earlier value may be nurtured until more fully fledged meaning is researched and re-established, and new (or old) sets of ideas and discourses becomes possible (again). Older meanings reinvigorated cannot take exactly the same form as they did previously as new circumstances are in play and it is never possible to reconstruct the past entirely. Historical imagination is always necessary in constructing an image of the past.

In the re-emergence of older ways of meaning through the nurturing of long lost traces and the excavation of former value, invisible histories become visible and new understandings become possible. These new understandings can illuminate present positions in history and culture, and deepen contextual and specific knowledge. Where old injustices have been covered up, the bringing to visibility of acts, ideas, and events from the past can enable the recasting of the present. As long as the material traces remain, there is still this possibility.

This chapter examines a single complex object and, through a discussion of its history, suggests that the meaning of an object is never single or unified. I suggest that objects are made meaningful within diverse interpretive frameworks, and that meaning is at least in part due to the purposeful sensibility of the meaning-making subject.

Hinemihi at dawn

On 9 June 1995, at 4.45 a.m. in the grounds of Clandon Park, a National Trust property near Guildford, Surrey, England, a remarkable ceremony took place in front of a Maori meeting house called Hinemihi. The ceremony was *Te whakatapua o nga taonga whakairo o Hinemihi ki Ingarangi* ('the blessing of carvings for Hinemihi meeting house in England'). As the sun rose, Lord Onslow, the New Zealand High Commissioner (whose family originally owned Clandon Park), and the National Trust Administrator were challenged by three warriors wearing flax kilts from Ngati Hinemihi.[9] *Kuia* (women elders) from Ngati Hinemihi called the participants in the ceremony on to the *marae*[10] in front of Hinemihi, and *kuia* from the London Maori Club, Ngati Ranana, responded.

The Maori ceremony,[11] with its traditional rituals of encounter – *wero* (challenge), *karanga* (welcome calling), *tangi-nohonga* (moment of silence for the dead) and the *whaikorero* (speeches) were followed by the *karakia whakatapua* (blessing service) and the *hongi* (greetings).[12] Hinemihi, representing an important female ancestor of the Te Arawa tribe, was lit up with a golden light from within. Framed portraits of tribal ancestors hung on the front wall, close to their carved relations. The *koruru* (carved head) of Hinemihi o te Ao Tawhito (Hinemihi of the Old World) herself presided over the proceedings from the gable of the house (Figure 3.1).[13]

In the speeches that formed part of this ceremony, certain cultural discontinuities became visible. It wasn't only that many of the speeches were in Maori so that the British participants could not understand the proceedings. Profound differences in world-view became apparent in the language used and in the way in which Hinemihi was named and presented. National Trust officers talked about the privilege of 'looking after these works of art in our care', but Hare Waikingi, one of the Maori elders, spoke of the meeting house in quite other terms. First, as he strode backwards and forwards, carrying a carved walking stick,[14] he referred to the Hinemihi as 'she'. He addressed the house as though she were a living person, and described how all those Maori living in or visiting England

Figure 3.1 The blessings ceremony at Hinemihi, 9 June 1995.

should come to see her when they were sad or homesick, as though they were visiting a homely and nurturing elderly female relative. He further described Hinemihi as a 'symbol of unity', comparing her with the eye of the needle, through which white, red and black cotton might pass to achieve unity. In an explicit reference to white, black and hybrid peoples, he positioned Hinemihi, the ancestor figure, as a point of conjuncture for the past, the present and the future.

Hare Waikingi went on to say 'We will leave her here for this purpose, and not take her home. Our children will come to visit her in the new century to maintain the unity which she represents today.' The emotional and spiritual feeling in the words, and the sense that the carved *whare nui*[15] (meeting house) is the bearer of these feelings, is in stark contrast to the understanding of the meeting house as merely 'a work of art'. In Western terms, a work of art is inanimate, and does not have overtly personalised relationships back to the past or forward into the future. A work of art is to be cared for, it doesn't care for us.

In Western art history it is not seen as necessary to talk to paintings or sculptures in order to discover and elaborate their meanings. Maori, on the other hand, believe that their *taonga* (treasures) must be surrounded by *kōrero* (talk) that both clothes them and that enables the treasures to mediate the links between the living and the dead.[16] The histories of the *taonga* stay alive when they take part in gatherings and ceremonies and are talked over, touched, and wept over.[17] Each treasure is understood as a fixed point in a tribal network of names, histories and relationships. Individual objects 'belonged to particular ancestors, were passed down particular descent lines, held their own stories and were exchanged on memorable occasions'.[18] Meeting houses, which are particularly rich and elaborate treasures, are understood as spiritually animate mediators between the past and the present, which through genealogies and narratives locate individual subjects within tribal networks, and which give them 'a place to stand' in the present-day.[19] This is achieved through cultural rituals in combination with the architectural and decorative structures of meeting houses which physically embody complex cosmological and genealogical systems.

As part of his formal response to the Maori speeches, Lord Onslow recalled playing in Hinemihi as a child. To him, the meeting house had been a garden summer-house to run in and out of at will. There was little indication that the house might be more significant seen from a different cultural framework. Jim Schuster, a member of Ngati Hinemihi, who had been involved in the production of the new carvings, felt differently, and told one of the news reporters present: 'It's hard to describe that deep inner-feeling I get from the knowledge that the ancestral house is completed and whole again.'[20] The Maori minister blessing the carvings described the light rain that fell after the ceremony as expected – it always happened at ceremonies such as this and 'was the ancestors weeping for us'.[21] During this ceremony, Hinemihi was seen from a range of perspectives, as a garden folly, a work of art, an ancestral house, and a spiritual mediator between people today and their ancestors.

The disjunctions and dislocations in these views of Hinemihi are rooted in different ways of knowing. Nietzsche pointed out that 'the perspective decides the character of the "appearance"'.[22] According to the epistemological perspective from which the house was being viewed, and the values that were being used to construct that view, Hinemihi would look different – a different object would in effect be seen, experienced and spoken about. We can see Hinemihi as an accumulation of discourses, both a stimulus for and a repository of knowledge, gazes, behaviours and feelings. An analysis of elements of the story of Hinemihi will reveal the connections, encounters, supports, blockages, plays of force, and strategies that at any given moment have produced an interpretation of Hinemihi that has seemed, at least to those producing the interpretation, self-evident and obvious. As Nietzsche indicated, our values are interpreted into things. There are no limits to the ways in which the world can be interpreted, but control and imposition of meaning offers control over the world: 'To impose upon becoming the character of being – that is the supreme will to power.'[23] Thus the different interpretations of Hinemihi expose a broader field of conflict – the struggle to impose and maintain truth and rationality, an unequal struggle that has taken place over the last 200 years within the framework of colonialism.

The meanings of Hinemihi have been construed in a range of contexts, varying in both time and space. This chapter partly reconstructs some of those meanings. A version of the story can be told first in outline. The only complete Maori building in Britain, Hinemihi o te Ao Tawhito stands in the grounds of Clandon Park, Surrey.[24] Built in Te Wairoa, near Rotorua, New Zealand, in 1880, and opened in 1881, the *whare nui* acted as a religious and community centre, and was used for tourist entertainment until it was all but buried in the cataclysmic eruption of Mount Tarawera on 10 June 1886. Left for derelict, in 1892 Hinemihi was bought for £50 by Lord Onslow, the retiring Governor of New Zealand, and shipped to his family home at Clandon. Here the *whare nui* was used at first as a boathouse. During the First World War, Clandon Park became a military hospital for soldiers from outside Britain, many of whom were from New Zealand. In 1917 soldiers from the Maori Pioneer Battalion were involved in the removal of Hinemihi to a more appropriate position closer to the big house.[25] In 1978 Hinemihi was restored by the National Trust, which had meanwhile taken over responsibility for Clandon Park.

The meeting house at Clandon Park was verified as Hinemihi[26] by Bernie Kernot in 1976.[27] Kernot commented in detail on the house and its assembly. He pointed out that the house had been foreshortened, that the doorway, window and front wall and their associated carvings were missing, and that it had been incorrectly re-assembled. He also pointed out that it was one of the oldest meeting houses still standing and one of the few to survive from the 1880s. He credited the Onslow family for preserving the house, while many in New Zealand had been allowed to rot out of existence. He suggested that Hinemihi should be returned to New Zealand as a national monument, to be returned to its original owners as guardians on behalf of the nation. In the event of this not being possible, he suggested that every effort be made to have the house restored under the direction of a qualified carver.[28]

Shortly afterwards, it became clear that the house would not be returned to New Zealand. Kernot reported that the New Zealand Department of Foreign Affairs had been contacted by contractors employed by the British National Trust for help in restoring Hinemihi. It was clear from the contractors' report that there was little understanding of the house as a cultural object as distinct from a collection of carved posts and painted scroll designs to be restored. Kernot insisted that it is Hinemihi the house as a whole which should be restored and makes a plea that the New Zealand government should take responsibility for funding this.[29] Kernot noted calls for the return of Hinemihi from Ngati Tuhourangi,[30] some of whom visited Clandon Park later, in 1986. Appeals for the return of Hinemihi may have been modified by the fact that two new houses with this name have been built fairly close to the site of the original Hinemihi.

In 1992, John Marsh, director of the New Zealand Maori Arts and Crafts Institute at Rotorua, and a direct descendant of Hinemihi, visited Clandon Park. The front wall, with door and window, had been rebuilt, but the carvings that would originally have been there were missing. A plan emerged to reproduce the lost carvings around the door and the window. In 1993, Jim Schuster, headmaster of Whangamerino school at Rotorua, a carver and descendant of Hinemihi, visited Clandon Park to take measurements for the new carvings. A few days earlier some large carvings had been found in the attic at Clandon Park, which, with the help of early photographs of Hinemihi, were identified as some of those belonging to the missing front wall. Some, however, were not found, and so new carvings were made in Rotorua by descendants of the original carvers, to complement the old ones newly rediscovered. Jim and Cathy Schuster and other members of Ngati Hinemihi attached the new and old carvings, and refurbished and repositioned other parts of the house immediately prior to the blessings ceremony on 9 June 1995. This was exactly 110 years since the night of the cataclysmic eruption.

Building Hinemihi at Te Wairoa

Hinemihi o te Ao Tawhito stands in the grounds at Clandon Park, the home of the Onslow family, now owned by the National Trust. In comparison with the grand eighteenth-century Clandon, Hinemihi is tiny. With her English thatched roof, she does indeed have the air of a quaint summer-house, standing quietly under a large tree.

In Britain, most people are not familiar with any aspect of New Zealand history, and certainly do not know how to read or decode a Maori meeting house. In New Zealand, however, efforts have been made since the 1950s to grasp the complex meanings of these structures. Until fairly recently, writers on Maori culture assumed that an unchanging and standardised way of life had prevailed in New Zealand for many hundreds of years, only to be disrupted during the nineteenth century with the impact of colonialism. Many cultural practices which in fact originated in the nineteenth century were assumed to have been part of pre-contact New Zealand. One such cultural element was the carved meeting house.[31] More recently, it has been acknowledged that meeting houses are a relatively late phenomenon.

The basic design for what is now known as the Maori meeting house can, in fact, be traced back to the twelfth century.[32] However, the fully carved meeting house is a nineteenth-century developent, emerging in response to the advent of Europeans. A more settled life-style, the need to house large groups of people to hear the message of Christianity, and the desire to make a strong statement of cultural identity were some of the pragmatic and symbolic reasons behind the development of the full concept of the carved meeting house.[33] By the end of the nineteenth century, the meeting house and its *marae* formed an integral part of the village, surrounded by the houses of the people of the village.

Meeting houses are large rectangular buildings (perhaps 80 ft long by 30 ft wide by 20 ft high), with a gabled roof and a front porch. The size and degree of decoration of the meeting house makes a statement about the *mana*[34] of its tribe or owner group.[35] The '*marae*' is an ambiguous expression which refers both to the secular ceremonial ground in front of the meeting house, which is the centre of political debate and oratory, and to the complete complex within which the meeting house and the ceremonial courtyard (sometimes called the '*marae atea*') stand. This complex today in New Zealand might consist of a meeting house, the ceremonial courtyard, a dining hall, and other small buildings set in about an acre of land.[36] The majority of contemporary *marae* are rural, but some urban *marae* have been built, although here space is much more restricted, and new ways of using the available facilities have had to be devised.[37]

Hinemihi was commissioned and paid for by Chief Aporo Te Wharekaniwha of the Tuhourangi tribe and formally opened in 1881. One of the forces behind the need for a new large building was the development of the tourist trade. Te Wairoa was the starting point for a visit to the already legendary Pink and White Terraces (Figure 3.2).

Figure 3.2 A group of people in front of Hinemihi at the time of the tourist period before the eruption in 1886.

Photo by kind permission of the Rotorua Museum of Art and History Te Whare Taonga o Te Arawa, Rotorua, New Zealand. Reference number CP 116.

The Pink and White Terraces, Otukapuarangi and Te Tarata, of Lake Rotoman-hana, close to the sacred Maori mountain, Mount Tarawera, were regarded as the eighth wonder of the world by European travellers; large areas of pink and white silica deposits, they formed step-like accretions interspersed with pools of warm water where bathing could take place. James Froude visited New Zealand in 1885 and described the natural phenomenon that he and other tourists and travellers came to see:

> [the] White Terrace in all its strangeness; a crystal staircase, glittering and stainless as if it were ice, spreading out like an open fan from a point above us on the hillside.[38] . . . The Pink Terrace . . . was narrower, and

was flushed with pale-rose colour . . . The crystals were even more beautiful than those which we had seen, falling like clusters of rosy icicles, or hanging in festoons like creepers trailing from a rail. At the foot of each cascade the water lay in pools of ultramarine . . . in the deepest of these we were to bathe . . .[39]

The entrepreneurial opportunities presented by this enthusiasm were astutely exploited by the local Maori group, Ngati Tuhourangi.

In addition to the commercial use of the meeting house, Hinemihi would have represented a strong statement of tribal prestige. By the 1880s, the carved meeting house had replaced carved war canoes as the focus of group pride.[40] Wero Taroi of Ngati Tarawhai was Hinemihi's main carver.[41] Other carvers involved with the work were Tene Waitere, Katene Waiana and Inia Hohaia.[42] Wero Taroi was a recognised master carver. He was born in the early years of the nineteenth century at a time when Ngati Tarawhai were well known for the making of elaborately carved war canoes, powerful symbols of tribal identity, pride and territory. By the 1860s, at the time of the musket wars, war canoes were becoming obsolete, and many groups were beginning to build carved meeting houses to maintain and assert their *mana*.[43] The carving of Hinemihi was one of Taroi's last commissions, as he died in the early 1880s. In many ways, Taroi set the pattern for most sub-sequent Te Arawa carving, and for what ultimately would be seen as a national 'Maori' style, to be taught at the Rotorua School of Maori Arts in the 1930s and 1940s.[44] The work on Hinemihi was one of the early commissions for Tene Waitere, who would go on to work until the late 1920s.[45]

At the time when Hinemihi was being built, it was already clear that Europeans had certain expectations of what they thought 'Maori art' should be. The writings of the early visitors such as Anthony Trollope, who visited New Zealand in 1872, established expectations for European travellers. Missionaries and colonial administrators had also played a part.[46] Although this trend was to increase in the years up to the end of the century and later, by the 1880s tourists, government officicials, and collectors had already made it plain that they wanted to see artefacts that were 'authentically Maori'.

The Te Arawa had made a rapid transition to the new world of Christianity, metal tools and a cash economy. From as early as 1850, payment in cash replaced the exchange of valuables for Ngati Tarawhai carving,[47] and by 1871 a system of payment for visitors to the Hot Lakes had been devised by Ngati Tuhourangi and was rigidly maintained.[48] During the Land Wars of 1860–1872, Te Arawa fought on the side of the Colonial Government. In an enterprising and politically aware context, it would be likely that an astute Chief Aporo, in building Hinemihi partly to cater for a growing and potentially very profitable tourist market, would want a product seen as 'authentic'. That Ngati Tuhourangi was extremely successful in developing and managing the tourist industry can be seen from the story that Hinemihi became known as 'Hinemihi of the Golden Eyes', the *paua* (abalone) shell eyes of the carvings being replaced by golden sovereigns.[49]

Hinemihi was built in a region of the North Island that had been the home of carvers since earliest times. Ngati Tarawhai had managed to maintain their own distinctive carving style since pre-European days, although since the 1830s this had developed in a hybrid social context, an amalgam of old Maori, missionary and trader-settler culture.[50] The carvings produced in this mixed environment were seen, even in the 1880s, as 'traditionally Maori'.

However, Ngati Tarawhai carving did indeed reach back to early nineteenth-century Maori culture. In choosing Wero Taroi as the main carver, Chief Aporo was both employing the best and the most experienced person, but also a man whose personal experience linked him to the old ways. Wero Taroi's teachers would have used stone adzes and greenstone blades for their work, although he himself used metal tools; Taro's earliest carvings were on war canoes, cultural artefacts that linked to earlier times and that symbolically expressed much of Maori tradition.

Interpreting cosmologies and histories

The meeting house as a cultural phenomenon consists of a complex assemblage of elements from several different art forms. These include carving (*whakairo rakau*), painting (*kowhaiwhai*), woven latticework (*tukutuku*), and architecture (*te whaihanga*). Both men and women are employed in the production of the house: men produce the carvings, and women the latticework *tukutuku* panels that fill the spaces between the carvings; both men and women (at least latterly) work on the *kowhaiwhai* scroll paintings on the rafters and ridgepole. The various elements of the house are intended to work together as an assemblage, in combination with cosmologies, mythologies, genealogies and ritualised customs and modes of behaviour.[51]

Maori cosmology is rich and complex and provides mythic descriptions and explanations which are still of relevance today.[52] Embodied in the architectural structure and in the carved, painted and woven elements of the meeting house are creation and other myths, relationships of the past to the present, and behaviour codes that place the subject today in cosmological space. The cosmological models are not static, however, but have changed as other explanations, particularly those of Christianity, have been incorporated. As cosmological models have inflected, so the representation in the meeting house has changed.[53] Genealogies are represented through the carved figures that are placed in the large veranda that acts as a porch, and inside, against the walls and as parts of the posts that hold up the ridgepole. The choice of which of the tribal ancestors to include in the representational scheme depends on the communicative function of the house and other contingent criteria.[54]

The meeting house can be seen as an exemplary 'site of interpretation'. Kernot has demonstrated how Christian elements have been built into a new meeting house, Ngatokowaru II, in such a way that speakers wishing to emphasise the Christian influence in the past of the owner-group may refer to the carvings of Bishop Hadfield and Father Delach, and the *tukutuku* panels that 'quote' those in a Christian church. However, those speakers who feel that it is the old Maori aspects of the past that are important refer to the large range of ancestor figures that are presented in a more stereotypically Maori way.[55] In any structure as complex as Ngatokowaru II, or Hinemihi, there are many systems of meaning operating. A multidimensional and fluid space of meaning is opened up which is constituted through the articulations of the fixed material elements with the social and psychological characteristics of the subjects, both speakers and listeners, within the space.[56] Meaning becomes a dynamic process rather than a fixed value.

Maori cosmology and genealogy is known through speech; it is oral rather than inscribed in fixed texts. It is learnt largely through listening on the *marae*,[57] as books on tribal histories are still rare. Speaking on the *marae* is seen as creative: thus discourses are not static, but may be construed to suit the specific context or the specific speaker. Different aspects of the kin group history may be presented according to the occasion, or to relate to the specific participants. Emphases will vary, and some aspects of a story may be omitted according to who is listening.[58] Different versions of the myths through which the Maori world is represented may be offered. The distinctions between verifiable events, the fictive and the symbolic, become blurred.[59]

An oral tradition leads to an understanding of history as a recitation of the deeds of the ancestors. The art of genealogy (*whakapapa*), a major aspect of Maori scholarship, enables the linking of people living in the present with immediate ancestors, tribal and sub-tribal founders, migrating ancestors, culture heroes, and ultimately Rangi and Papa, the sky-father and earth-mother, and with their offspring, the departmental gods. With colonisation, *whakapapa* became of increasing political importance. Land claims, both in the nineteenth century and today, depend crucially on the ability to demonstrate continuity of ownership.[60] Ngati Hinemihi are able, as are many Maori people, to cite their ancestors back through Hinemihi to Ngatoroirangi, Priest of the Te Arawa canoe.[61] Thus John Marsh identifies Hinemihi by showing her lineage from Ngatoroirangi to himself.[62]

In analysing traditional meeting houses as models of the old Maori cosmos, it is important to bear in mind the extent to which both the cosmic model and the meeting house structure can be modified as contingent elements change. However, as Neich suggests, in some areas of more conservative groups, such as Te Arawa, the traditional meeting house model may be retained as an ideological commitment to a traditionalist cosmology.[63] It has already been posited that with the building of Hinemihi at Te Wairoa by Ngati Tarawhai there were a number of good reasons for building a house that could be seen as 'authentically Maori'. Hinemihi, even today, has many of the characteristics of older meeting houses, and it is certainly possible that Hinemihi can be seen as embodying a model of the traditional Maori cosmos.

Maori cosmology locates the past time to the front, where what is known can be seen, while the unknown future lies behind and is invisible. The past is therefore continually in view and the present changes into the past as each event occurs.[64] Maori walk backwards into the future, looking back for support and direction from the past, which becomes more distant the further away it is from the present.

This reversal of the Western way of explaining historical times combines with an understanding of history as the experience of ancestors. Overlooking the past from the present means that the ancestors are always to be seen, and as a result they are spoken of as continually present. The past thus nurtures, supports and informs the actions of the present.[65]

The cosmic model is produced through the arrangement of internal and external forms of the meeting house, but the placing of the house in the landscape is also symbolically significant. The meeting house and the *marae* complex in the landscape can be seen as a cultural ordering of spatial relationships. Where possible, the meeting house faces elements of openness such as the sea or open landscape, and is backed by elements of enclosure, such as hills, mountains and bush. The open and closed elements in terms of Maori cosmology relate to the distinction between Aotearoa/New Zealand and Hawaiki. Hawaiki is the mythical homeland across the ocean, the source of food, fish, greenstone and *mana*, from whence the Maori came in the ancestral migration canoes, and to which the dead return.[66] New Zealand is the site of present existence, for many Maori a site of continuing struggle.[67]

Whether by accident or design, Hinemihi today stands looking outwards over the open space of the garden of Clandon, with her rear to dense bushes. Away to the right of the house is the lake. In this sense, Hinemihi complies with the cosmic system, but of course the ground on which she stands is alien ground in a foreign country. She also faces the large eighteenth-century Clandon against which she is dwarfed.

The front of a meeting house is the more public and important part, with the rear of the house being reserved as a more private domain. The front of the house and the *marae atea* is sometimes related to the world of life and light, while the rear of the house is related to the world of darkness and death. When visiting Hinemihi at Clandon, the back of the house is not at all in evidence from the outside. The visitor approaches the meeting house by walking along one of the side walls of Clandon, and then across a large lawn to arrive at Hinemihi immediately in front of the porch, on what is effectively the '*marae*'. The *amo*, or carved side-posts[68] standing to each side of the porch, act as frames for the experience of looking at the six ancestor figures and the other carvings in the veranda itself (Figure 3.3).

The names of all the six ancestor figures are no longer certain, although at the time when Hinemihi was built these were recorded.[69] Some of the carved figures have names etched into the surfaces; Rotopopa and Roto-tanga-te are not known, but Pikiao is a well-known and famous ancestor of the Te Arawa.[70] The six figures are deeply carved with highly decorated spirals, slanted eyes inlaid with shell, and protruding tongues. It is possible that these figures in the porch represent people of greater antiquity than those inside the house, as they are closer to the mythic past, which stretches in front of Hinemihi. At the apex of the gable is a *koruru*, a carved mask, possibly representing Hinemihi herself, and above this a carved figure of a tattooed man wearing a European-style hat. Both Hinemihi and the male gable-figure are fully tattooed, although women are usually only tattooed on the lips and chin.

Figure 3.3 The left-hand *amo*. The 1934 Reserve Bank of New Zealand featured the right-hand *amo* on its one-pound bank note. These were in circulation until the 1960s (see Gallop, 1998: figs 39a and 39b).

Photo Eilean Hooper-Greenhill.

The veranda, or porch, of a meeting house acts as a threshold zone, not only between outside and inside, but as a transition from tribal, economic, and social collaboration to family solidarity and group identity on the inside.[71] The doorway (Figure 3.4) is a threshold or boundary between the world of myth embodied in the actual space of the porch and the metaphorical space of the landscape, and

Figure 3.4 The doorway and the porch of Hinemihi.
Photo Eilean Hooper-Greenhill.

the world of history represented within the house.[72] The carved lintel (*pare*) above
the door has a special meaning relating to the move both from the past to the
present and from the external social world to the internal family framework. In
traditional meeting houses, the carved figures were always female, and in the older
carvings, explicit reference was made to the genitals. The *pare* is acknowledged
as the most *tapu* carving in the house, through the dense symbolism of sexual
womanhood, which is associated with both birth and death, with the lifting of

tapu,[73] and with vitality and pleasure.[74] The function of the carved female figures is the mediation of the dangerous liminal zone between the world inside and the world outside.

The original *pare* of Hinemihi has been lost.[75] The *pare* which is now set above the door is a replica of the original carving, reproduced from photographs. Three figures are represented. Their gender is not obvious; explicit renderings were avoided following European contact, but it is likely that they, following tradition, are female. The face of the central figure is fully tattooed in a style very close to that of the head of Hinemihi on the gable. The central figure is still, with her hands clasped on her knees, her eyes calm and her mouth closed. The two side figures are apparently moving, with arms raised above their heads and their faces in the ritual grimace of the *haka*, their eyes round. The two side figures may be holding up the heavens.[76] They may be dancing. The elaborate gestural codes that are frequently found in Maori carvings are not well understood. In all cases, the three figures have three fingers. The number three, repeated in material form, has been suggested as having a Christian significance, linked to the idea of the meeting house as a symbol of unity.[77] As the Blessings ceremony showed, this is one of the ways in which Hinemihi is seen today. The complex integration of old Maori mythology with imported Christianity can perhaps be glimpsed.

The three figures are carved in higher relief than the background, which is made up of layered curving snake-like shapes (*manaia* figures), repeated in a symmetrical way on each side of the lintel. The three figures may represent the emergence of people and gods from the original primal chaos, that may be suggested by the disembodied fragments that move in the spaces behind the figures. The central figure both separates and links the two figures on either side. This, too, may refer to the unity and separation of the elements of the mythical and the material world. Given that Maori carving is interpreted through speech, this *pare* offers a number of avenues for elaboration.

In addition to the six ancestor figures and the door lintel, there is one other important element of the porch. This is the ridgepole, which also carries a symbolic meaning. Through the painted rafters (*heke*) it physically links the founding ancestor with the descendants represented in both the porch and the body of the house. The length of the ridgepole stretches from the back of the house, which represents the most recent present, through the porch to the gable, which represents the most distant past. This continuity expresses the continuity of past and present in the tribal group. Papa and Rangi, the gods of creation, are frequently represented on the part of the ridgepole that projects into the porch of meeting houses, thus linking the ancestors of the tribe back to the dawn of time. Most of the ridgepole of Hinemihi has had to be replaced. It became damaged during the night of the eruption, and the only remaining original part is the section over the porch. Here there is a large carving of Rangi and Papa, lying opposite each other, re-enacting the conception of the world. A reference to European culture is made in the carving of the feet which are encased in boots[78] (Figure 3.5).

Figure 3.5 The carvings above the porch. Unusually, the feet are shod in European boots. Photo Eilean Hooper-Greenhill.

Within Hinemihi there are several carvings. There are no carvings on the wall panels, as is the case with many meeting houses, but at the front and the back of the house there are carved posts, and also a carved centre post. The post at the back represents a well-known Te Arawa ancester, Tutanekai, who is recognised because he holds a flute. The story of Tutanekai is a romance: Tutanekai, a young man of low birth, and Hinemoa, a young woman of high birth, loved each other but could not come together owing to their difference in social status. Each night

Tutanekai, who lived on a island, played his flute to express his love and his sadness. Hinemoa could hear the flute, and eventually swam across the lake to claim Tutanekai as her husband.[79]

The identities of the figures carved on the central and front posts are not known. An unusual small relief panel, which shows an embracing couple, is currently hanging in the house.[80] Climbing down the central post is a carved lizard, 'Kataore', a pet *taniwha*, or monster, of Hinemihi, which has become a symbolic guardian (*kaitiaki*) of her descendants.[81]

Traditionally the internal space of meeting houses is divided in terms of groupings of associated major binary divisions: thus the side of the house with the window, the left side of the house when inside looking out, is called the important side, is *tapu* and associated with men, visitors, and death. The side with the door is called the unimportant side, is *noa*[82] and associated with women, hosts and the living.[83] The internal spatial arrangements combine with the external orientations of front and back, left and right, to construct a space that relates the past to the present, men to women, hosts to visitors, and that regulates behaviours accordingly.[84] Much of this cosmological framework is interpreted as positioning men as strong, virile, lucky, and powerful, while women are placed in opposition as weak, listless, unlucky, and related to witchcraft.[85]

In addition to the cosmological model, meeting houses also serve as genealogical models. The whole house represents the founding ancestor of the group owning the house. Most houses represent male ancestors, and the Hinemihi meeting house is unusual in being named after a female ancestor. Visiting speakers on the *marae* greet the house by this name and address the house as a living person, as was the case at the Blessings ceremony.

The structure of the house represents the body of the ancestor. The carving at the apex of the bargeboards is usually the face of the important ancestor, the bargeboards the arms, the ridgepole (*tahu*) the backbone, supported on the central post, the *poutokomanawa* (heart-supporting post); the rafters (*heke*) represent the ribs, and the interior of the house, the belly (*po*) or bosom. People entering the house are entering the body of the ancestor, or the heart of the tribe. Thus, when the kin group assemble in the house, the living and dead are joined together in the belly of their ancestor.[86]

In Hinemihi meeting house, Hinemihi, the founding ancestor, is possibly represented on the gable, at the end of the ridgepole. In the porch, *heke* carry the lines of genealogical descent from Hinemihi to what are probably succeeding ancestors. Inside the house, Kataore (the lizard) refers to Hinemihi, and Tutanekai is one of the culture heroes of Te Arawa. Thus, after complete dismantling, and reconstructing at least twice in an alien environment, Hinemihi is still susceptible to a reading based on some aspects of the traditional Maori cosmos and, although much of the significance has been lost, is still capable of acting as a genealogical model for Ngati Hinemihi.

However, these messages from the past are in themselves problematic. Ideas about the past, and the way in which the past is thought to have been, become part of the system of ideas that affect present-day behaviour.[87] Thus on the *marae*, the roles that men and women are generally permitted, and the forms of behaviour that are required, are constructed and controlled through the cosmologies and genealogies that are invoked. Given that women are traditionally not permitted to speak on the *marae*, where these myths and historical narratives are constructed, the view of the past and present which is construed is inherently patriarchal. For many Maori today, the power of the *marae* is still strong, influencing both views of the self and life-possibilities. For many women, this may still mean limited aspirations.

It has been suggested that the duality of the past and the present is one in a series of oppositions that structure the old Maori world. Some other oppositions are *tapu/noa*, left/right, male/female, and death/life.[88] In developing a very elegant structuralist analysis to explain the traditional Maori cosmos, Salmond has produced an explanation that has been very influential.[89] Much of the analysis is indeed very helpful in decoding the symbolic system of a complex artefact, but, in common with much structuralist thinking, there is a danger that the seductive symmetry of the argument can lead to the presentation of an over-structured picture. Although ideal representations can be constructed, the question arises of the correspondence with lived reality, which is never as tidy and unproblematic as many structuralist analyses suggest. The view of the subject within structuralist analysis is underdeveloped: subjects are seen as passive, manipulated by social structures, rather than as active negotiators within articulations of the social. Subjects are further theorised as unified and transcendent, rather than as fragmented and constituted through action.[90] In addition, the relationship between the systems of the past and their use in the present is not simple. As Kernot says: 'Only from long discussions . . . did I become aware that the traditional semantic structure based on concepts of tapu and noa, ora and mate[91] has less meaning for some than it does for others.'[92]

The earliest writers on 'traditional' Maori culture were European men; some of the more recent writers have revived the early work in order to reassess or reinterpret it.[93] However, it is significant that although some of the early twentieth-century ways of explaining the Maori histories and cosmologies have been radically revised,[94] the relative positioning of men and women in both the old and the new worlds has not been subject to the same scrutiny. Thus the vast majority of discussions on the significance of meeting houses is underpinned by the general cultural view that men are *tapu* and women are *noa*. The meanings of each are complex and multi-layered: *tapu* is sacred, positive, restricted, strong; *noa* is 'not *tapu*': thus profane, negative, unrestricted, destructive, passive.[95] Although there are ways in which the multiple associations of these divisions could be interpreted which would emphasise different forms of powers, this rarely happens, with the result that women, and the female principle, are consistently seen as weak, inferior and secondary.

Tapu is an ambiguous concept which can be applied equally to high descent, ritual and sacred knowledge, and to death, menstrual blood and filth.[96] Salmond discusses how European ethnographic scholars found the logic of these combinations problematic, although she points out that Maori speakers do not find them difficult. Foucault[97] shows how classifications reveal rationalities and how some classifications, for those outside the system of rationality that underpins them, are impossible to think about. During the nineteenth century, male Europeans found much that was impossible to think about, both at home and in the colonies, especially in relation to women, who by the middle of the century (at least in bourgeois circles) were confined to the domestic sphere and were effectively deprived of legal and public existence.[98] Neich[99] points out that *tapu* and *noa* are rarely absolutes, but work in complex and sometimes contradictory ways. In a structuralist analysis which searches for binary pairs, divisions and distinctions are frequently made more clearly than would otherwise be the case. A structuralist approach identifies binary pairs, one element of which is always privileged.

As an exemplary site of interpretation, meeting houses still stand as material resources for stories, myths and histories. It would probably be possible to read Hinemihi in such a way as to emphasise female powers. The founding ancestor herself is female, and she gathers her descendants into her nurturing womb. In order to re-enter the dark and mysterious space of origination, we must subject ourselves to the cleansing power of the densely symbolic sexuality of woman. Within the body of Hinemihi, Kataore, the ancestor's familiar, climbs down the central post to greet us. At the rear of the house, Tutanekai plays his flute, calling his princess to him. Explanations are not static, but are subject to variation according to the contingencies of the occasion of interpretation.

Meeting houses, including Hinemihi, were built in the past, and are still built today to mediate between past and present, secular and sacred, life and death, but these relationships can only be fully understood from within an intimate knowledge of Maori myth, legend and history.[100]

The politics of tourism in the 1880s

European tourists during the second half of the nineteenth century found the complex symbolism of the meeting house impossible to perceive. They were given little help by their guides who seemed eager to meet European expectations of viewing primitive peoples living incomprehensible lives. Anthony Trollope describes an incident when he visited the Hot Lake area in 1872. At Ohinemutu, on his way to Te Wairoa and the Terraces, he saw a 'whare', and next to it 'a huge war-canoe, capable of carrying some sixty men at the paddles'. The *whare* he describes as 'a long, low room, with high pitched roof, with an earthern floor, and ornamented with grotesque and indecent carvings'. Trollope states: 'I may however, as well say that I doubt whether I should have discovered the indecency had it not been pointed out to me.'[101] He is expected to construe the carvings from within this particular frame of reference. He was accompanied on his travels by Captain Gilbert Mair, and two orderlies, one Maori and one European.[102] It is impossible to know who pointed out the 'indecency'.

Writing about his visit, James Froude described a meeting house at Ohinemutu (possibly the same one as seen by Trollope) as 'a Maori temple . . . the doors outside and the panels of the walls within ornamented with hideous carved monsters, the tongues hanging out of the huge gaping mouths, and slips of mother-of-pearl glittering in the eye-sockets . . . the old "joss-house" now answered the complex purpose of school room, land court, and religious meeting house'.[103] The language used here is indelicate: 'hideous', 'monsters' – 'gaping', 'glittering'. The only architectural and conceptual model for the meeting house that Froude can call on is that of the 'joss-house', a space in the minds of Europeans inhabited by the drugged and unpredictable Chinese. Through statements such as these, through interpretations of the artefacts as ugly, barbaric, and incomprehensible, Maori are constructed as 'other'.[104]

The constructing of 'the other' as aggressively sexual is deeply imbedded in colonial discourse;[105] the label 'indecent' is applied so frequently to cultural artefacts in the colonial discourse that it becomes clear that this is one of the expected features, indeed one of the 'attractions'. Part of the experience offered at Te Wairoa was the opportunity to see 'native dances' in Hinemihi. Froude, for example, was invited on his visit in 1885 to see some 'native dances by torchlight' which 'the gentlemen often prefer',[106] but declined. The fascination of some male Europeans with invented exotic sexualities had been observed and exploited in itself and was becoming a commodity.

The involvement of the Te Arawa tribe, including Ngati Tuhourangi, in tourism needs to be seen in the context of the social and political climate of the time. The 1870s and 1880s were a period that saw the establishment of British institutions that were designed systematically to disadvantage Maori. The initial period of European contact had been to the mutual advantage of Maori and visitors, as traders, whalers, sealers, navigators (who were to turn out to be the advance party of colonisation), were welcomed by the people of the land because of the wealth of material goods that they brought with them.[107] Missionaries arrived in 1814, to be followed by the settlers of the New Zealand Company, and Captain William Hobson. However, colonisation is about land and land ownership.[108] In 1860, very nearly all the North Island was still in Maori hands. However, between 1861 and 1881, the Pakeha population increased from 100,000 to 600,000.[109] By the turn of the century all the best land across New Zealand had been alienated with only two million hectares remaining in Maori ownership.[110] *Pakeha* (whites) owned 24.4 million hectares. By the turn of the century Maori were impoverished, chiefly authority was marginalised and numbers were down to 45,549.[111] By 1905 the use of the Maori language in schools was virtually prohibited.[112]

Colonial techniques such as taking advantage of tribal divisions, deceit, and the establishment of systems of governance that attempted to destroy Maori culture were supported by British attitudes which revolved around pseudo-speciation, the mental process whereby the humanity of the intended victim of exploitation is denied.[113] The *Taranaki Herald*, discussing Maori people, for example, told its readers in the 1850s: 'We are at liberty at any time and place to do our best to extirpate them as [we should] any other animals of a wild and ferocious nature. Their lives and land are forfeit'.[114]

Similar attitudes are in evidence in some of the visitors to Te Wairoa and the Terraces, where the entrepreneurial flair shown by Ngati Tuhourangi was bitterly resented by many of these early tourists.[115] The organisation of a range of different types of event and experience that together offered a view of a natural wonder and also an indigenous culture did not fit well with the colonial attitudes of superiority that some travellers brought with them. Colonial travellers wanted to have their 'natural' superiority confirmed through viewing marvellous things, but also through seeing people that they could denigrate as inferior. This led to some ludicrous and illogical comments, as Europeans tried to impose their values on what they actually saw.

George Augustus Sala, foreign correspondent for the *Telegraph*, visited Rotomahana on 24 November 1885. He describes Ngati Tuhourangi as 'astute savages' who are 'continually loafing about the Terraces, and who are mainly very old people and children', and who make a good living 'out of tourists' bakshish'.[116] The contradictions in this statement are manifest. Tuhourangi were 'astute' but also 'savage'; they 'loafed about' but also managed to exploit tourists; and they were mainly either very old or very young while they managed to 'make a good living'. The resentment at having to comply with Tuhourangi organisation is clear in Sala's comparison with similar experiences on the tourist itinerary in other parts of the world:

> Just fancy the manner in which Americans, or in which the Frenchman would act if the Indians in a western 'reserve', or the Arabs in Algeria, insisted on the payment of so many dollars or so many francs before a photographer could be suffered to do his 'spiriting'. Short work would be made of the demands – and the demanders, it may be opined.[117]

Hinemihi is here placed within an international system of racial hierarchies which sustains Europeans as leaders, and places colonial people together as those subalterns who sustain this 'natural' leadership position.

Disruption, displacement and new frameworks for meaning

The webs of cosmic, economic and social relations that structured the meanings of Hinemihi in New Zealand in the late nineteenth century were abruptly changed on the night of 10 June 1886 when Mount Tarawera erupted, destroying the Pink and White Terraces, and wrecking Te Wairoa.

The *New Zealand Chronicle* for June carried a number of reports and accounts of the event including the following from H. Dunbar Johnston in Rotorua, dated and timed at 10 June, 8.52 a.m.:

> We are in the midst of a terrible convulsion of nature. The extinct volcanic cones of Tarawera and Rutahia burst into activity between one o'clock and two o'clock this morning. There was a constant succession of earthquakes until about five o'clock, and the thunder and lightning became almost incessant, and still continues. Immense volumes

of flame and smoke issue from the cones, and steam from the locality of the White terrace. Showers of dust and grit reached here a little before six o'clock, but a fortunate shift of the wind has since diverted them.[118]

A telegram sent by Roger Dansey, the postmaster at Rotorua, conveys the character of the event seen from a few miles away:

> We have all passed a fearful night here. The earth having been in a continual quake since midnight. At 2.10 a.m. there was a heavy quake, then a fearful roar which made everyone run out of their houses, and a grand, yet terrible sight for those as near as we, presented itself. Mount Tarawera, close to Rotomahana, suddenly became active, the volcano belching out fire and lava to a great height . . . A dense mass of ashes came pouring down here at four o'clock a.m., accompanied by a suffocating smell from the lower regions. The immense black cloud . . . was one continual mass of electricity all night, and is still the same . . . Judging from the quantity of ashes and dust here, I fear serious results to people at Wairoa and all the natives around Tarawera Lake.[119]

At Te Wairoa the village was demolished. Approximately 150 people died. The newspaper reports concentrate on named European families, the Haszard family (Mr Haszard was the schoolmaster) and the McRae family (Mr McRae owned the hotel). Ngati Tuhourangi are unnamed numbers – '80 Maoris have perished'.[120] As one of the largest structures in the village, many people ran to Hinemihi when the mud and ashes began to fall. Exact numbers of people who sheltered in the meeting house are not known, but there were possibly as many as fifty, including one of the carvers of Hinemihi, Tene Waitere, and his wife and daughter.[121] The long tourist benches were used to prop up the roof to stop it falling in.[122]

For the small Maori community at Te Wairoa, the results of the eruption were catastrophic; many people were killed, and tribal lands and livelihood were devastated. Survivors from Te Wairoa moved to other locations nearby. Hinemihi was left, her walls buried up to the roof in mud, ash and debris from the eruption (Figure 3.6). Five years later Hinemihi was bought by William Hillier, 4th Earl of Onslow, who wanted a souvenir to remind him of his four years as colonial governor.[123] A meeting house is relatively convenient for collection and removal as it is possible to dismantle the carvings and transport them as individual pieces. Hinemihi was purchased from Mika Aporo, the son of Chief Aporo Wharekaniwha, the original commissioner of the building. A deed of sale legitimising the removal hangs in the 'Maori Room' at Clandon Park. This is signed by Mika Aporo and M. Jean Camille Malfroy, a French engineer who acted as agent for Lord Onslow:

> Received from Mr. C. Malfrey pen cheque the sum of twenty-five pounds stg (£25. 0. 0) being half the purchase money for 23 pieces of Maori carving originally part of the native meeting house at Te Wairoa and known as 'Te Hinemihi' which I have this day sold to his excellency the Governor Lord Onslow for the sum of fifty pounds sterling (£50.0.0) the

balance of which is £25.0.0 together with the sum of three pounds stg (£3.0.0) for the carriage from Rotorua to Oxford to be paid to me upon my producing a receipt from the Railway Station Master at Oxford to the effect that the said 23 pieces of carving have been duly delivered to him for transmission by rail to Auckland.

Signed Mika Aporo

Mika Aporo's signature is date-stamped 21/1/92 and witnessed by the interpreter:

Witness to signature of Mika Aporo after the above had been duly interpreted to him in the Maori language and he duly appearing to understand the meaning and purpose of the same also witness to the payment pen cheque to Mika Aporo the sum of £25.0.0

(R. Dansey)
Licensed Interpreter

Written sideways next to the the initial statement is a statement confirming that the balance of £25.0.0 was also received, on January 29th 1892.

Hinemihi was dismantled, loaded on to a bullock-cart and driven to a railway station at Oxford (Putaruru). From here the journey continued by rail to Auckland, and then by steamer to England, where Hinemihi was erected, without the front wall, by the lake at Clandon Park, to serve as a boathouse. In 1917 she was moved to the present site, and in the late 1970s restoration involved the installation of a damp course, cleaning and repainting of the carvings, and re-erecting the front wall.

Figure 3.6 Hinemihi after the eruption at Te Wairoa.

Photo by kind permission of the Rotorua Museum of Art and History Te Whare Taonga o Te Arawa, Rotorua, New Zealand. Reference number OP 2973.

How can we assess the structures of meaning that enmesh Hinemihi today? Although it is clear that it would be impossible to explore fully all possible meanings, two broad perspectives from which meaning may be constructed can be identified. They are, firstly, the framework of ownership, secondly, that of the present-day Maori community in Britain.

Hinemihi is owned by the National Trust. This is unequivocal. The bill of sale demonstrates that the meeting house was alienated by purchase,[124] and it is clear the National Trust will not be relinquishing this control. Requests for repatriation in the 1980s were met with a firm refusal. The structures of ownership are fully visible as encoded in the press reports of the Blessings Ceremony: 'The National Trust handed over the property for around two hours to allow nearly 30 members of Ngari [*sic*] Hinemihi, from Rotorua, to present a gift of new wooden carvings to decorate Hinemihi'.[125] The architectural and territorial configuration at Clandon within which Hinemihi is placed clearly reveals the legal framework of ownership and also establishes a cultural and interpretive hegemony within which dominant meanings will be made and against which alternative meanings of Hinemihi must be construed.

Hinemihi stands in the garden of Clandon, the Onslow family residence, which was built in the early 1730s for the second Lord Onslow by the Venetian architect Giacomo Leoni. A baroque eighteenth-century English stately home, the house has huge ornate formal rooms, a state bedroom, and a two-storeyed marble hall with elaborate plasterwork and large chimney-pieces by Rysbrack. Both the hall ceiling and the marble chimney-pieces are decorated with mythological scenes. The hall ceiling is covered with relief stucco-work scrolls, drapes, and garlands, much of which is supported by cherubs and 'slaves', based on Michelangelo's slaves in the Sistine Chapel. The central relief represents Hercules and Omphale and the four figures in the corners are Virtues.[126]

These references place Clandon firmly within the cultural frame of European humanism, which claims its legitimation from ancient Greece and Rome. Over the west and east doors of the marble hall are busts of negroes, apparently alluding to the Jamaican origins of part of the Onslow fortunes.[127] The references to slavery in the ancient world and to the African slave trade of the modern world, included as incidental motifs in a decorative scheme intended to demonstrate the cultured sophistication of the Onslow family, show all too clearly how European humanism constructed its values through exploitation and exclusion. These references to dominated others are probably invisible to many who visit Clandon Park. In the same way that the classical myths subsume their exploited lives into the humanist tradition, so the huge and elaborate structure of Clandon dominates and subsumes Hinemihi, reducing the complexity of a different world of myth and history to a small, somewhat exotic, garden collectable – a conversation piece along with the grotto, parterre and Dutch garden.

At Clandon one room – the Onslow Room – is set aside as a museum of family history, intended to house changing temporary exhibitions. This room is small, and was originally a study and dressing room. It is flanked by the State Bedroom and the Library, large and weighty rooms, with sumptuous furnishings, precious objects, and historic books and portraits. The first exhibition in the Onslow Room was set up to coincide with the Blessings Ceremony, and displayed the Maori and other New Zealand collections of the Onslow family. These included two cases of stuffed birds (now extinct), a feather cloak, some greenstone ornaments, two whalebone clubs, a carved walking stick, some photographs (some of Hinemihi immediately after the eruption), and of course the bill of sale for Hinemihi. This exhibition commemorates the 4th Earl of Onslow's Governorship of New Zealand, 1888–92.

It is, of course, reasonable to display these mementoes as a very small part of the Onslow family history. However, the effect of this is to destroy the original significance of the artefacts within a Maori cultural context as *taonga* with their own place in a tribal network of names, histories and relationships, animated by *korero* (talk).[128] Instead, the *taonga* become insignificant, co-opted into a larger display of artefacts designed to demonstrate the superior culture and life-style of both a specific aristocratic family and the British aristocracy in general.

The cultural significance of Hinemihi and the other Maori artefacts is invisible to visitors to Clandon, unless they bring some relevant knowledge with them. There is little information in guidebooks, interpretive panels or labels. The powerful and coherent materialisation of Western culture in the architecture of the house, the layout of the gardens and park, and the furnishings and decorative schemes of the house interior form a complete and compelling narrative, with little to disturb its ideological hegemony. However, Hinemihi maintains a material existence in the garden, as do the Maori *taonga* in the house, and as long as this remains the case the possibilities for the activation of alternative and more complex frameworks of meaning exist.

An alternative perspective from which Hinemihi might be viewed is that of Maori people within Britain in the late twentieth century. On 2 July 1995, a performance by Ngati Ranana, the London Maori Club, was held in front of Hinemihi. As a preliminary to the programme of songs and dances, a Master of Ceremonies greeted the audience and the ancestors they brought with them. During the concert, he discussed *whakapapa* (genealogy) and pointed out its importance to the audience.

These and other references to Maori cultural pathways constitute a way of enacting Maori identity, and through enactment both creating and confirming it. Butler has shown how gender is not given, but is constructed through performative acts,[129] and in much the same way it is possible to see how cultural identity can be established and reinforced through the stylised repetition of performative acts. In taking part in the posture dances, and in singing, Maori people in Britain act out their Maoriness and reaffirm their relationships to their past. Through performative acts Maori treasures are kept alive, and their histories reactivated by being touched, wept over, and talked over and by taking part in gatherings and ceremonies.[130] Carrying out the two ceremonies with Hinemihi in the summer of 1995 reactivated her cultural significance for some of the Maori participants, and in so doing reinforced their identity as Maori.

For one of the *kuia* involved in the ceremonies it was important, for example, to have people there who 'knew what had to be done' in terms of *karanga* (welcome calling). It was also important to bring the young Maori people in Britain to the *marae* at Hinemihi to pass on the cultural tradition. The use of the Maori language was crucial: although English was necessary in order to earn a living, the Maori language expressed identity, gave a cultural grounding, and was needed to describe the past.[131]

Salmond suggests that it is possible that Maori people in New Zealand today are able to hold two worlds within their mental schema – a European way of explaining the world that holds good in European situations, while in Maori situations the Maori cosmology, with its different concepts of time and space, comes into stronger focus.[132] This 'ethnography of occasions',[133] a hybrid construction of the self, is one way of establishing personal identities within a complex post-colonial world.

John Marsh, visiting Hinemihi from New Zealand in 1992, explained how the carvings 'tell a story of our past'; he was afraid that his reactions to reading the carvings might have been too much to control. However, he found he was unable to read many of them.[134] This openness to spiritual and emotional experience, and readiness to respond to the genealogical stories, is one manifestation of an 'ethnography of occasions'. Some members of the group with John Marsh did indeed feel links back to their relatives sheltering in Hinemihi during the eruption: 'We could hear their screams and feel their pain. They are still present in Hinemihi'.[135]

Figure 3.7 Hinemihi at Clandon Park today.
Photo Eilean Hooper-Greenhill.

During the nineteenth century, in New Zealand the meeting house was a place for oratory, for affirming genealogies, and for confirming relationships and affinities. In post-contact New Zealand all of these became intimately bound up with questions over land ownership. As Maori land was taken out of their owner-ship, and as Europeans laid out towns which developed into the twentieth century, the *marae* and meeting house became a special place for specifically Maori activities, a special space to celebrate and confirm Maori identity, a symbolic place which visibly stated the survival of *Maoritanga* (Maoriness).[136] For Maori people in Britain today, Hinemihi still has the potential to perform this function (Figure 3.7).

At the present time, Hinemihi is in the care of both the National Trust, who retain legal title, and Ngati Hinemihi, who have agreed to leave her at Clandon as witness to cross-cultural partnerships such as this one.[137] As Hare Waikingi said: today Hinemihi can act as a symbol of unity.

Hinemihi, a cultural artefact, can be placed within a range of contexts and viewed from a number of perspectives. The meaning of the object is constructed and reconstructed as the frameworks for interpretation and the interpreting subjects change. Meaning is dense and multi-layered; not all can be mobilised at any one time. The selection of ideas to be expressed, the perspective from which these ideas are presented, and the knowledge these ideas both embody and produce construct the meaning of Hinemihi in different ways. Hinemihi may be placed within a range of discourses, each of which will speak her differently.

4

Words and things
Constructing narratives, constructing the self

Knowledge and power

The previous chapter presented an in-depth case-study of one object. From this it was proposed that the meanings of objects are constructed according to the perspectives from which they are viewed and in relation to the discourses within which they are placed. Hinemihi meeting house was seen to be understood from a number of points of view, and a brief discussion of the implications of two of these will introduce some of the themes with which Chapter 4 is concerned.

On the one hand, Hinemihi was described as 'a work of art'.[1] Objects placed within this discourse become subject to analysis as part of the discipline of art history, and may therefore also find themselves considered as part of the art market. They will be the target of connoisseurship, of expert specialist knowledge, and will be judged in aesthetic and stylistic terms. The perspective is formal, impersonal, related to a specialist field of knowledge and publicly available. Within a discourse of this nature, the other objects that would form part of the context of meaning-construction would be other works of art. These might be, for example, other Maori carvings, or wood-carvings from other parts of the world, such as Nigeria; the typical curvilinear surface carving might be compared to that of Celtic stone crosses. The comparative objects will be selected from a world-wide panorama of objects that have similar formal structures, and that can be subject to similar aesthetic judgements. This discourse forms part of the modernist Western view which is based on judgements that are given the status of universality.

Hinemihi was also described as an object which 'tell[s] a story of our past'.[2] This is the same object seen from within a personal biographical framework. It is placed within family histories concerning the activities of siblings, parents and ancestors. The discourse has an intimate, private emphasis. It is formed from the memories and feelings of individuals. It is not judgemental, but based on unconditional acceptance. The other objects likely to be referred to within this discourse are other family treasures and mementoes, which come together because of family associations. This family discourse links with broader Maori histories and cosmologies, specific cultural ways of interpreting the world that are not well known outside New Zealand.

The knowledge of Hinemihi is therefore positioned and the epistemological character depends on the standpoint of the knower. Individual objects, particularly those relating to people and history, can be viewed in different ways. It is at this point that the argument becomes complicated and the issues become part of the politics of culture. There are political implications to these ways of knowing. Where meaning is multiple, but where a single meaning is insisted upon, questions must be asked as to who is advantaged by the meaning made available, and whose history or culture is denied by being suppressed? Questions of knowledge are also questions of power.

Individual objects are polysemic, have multiple meanings, and are susceptible to being placed in many different groupings. As we saw in Chapter 2, groupings of two- and three-dimensional visual culture make statements about histories, cultures and identities.[3] The choice of objects collected, their placing in groups or sets, and their physical juxtaposition construct conceptual narratives and present visual pictures. Assemblages of objects produce knowledge, and this is one of the most vital functions of museums. However, museological narratives are embedded in other social narratives, and while museums and collections generate specific stories that are at one level unique to the particular museum, at another level they have deep connections and are themselves partly formed by stories that are written elsewhere.

This chapter examines two people and their writings and collections. The collections interrelate in that they are both of similar material, were collected at roughly the same time and come from the same part of the world. However, the contextual circumstances of the collections are widely different, and the resultant uses and meanings made of the collections at the time of collection and today are also very different.

Both collectors used their objects to construct their self-images, and they also wrote about their collections as part of their lives. Comparison of these two examples of the writing of identities through words, images and things enables the examination of the positioned production of meanings, and the ways in which these meanings articulate and are shaped by different forms of power. It also illustrates some of the routes which objects take on their way into and out of museum collections, and suggests some of the diverse ways in which they may be used within museums.

An image of the past in the present

There is a photograph of a young woman in the Russell-Cotes Art Gallery and Museum, Bournemouth, on the South coast of England. It was exhibited in 1992 as part of the exhibition 'Images of People', although it had been in the museum for a long time before this. The photograph shows a young woman, inclining her head with her eyes downcast, looking 'demure and submissive', as the label for 'Images of People' suggested. Her hair is long and loose, she is wearing a black and white feather, a cloak that might be made of feathers or long hair, and on a

Figure 4.1 Makereti as a young woman, looking 'demure and submissive' as the label stated for 'Images of People'. How did this photograph join the collection at the Russell-Cotes Art Gallery and Museum in England?

Photo by kind permission of the Russell-Cotes Art Gallery and Museum, Bournemouth.

ribbon around her neck is an unusual pendant. She is in her early twenties (Figure 4.1).

The face of the young woman is striking. She is very beautiful and a half-smile is on her lips. With her eyes almost closed, and one shoulder bare, she looks as if she is dreaming of sensual pleasures. The woman is posed to be gazed at, and the appropriate gaze should be male. She personifies the alluring exotic beauty of the South Seas. This is an image that has been composed to appeal to others, that positions the young woman as something to be desired. Who is the woman?

Who took the photograph? And for whom? How did it come to be in the museum?

On the back of the photograph there is a name. It says 'Mrs Staples-Browne'. Handwritten in ink are the words: 'Maggie Papakura was a guide at the thermal springs at Arikarewe [*sic*] near Rateria [*sic*] North Island of New Zealand. She married an Englishman and became Mrs Staples-Browne'.

There is little information in the museum archives about this image, although the woman is mentioned in the museum *Bulletin* in 1928. The bulk of this issue of the quarterly *Bulletin* is taken up with a long discussion of 'The Maoris of New Zealand', which gives background and context to the collection in the museum. Maggie Papakura is described as a Maori queen, the daughter of a long line of chiefs stretching back for thirty-two generations. It is pointed out that she came to England in 1911 and was involved at the White City, London.[4] The article then goes on to quote Maggie Papakura:

> 'Before I came I seemed to know England, for I had learnt your language, your history, your geography is my home. There is the beauty of your country, the peaceful meadows, the streams, the grey, silent old buildings! They spoke to my heart. They were like the dreams of my girlhood come true – my girlhood, when I wandered all alone in the wilds around my native village far away in New Zealand, with no companions but the trees and the birds. My mother knew not a word of English, even to her death, but she saw that I should have to know the language of the "pakehas" or white folk. So she sent me to an English school. But she did not wish me to forget all that was beautiful in the old Maori ways and thoughts.'

The exhibition in 1992 where this image was displayed represents one of the ways in which the staff of the Russell-Cotes Art Gallery and Museum have set out to review the museum, its history and its collections critically. The collections and lives of Merton Russell-Cotes and his wife Annie form the basis for this investigation. This exhibition was very specific in its aims, both in introductory texts within the display itself and in accompanying materials. The questions asked by the exhibition included:

> How do objects from places as different as Japan, Africa and New Zealand come to be in a Victorian house and museum in Bournemouth?

> Whose viewpoint is put forward in the displays?

> What were the attitudes of the collectors and do they still affect us today?[5]

Some of the other questions raised by the exhibition focused on whether and how meanings have changed over time, and how museums can show how people are involved in shaping their material world and in negotiating social relationships.

Merton Russell-Cotes visited Hinemihi meeting house as part of his tour of New Zealand in 1886; some of this chapter discusses his reaction to what he saw.

Makereti's story

In 1928, Maggie Papakura, Makereti, was in Oxford writing her book *The Old-time Maori*. It was two years before she would die unexpectedly, aged 58. The photograph displayed in 'Images of People' also appears in *The Old-time Maori* with the following caption:

> Makereti about 1893. In her hair a feather of the huia bird, black with white tip, worn only by chiefs. Round her neck a greenstone TIKI whose name is Te Uoro. It has been buried with ancestors and dug up after a lapse of thirty years at five different times, and is over five hundred years old. The shoulder mat or cloak is of golden-brown kiwi feathers, worn only by chiefs, with a border of white pigeon feathers. I do not remember seeing this cloak among the regalia which she brought to England.[6]

The woman depicted in the photograph is a woman with multiple identities, which are signalled by the floating character of her names. Makereti constructed her own image in a complex and frequently contradictory liminal space between traditional Maori culture and values, new entrepreneurial Maori approaches, and the English land-owning class, which before the First World War still retained many nineteenth-century characteristics. Name changes and the resulting ability to disguise, cover, reinvent, and recover the self is one technique that is open to being used by some women within patriarchal societies in order to slip between and subvert pre-designated categories of being. Makereti's many names (Maggie Papakura, Margaret Thom, Makereti) denote her complex story and illustrate the interplay of ethnicity, gender and cultural politics.

Makereti was born Margaret Thom in Whakarewarewa village in 1872. Her mother, Pia Ngarotu Te Rihi[7] was a high-ranking Maori woman from the Te Arawa tribe and her father, William Arthur Thom,[8] an Englishman recently retired from the Indian army.[9] For the first ten years of her childhood she was brought up by her 'old people', her mother's aunt and uncle, who lived in a remote area in a way very close to a traditional Maori life-style. She learnt the old Maori ways of hunting with bird-snares, harvesting berries and fruit, and was tutored in genealogy, and women's arts of weaving, dancing, song and story.[10] At the age of ten, in 1882, she began more formal schooling, spending one year in school at Tauranga, before being sent for three years to the college for Maori girls at Napier. While she was there, in 1886, Tarawera erupted.[11]

Makereti must have returned to her family at Whakarewarewa, as the survivors from Te Wairoa came there to live because their own village had been buried by lava. As the Tuhourangi people from Te Wairoa re-established themselves at Whakarewarewa, some negotiation was necessary with Ngati Wahiao, the group of families (*hapu*) already living there.[12] However, together, they employed their entrepreneurial skills by setting up a new tourist destination in the thermal valley, and by 1894 the new railway was bringing in thousands of visitors in the summer months. A section of the thermal area was bought by the New Zealand government, who began to lay out a town, Rotorua, that would cater for the visitors.[13] Tuhourangi refused to allow access to the geysers except through the village at Whakarewarewa so that guiding could only be carried out by the women of the village, and so that payment would go to the families rather than the government.[14] Anyone who could speak English was especially useful. Margaret Thom and her sister were sought out as interpreters.[15]

The Maori form of Margaret is Makereti. She re-named herself 'Papakura' after a nearby thermal geyser at Whakarewarewa, when asked by a tourist whether she had a Maori surname. 'Maggie Papakura' worked as a tourist guide between 1890 and 1910. She was fluent in both Maori and English, and from her early education in both communities was able to move easily between both cultures.[16] She became a very successful and well-known guide, writing her own book, *Maggie's Guide to the Hot Lakes*, and organising a cultural entertainment group with her sister Bella.[17] Together with Te Arawa chiefs such as her uncle Mita Taupopoki, she became an advocate for Maori culture, using her social position to lobby politically for Maori hunting and fishing rights, and becoming active in health issues such as alcohol consumption.

Makereti was also energetic in promoting Maori culture,[18] and gathered a collection of artefacts of her own to show to tourists and visitors. In 1910 she opened a carved house, Tuhoromatakaka.[19] The cultural entertainment group was invited to set up a 'model village' at Clontarf, near Sydney, which would show weaving and other arts felt to be traditional. Tene Waitere and his team of carvers worked on the *whares* required. The success of this event led to an invitation to participate in the Coronation Exhibition at White City, London[20] the next year (1911), where the Clontarf model village would be rebuilt. The village included Tuhoromatakaka, which contained many of Makereti's private possessions, including Maori artefacts, cloaks and ornaments, and the greenstone Te Uoro.[21] Also in the village were an old carved storehouse (*pataka*), and many other buildings.[22] Makereti was accompanied to London by her uncle, Mita Taupopoki.

In 1907 Makereti had met an Englishman, Richard Charles Staples-Browne, while he was touring New Zealand.[23] She met him again in England, and married him shortly afterwards, becoming Mrs Richard Staples-Browne, living at Oddington Grange, Oxfordshire.[24] The marriage was dissolved in 1924 and Makereti moved to North Oxford. She established the largest space in her house there as the 'New Zealand Room', which, it is suggested, became a *marae*[25] away from home. She hung her capes of kiwi feathers, kereru (pigeon) and flax, and set out the ornaments, weapons and ornamented boxes, and a glass show case of huia birds. She entertained there every Thursday evening, and was visited by anthropologists, colonial students and others.[26]

By 1926 Makereti had enrolled as a Bachelor of Science student in the School of Anthropology at the University of Oxford.[27] She returned for a four-month visit to Whakarewarewa, where she discussed the writing project with her 'old people' who agreed to help her, and advised her on what to reveal and what to withhold, as some of the material could not to be made public. She began to work on the manuscript of her thesis and accumulated an enormous quantity of material. She was to present it to the Anthropology Committee on 7 May 1930. However, on

15 April 1930 she suffered a heart attack and died the next day.[28] Makereti was buried at Oddington Church in Oxfordshire.

Constructing the self through images, objects and words

Maori images and artefacts were central to Makereti in the construction of an identity both at home and in England. In New Zealand, cultural items were assembled both for personal and for more commercial public purposes, as Makereti developed her identity as a highly positioned member of the tribe, but also as she became well known to international tourists and as, to them, a symbol for the whole of Maori culture. Using artefacts, modes of dress that became recognisably hers, images of her extended family, and of course her carved house, Makereti put together a personality that suited her personal, tribal and commercial needs. On moving to England, she used the same techniques, and the same things, to perform her public identity as leader of the Maori cultural group at White City and succeeding entertainments on stages across the country, and later to sustain her private sense of self in her Maori room at Oxford.

A composite photograph from *The Weekly Graphic and New Zealand Mail* for 25 May 1910 shows the interior of the house Tuhoromatakaka, the artefacts in the house and Makereti herself. The photograph was taken by Parkerson, for *The Weekly Graphic and New Zealand Mail*. From the caption it seems that the occasion might have been at the time of the opening of the house.[29] It is impossible to know how much control Makereti had over the construction of this image, but it is in marked contrast to the earlier photograph held in the Russell-Cotes Museum (Figure 4.1).

The left-hand photograph shows the left side of the single room of the house, as it would have been seen from the doorway. The house is built as a traditional Maori *whare*, with walls of about 6 ft in height and a pitched roof. The walls are covered with framed pictures of people, presumably family and friends, with one or two short clubs hung among them. Ranged along the wall is the furniture: tables, chairs and a dresser with a display case containing birds on the top. The right-hand photograph shows the right-hand wall, and the end wall. Further chairs and a bookcase are set against the right-hand wall, which is also hung with many framed photographs, and at the back of the room is an iron bed. The chairs are draped with a variety of cloaks and mats. The roof is supported on painted rafters, and between their bases at the top of the walls are flat carvings. A carved post stands behind the bed, reaching up to the apex of the roof. At the front of the house is a further carved post (the heart-post, *poutokomanawa*) with, at its lower end, what appears to be a figure draped in a mat. The wooden tattooed head of the carving is visible, but the rest of the body is covered. There appear to be no windows set into the walls. Woven flax mats cover the floor.

In the left-hand image, Makereti herself is pictured in Tuhoromatakaka, in the *po* (belly) of her ancestors. Surrounded by the images, the cloaks, the carvings, her feet resting on *whariki* mats, she sits at a table writing. She is wearing a white long-sleeved blouse, with what looks like a cloak over her knees (perhaps acting as a skirt?), and the head-square that she wears in all her photographs apart from the very early ones; and she has a *tiki* round her neck. She is working: books are on the table next to her, and she is writing in a book.

A third photograph is superimposed between the two of the house. An oval encloses a close-up of Makereti standing next to the heart-post, her head resting against it. She wears the headscarf, the white blouse and the *tiki*, but wrapped around the shoulders is a feather cloak with strong triangular motifs, which can be also seen draped over a low chest in the left-hand image. This cloak belonged to her mother.[30] She looks calm, serene, confident. The central photograph is part of one that appears in *The Old-time Maori*, which was apparently taken at Whakarewarewa in about 1908.

The composite photograph is purposefully composed. It is harmonious: the design suits the subject. It reveals a considerable amount about the appearance of the house as it is seen from two angles, and shows the occupant both in her place within the house and in a close-up for further information about who (and how) she is.

The images construct a unified and integrated picture, and this relates closely to the overall impression of the house and its owner. Here is a woman at home in her culture, her home, her personal identity. She integrates elements of Western culture (the furniture, the frames, the Victorian display case) with elements of traditional Maori culture (the house itself, the mats, the clubs). The Maori objects, and the *whare*, are very strong aspects of the image, and clearly construct the Maori identity of the 'sitter'. She surrounds herself with the emblematic objects of her culture. She presents herself as Maori.

In contrast to the photograph of her when younger (Figure 4.1), Makereti seems here to be much more in control of the character of the image. She appears to have chosen how to present herself. She looks unique, herself. She is dressed soberly. In the distance shot, she is at work, writing, looking down, concentrating on her work. In the close-up she looks squarely at the photographer, unsmiling, her lips closed; confident, but not aggressive. In the photograph, her own unique life-story is created, with herself as the central character. It is a highly controlled and carefully crafted image, one prepared for public consumption, offering enough of the exotic and not too much of the personal.

The composite image of Makereti discussed above was produced slightly later than the photograph reproduced as Figure 4.2. This later image demonstrates her ability to partly take charge of the situation within which she found herself. Here again she looks boldly at the camera, and at the viewer, and while adopting the appropriate recognisably 'Maori' cultural signifiers of feather, cloak, *kotiate* (club), long flowing hair and bare feet, she folds her arms firmly across her body and looks down slightly sardonically at the photographer. She does not offer herself as a woman available for European consumption but as a woman who is well able to manipulate those male desires and to use them for her own ends, and the ends of her people.

Figure 4.2 Makereti takes control of her image as part of the tourist industry. She is 'on display'.

Photo by kind permission of the Rotorua Museum of Art and History Te Whare Taonga o Te Arawa, Rotorua, New Zealand. Reference number CP 69.

Nevertheless, in spite of her attempts at control, Makereti was enmeshed in a successful industry – that of producing the exotic South Seas maiden for the Western male gaze. By the turn of the century, a photographer, George Isles, had set up in Rotorua[31] to produce the images that would be used for the new fashion for postcards.[32] There were over two hundred examples for tourists to choose from, nearly all of which were photographs of the women of Tuhourangi.[33] These images were captioned: 'Black but beautiful', 'Maori belle', and so on. Several images of Makereti exist that may have been used as postcards, and she has not been as successful in all of them in subverting the genre to her own ends. And even where she was able to project a more active and stronger image, as in Figure 4.2, her photographs were susceptible to being read in the same way as many of the others that projected an exotic sensuality to meet the ready interpretation of the Western male. The colonial gaze easily associated Maori, 'that extraordinarily clever race', with Polynesia, and the 'beautiful suppleness . . . possessed by the Polynesians' with 'exhilarating relics of savagery'.[34]

Tuhoromatakaka was built partly to support the tourist industry that Makereti promoted and in which she participated. The house and the woman became the destination of the tourist gaze. It was the carvings of this house and many of the contents of the house that Makereti brought with her to England. According to Penniman, she brought all her possessions when she moved to England: the carved house and all its furnishings, the ancient carved *pataka*, greenstone and other ornaments, weapons, and feather and flaxen cloaks.[35] Tuhoromatakaka was erected at the Coronation Exhibition in 1911 and then, after her marriage, Makereti took it to Oddington Grange.

Te Awekotuku tells how Maori ancestral art, *Maori taonga*, holds many different meanings for Maori:

> The taonga inspire and confront; they relax and soothe; they provoke and energise; they empower and sustain. They convey memories from the past and make promises for the future. They tell us where we, as a people, have come from and where we are going to. They represent hope, fortitude and resilience: the survival of the spirit.[36]

The Pitt Rivers Museum in Oxford holds several lists of the Maori ancestral art that Makereti had with her in England.[37] They show the substantial collection that she had with her in Oxford to remind her of her people, home and culture. Her lists are mainly handwritten, although one is typed. They are not dated. The objects are grouped, classified and named, and each group or individual item is priced.[38] The lists give a good idea of the type and range of some of the material that Makereti brought with her from New Zealand.

Makereti describes the characteristics of a *tiki* (she wears one in her early photograph):

> A tiki would take from fifty to 100 yrs to complete.
> "   is the memorial of an ancestor
> "   conveys the 'mana' of the ancestor to the possessor
> "   is valued for 'mana' conveyed
> "   shows that the possessor is descended from men of rank
> "   was worn round the neck with plaited fibre and fastened at the back with bone button which was human or albatross
> "   was worn night and day
> "   was very 'tapu' and must not be seen by others.
> "   averted witchcraft and accident

Makereti used her collections; as far as possible and practicable they were integrated into her life. For example, she took some of her collections to the Pitt Rivers Museum where she gave a public lecture to the Oxford University Anthropological Society.[39] The main use made of them, however, was to create a Maori Room, a home away from home, where she invited her friends to see and talk about her collections:

> These it was her delight to show to her friends and to explain, and those of us who knew her can never forget the slight turn of her body which set the *piupiu* skirt curling and uncurling, or the graceful and intricate movement of the *poi* balls in the Canoe Song composed by her sister Bella, or the thrill of the motion of a weapon which she took from our awkward hands and held as it should be held. When she wore Maori dress, she became not only her former self, but all her people, and it was not only the chieftainess who stood before us, but the *tangata whenua*, the lords of the land. No people ever had a better ambassador and interpreter than the Maori had in her.[40]

These collections were also used to build the narrative of the Maori life-ways and customs that form the theme of *The Old-time Maori*. Makereti's book is an account of the traditional ways of life of Maori people. The writer herself is not visible, the book having been based on her intended dissertation as part of the Bachelor of Science degree in Anthropology at the University of Oxford.[41] However, the book is written from personal experience, and uses personal collections as illustrations and in discussion. The life described is the early life of the writer. Written from an insider perspective, the book takes issue with European explanations of Maori culture, while conforming to the disciplines of ethnography. It is an example of what has been called 'autoethnography'.

'Autoethnography' is a term borrowed from Mary Louise Pratt,[42] who uses it to refer to instances in which colonised subjects undertake to represent themselves in ways which engage with the coloniser's own terms. While ethnographic texts are a means by which Europeans represent to themselves their 'others', autoethnographic texts are those that 'others' construct in response to or in dialogue with metropolitan representations. *The Old-time Maori*, then is a form of 'writing back',[43] of response to European writing on Maori culture and history. The book is also unusual in that it is written from a female perspective rather than a male one.

As with texts, so with objects. Along with written representations which use words and sometimes images, the production of 'others' through displays of objects also conveys attitudes and values, perhaps even more powerfully. But those 'others' also used objects in their own purposeful ways. Makereti's house in Oxford can be seen as a form of 'writing culture' with objects, a material autoethnography.

Merton Russell-Cotes: the seeing man

Merton Russell-Cotes (1835–1921) was born in the village of Tettenhall, Staffordshire in the English West Midlands into the family of a wealthy iron-master. His early comfortable years were interrupted by the death of his father who died intestate. All the land and property passed to Merton's older brother who appears to have ignored any family responsibilities, the upkeep of Merton and his mother passing to the husband of an older sister. This eventually entailed a move to Glasgow, where Merton was obliged to rely on the goodwill and support of his uncle. As Merton grew up he met and later married Annie Nelson Clark, the daughter of a wealthy cotton manufacturer, whose inheritance underpinned Merton's ambitions and achievements.[44]

Annie and Merton had moved to Bournemouth by 1876, largely because of Merton's recurring bronchitis. He bought the Bath Hotel and, following the death of Annie's father a year later, embarked on a substantial refurbishment that enabled him to host elaborate events and generally claim a prominent position on the local political scene.[45] He was a controversial figure, however, and trouble at home seemed to precede his embarkation on lengthy journeys overseas.[46] One of these, from 1884–85, was a tour of Australia, New Zealand and Fiji. It had been planned that the tour would extend to San Francisco, New York and then home, but in the event the Russell-Coteses travelled on from San Francisco to Japan.

Collecting seems to have become a way of life for the Russell-Cotes. Merton began to collect paintings in his early twenties, frequently buying works from the Walker Art Gallery Annual Exhibition in Liverpool. Running out of space at home to hang the works, Merton left the work in the Gallery. Prior to his 1884–85 travels, he entrusted the works, then numbering more than 200, to the Liverpool Corporation. On his return, he was pleased to see many on display. Later, some, at least, of the works circulated among local authority art galleries as the Russell-Cotes loan collection. Eventually, the organisation of this circulation became too demanding, and some of the work was retained for the collection in Bournemouth, while the rest was sold at Christies on 11 March 1895.[47]

The collection at Bournemouth contained those paintings that were not sold, but also contained other items. Where the art collection comprised what Merton called 'the modern British School of Art',[48] both Merton and Annie also collected 'curios' on their travels overseas. Annie's interests focused on natural history and ethnography.[49] Collecting seems to have taken the form of acquiring souvenirs as and when possible. There is no evidence that the collecting was systematic or planned to any large degree; the enormous amount of material collected on the visit to Japan, for example (over a hundred cases of 'curios'[50]) was acquired on the off-chance, the journey there being more or less by accident.[51] The collections reflected the whims and tastes of their collectors.[52]

Russell-Cotes refers to himself as 'an ordinary tourist in search of health'.[53] Tourism has been identified as one of the key structures of consciousness associated with modernity.[54] During the nineteenth century, health, culture, leisure, amusement and recreation were viewed together. If tourism was efficacious in restoring the body and cultivating the mind, Russell-Cotes also used his travels to proclaim himself as a man of science, and to justify his involvement in the learned societies of the day.[55] As Colley suggests, tourism was one way of proclaiming who one was.[56]

Russell-Cotes' autobiography, *Home and Abroad – An Autobiography of an Octogenarian* was published privately in two volumes by Merton and Annie's son Herbert in 1921, a few months after Merton's death. This book is a conventional autobiography. Written in 1921, when the writer was 86, it gives an account of his life, focusing on the people he knew and their social, political and cultural connections. He spends a considerable amount of time describing his travels, including his journeys to Australia and New Zealand. He also describes what he sees on his travels from a personal perspective, but he is not, of course, commenting on his own culture. Rather, he is a perfect example of Mary Pratt's 'seeing man', that European male subject whose imperial eyes passively look out and possess[57] (Figure 4.3).

In the section of the work that concerns us here, Merton describes his travels in New Zealand in 1885 from a perspective of more than thirty years. Some of the work is based on the diaries of his wife Annie, whose pocket book he refers to and quotes frequently.[58] How much, however, cannot be entirely resolved as these diaries have since been lost.

In 1884, Merton and his wife embarked on a lengthy trip to Australia and New Zealand. The section describing the New Zealand visit occupies some sixty pages. It can be roughly divided into three sections: the first gives a general background to New Zealand and describes the early part of the trip from Dunedin to Auckland; the second describes their impressions of Ohinemutu, Rotorua and Te Wairoa; and the third describes the visit to the Pink and White Terraces and the area known as the Hot Lakes. It is clear that the highlight of the New Zealand tour was the visit to the new tourist destination of Te Wairoa, where Russell-Cotes witnessed a 'Haka dance'[59] in Hinemihi, and viewed the Terraces. The visit of Annie and Merton Russell-Cotes took place at the end of the first period of tourism at the Hot Lakes, one that lasted from the 1870s to 1886, when Mount Tarawera erupted. The Russell-Cotes followed the same itinerary as other earlier visitors. Te Wairoa was the location from which the trips to Tarawera and the Terraces and the Hot Lakes began.

Annie's diary for Wednesday, 27 May 1885 is quoted by Merton: 'On our way from Tauranga by coach to Ohinemutu. Dr. Ginders [the Government official] says the Maoris have what they call a "Whari-puni".'[60] Annie's description tends towards ethnographic detail. She comments on housing and other buildings (*whari-puni* and storehouse), clothing, and customs such as riding – 'the Maoris are great riders' – and playing with an oval-shaped ball, composed of a bullrush tied to a string about four inches long. 'They play by throwing it first on to one shoulder and then another, clapping their arms and making a regular beating noise something similar to the beat the niggers [*sic*] make with their feet'.[61] Annie mentions some 'Fiji mats' and some 'Belgian blankets'. One 'very handsome woman' found baking scones 'kindly offered us some'.[62]

Figure 4.3 Annie and Merton Russell-Cotes on the occasion of their Golden Wedding.
Photo by kind permission of the Russell-Cotes Art Gallery and Museum, Bournemouth.

From Tauranga the Russell-Cotes travelled to 'the old native village of Ohinemutu'
near Rotorua. Merton describes:

> The 'whari-puni' (literally, the 'sleeping house') [which] is the public hall
> of the 'hapu' or sub-tribe, where visitors from other tribes are entertained
> and where important meetings of all kinds are held . . . Horrible goggle-
> eyed monsters – the ancestors of the tribes – writhe and twist and twine
> amongst each other with bewildering intricacy of design, whilst in odd
> juxtaposition with such uncouth conceptions may be seen a simple and

tasteful scroll border, rivalling in design and execution the delicate tracery of an Etruscan vase. Every beam, indeed every available wooden surface, is rich with massive carving or intricate tattooing.[63]

Russell-Cotes uses some of the negative language employed by some of his fellow English visitors in the 1880s, which has been described in Chapter 3,[64] but also adds some appreciative comments. The writing in the book as a whole is inconsistent; it speaks in many different voices, and more than one style can be found in the writing. There is a marked difference in tone, for example, between the references to 'horrible goggle-eyed monsters', above, and the excerpts quoted by Merton from Annie's diary, who appears to have a genuine interest in what she sees. She has obviously discussed the ways of the people she is observing with the government official:

> The Maoris are beginning to put glass in their windows at Ohinemutu, where we saw some women squatting and washing clothes in the warm lake; no need there to make fires or boil water for any purpose . . . When a chief dies they hold a Tangi or Wake, much like the Irish Wake. They send for the neighbouring tribes, and the body is kept until these all gather together . . . they make a present to the tribes who come to the funeral, and my informant told me . . . A grand procession goes out to meet the visiting tribes, the young girls dressed in white . . .[65]

The greatest detail of the New Zealand account is reserved for the visit to Te Wairoa. By the time of the Russell-Cotes' visit, Te Wairoa had become the centre of a busy tourist trade. The Reverend Seymour Spencer had established an Anglican mission here in 1844, introducing European agricultural and horticultural techniques.[66] During the 1860s, the settlement developed as the main point from which to service tourist visits to the White and Pink Terraces. The tourist experience was managed carefully and very successfully by the local Maori tribe, Ngati Tuhourangi, who owned the land. The members of the tribe controlled access to the Terraces, using their own whale boats. The young men were rostered on the boats,[67] while the women acted as guides. Fees were charged for being rowed the nine miles from Te Wairoa to Rotomahana; stops were made on the journey at Moura, where food was bought. Fees were also charged at the Terraces, for making drawings or photographs,[68] and for specially arranged performances of the *haka* in Hinemihi.[69]

Merton Russell-Cotes describes what he calls 'the Haka dance performed by the natives of the village. It is similar to the Hulu-Hulu dance in Hawaii.'[70] He devotes three pages to describing the *haka* that he observed within the 'whari', which is worth quoting at length:

> At Wairoa,[71] the staple amusement is the Haka dance performed by natives of the village . . . The young men and women retire to their toilet, and come forth by and by arrayed in 'evening costume' – the women dressed in white, with a shawl or sash of some gay colour wrapped artistically around them, and the young men in tweed trousers and cotton or woolen shirts! The master of Ceremonies was a powerful and athletic

young fellow of twenty-six or thereabouts, who made all the arrangements of the dance, assigned the dancers their places, indicated the proper gestures, and conducted the music.

Presently the dancers, thirty men and thirty women, trooped in and arranged themselves in two rows along the vacant side of the building – the women in front and the men behind. They seemed to be arranged pretty well in order of merit, the best dancers being towards the top of the whari, so that their virtues are brought well under the eyes of the visitors, the row tailed off towards the door, where the worst dancers were out of the direct line of vision and veiled in a judicious gloom. The dancers in their places, a short time of preliminary chatter followed, and whilst the women adjusted a scarf or put some other finishing touch to their toilet, we had time to observe the extraordinary variety of physiognomy in the row of brown beauties. Some were of large and masculine build, but comely, tattooed on the nether lip, and if it had not been for the laughter in the face, looking somewhat fierce – such women, one would think, as in bygone times might have taken or held a pah, when pahs were worth the taking. Some were delicately formed – some even fragile and approaching the European standard of beauty, wearing a look of sadness in the rare moments when the face was in repose – but for the most part seeming to enter into the work of the evening with zest and spirit. Towards the tail end the beauties were very decidedly *passées*, and appeared to be worn out with family cares and to find but little joy in their mirth. Some of the dancers looked self-conscious and modest, some looked arch, some had the brazen look begotten of many hakas, whilst some were so absorbed in the business of the evening as to be oblivious of everything else.

The MC straightened himself up – all eyes looked to him: he raised a low whining chant in monotone: bodies and limbs and facial muscles began to move in a series of rhythmical contortions. Ever and anon the chant of the leader swelled into a hoarse and guttural chorus, ending in a series of indescribable sounds, which seemed to come from far down the throat, half sighs, half grunts. Gradually the motions quickened. The bodies of the dancers turned now to this side, now to that, but always in a state of intense agitation, seemed to be animated by one spirit, so perfectly simultaneous were their gestures. The arms, moving in rhythmic motion to the chant, went through a variety of pantomimes. At one time they moved as if working a pair of oars; then the arms worked as if holding the reins of a galloping horse, and then again they were held rigid as a bar of iron – only the fingers quivering so rapidly that their outlines became blurred.

. . . Now they stood, now on their knees, now bent to this side, now to that; their voices became louder, harsher, and full of a fierce glee; their heads wagged violently; their tongues lolled from their mouths; nothing of the eye but the white was visible, and the whole face had a look truly diabolical. This extraordinary dance then came to an end, with a rapid and telling pas de deux between the leader and premiere danseuse.[72]

91

Hinemihi meeting house is the context within which a complex and multi-layered colonial ritual is played out. The description of the performance of the *haka* in Hinemihi shows Tuhourangi adapting their cultural forms to meet the requirements of tourism. These adaptions proceeded rapidly through the late nineteenth century. By the beginning of the twentieth century, dancers were performing wearing the *piupiu*, the flax skirt that had already become the 'traditional' dress of Maori, and were using a limited range of 'traditional' artefacts such as *poi* balls and *taiaha*. This would represent a move 'from clothes to costume'.[73]

In 1886 in Hinemihi, the *haka* was not as developed or stabilised a tourist commodity as it later became. The clothes worn were European rather than 'traditional Maori'. *Poi* were not used. Although later to become almost synonymous with the tourist rendering of the *haka* and other dances, *poi* were not introduced into the thermal regions until 1901.[74]

Russell-Cotes describes the performance at a level of detail that is surprising after more than thirty years. Perhaps he used some of his wife's notes, or some other source.[75] The description, presented as his own whatever its origin, suggests Merton's involvement in and relish of the experience. He appears to approve the levels of skill involved, and the flair of the dancers, but some of his descriptions use language that represent negative stereotypes. Faces and bodies move in 'rhythmical contortions'; the sounds are 'a low whining chant', 'a hoarse and gutteral chorus', 'loud', 'harsh' and 'indescribable'. Tongues 'loll'. Faces are 'truly diabolical'.

The account of the visit to the thermal regions is written (or assembled from a range of sources) as a tourist account. Passing through the area, the outward appearances of the people observed are described, as are the main sites and main tourist activities – travelling to the Lakes and seeing the *haka* in Hinemihi. The account is, as would be expected, from an outsider perspective – there is little appreciation of the cultural or economic situation of Maori in general, or Te Arawa in particular.

The performance of the *haka* must be seen in the context of a struggle to maintain some control over lives that were becoming more and more difficult to manage. The growth of the settler society, the establishment of a capitalist market economy, and the resulting colonialist hunger for both territorial and cultural control produced a crisis in Maori society. In 1886, the community at Te Wairoa was in turmoil as new values and new expectations, born of too rapid a move into a cash economy, clashed with long-established, much older forms of organisation.[76] The involvement in the tourist industry that this event in Hinemihi represents was a moment of vulnerable and fragile success that would be fractured on the eruption of Tarawera.

Writing the culture of the self

Makereti's book was written, as was Merton's, during the 1920s, and it describes the same part of New Zealand as that discussed above.[77] Her perspective is markedly different from that of Russell-Cotes. *The Old-time Maori* describes the traditional culture of Maori based on Makereti's own experience with her 'old people'. The book takes the form of an ethnography, but T. K. Penniman, her editor, tells us that:

> the village, was home . . . The genealogy of the village is her own genealogy, the record of marriages and births and the chanting of the Tohi rite over the children, the collection and cultivation of food, all represent the life of her own relatives as observed in her childhood and later years. The house was her own house, the objects which she described were her own.[78, 79]

This account can be compared with that of Merton Russell-Cotes, who visited Whakarewarewa in 1885, where he must have seen some of Makereti's family. Where Russell-Cotes observed from an external uninvolved position, Makereti's account is a very personalised one. Makereti is describing her life, her family, her relatives and the ways in which they organised their lives at around 1880 and earlier.

Makereti does not describe the ways that the tribe had adapted to cope with colonialism, and specifically tourism. She focused on older ways which she experienced as a young child living in remote circumstances with her uncle and aunt. She describes, from lived experience and deep cultural knowledge, a vibrant but straightforward and credible everyday life, a competent response to the environmental, geographical and social context of the time and place.

Makereti writes in part from a woman's point of view. She gives a great deal of detail of marriage customs and matters to do with conception, contraception, childbirth, feeding, weaning and caring for babies and bringing up and teaching boys and girls. She talks about illness and the epidemics brought by European contact, and about food. She writes: 'Much nonsense has been written about the starving Maori . . . I am writing enough in this chapter . . . to show that the Maori always had plenty of food . . .'[80] Detailed accounts of fishing, gathering fruit and berries, planting vegetables, and storing, preparing and cooking food follow. However, she also talks about matters which are not exclusively to do with women, such as building the carved houses, and weaponry.

The book engages constantly with European accounts of Maori life. Cook and Crozet are quoted describing the abundance of fish caught by 'the Indians', as Cook described Maori.[81] This passes without comment, but in other parts of the book, Makereti is very critical of people who pass judgement without fully understanding the cultural context: 'A person has to . . . understand all the Maori's customs, knowing why he does certain things and not others, before he can sit down and write about the Maori. Otherwise his criticisms lack understanding.'[82] 'The early writers spoke of things that they did not understand . . .' The *pakeha* did not know the customs or the language of the Maori, and judged the Maori according to European customs: 'The ignorant pakeha man or woman . . . often drew the wrong conclusions . . .'[83] An example is given: '*Herehere*, prisoners of war, are often spoken of mistakenly as slaves. In many cases these prisoners were men of high standing and exceedingly good looking. They were treated well by the chief, and indeed, often married into the tribe.'[84]

Makereti quotes an early writer (Nicholas, 1814–15), who is critical of the fact that plots for growing food were not always close to the villages. This he sees as a sign of 'insecurity' and 'barbarism'. In response to this, Makereti lists, for the next three and a half pages, the sites where vegetables were grown by her *hapu*, and the names of the tribes who worked these plots, such as Ngati Uruhina, N. Wahiao, and N. Hinemihi, all of the *hapu* of Tuhourangi. 'In the vicinity of Te Wairoa', she says, 'we had the following kumara[85] cultivations: at Punaromia, Opekarangi'. 'Perhaps I have said enough', she says, 'to show that other writers have not known or have failed to note the extensive plantations of the Maori, and so have failed to give a just account of their economic organisation.'[86]

In discussing the initial encounters between European traders and Maori, Makereti tells how some of the sailors who deserted their ships and wanted to settle down in a new land would be claimed by Maori as 'their pakeha', thinking that this would help in dealing with European traders. Some of the whalers who visited in the very earliest days shocked Maori people (even though, as Makereti says, 'he was called a savage'). Makereti condemns the 'drunken orgies, debauchery, filthy language, immorality, and vileness' of these sailors.[87] Sometimes the references are more humorous. 'Captain Cook is credited with having been the first to introduce the pig, and often when going on a wild pig hunt, people say: "We are going to hunt for Captain Cook."'[88]

Russell-Cotes' account focused on a lengthy description of the 'Haka dance'. Makereti had taken up the issue of the nature of the *haka* by responding to critical letters in New Zealand newspapers at the turn of the century.[89] She mentions *hakas* a number of times in her book, and from her references it is clear that a number of different dances, songs and events might equally be given this name. Thus, when talking about marriage customs, at the end of the ceremonies 'the entertainment began with the tangata whenua[90] doing poi dances and hakas'.[91] She also mentions *haka* which she and her playmates made up as children. These are clearly songs.[92]

She describes in detail a *haka* that she observed as a child on the occasion of a raiding party to avenge adultery (*taua puremu*):

> Long before daylight the stamping of feet could be heard keeping time to the takitaki, the leading song of a woman who led the taua party of a hundred people or more. There were the women in front. Then came the injured husband who was naked, with only two long plaits of torori (plaited tobacco leaf) hanging in front suspended from a cord of fibre which circled his waist. His face was traced with charcoal, he wore feathers in his hair, and in his right hand was his patu pounamu. The women had their skirts tucked up above their knees, and as they led the haka taua, it was a terrifying sight, yet a wonderful one.
> With movements of the body, pukana (eyes rolling) and tongue out, the taua party advance, all the while doing the haka movements led by the women, keeping rhythmic time with their feet and hands, and joining in

words repeated in answer to their leader – words appropriate to the hara (sin) committed.[93]

There is a considerable reference in the book to material culture, such as *patu pounamu* (short-handled greenstone weapon), *kotiate* (short-handled bone weapon), cloaks of *korowai*, *kahikiwi* and other feathers, and *whariki* (floor-mats).[94] Frequently these are pictured, with Makereti's own possessions being used as illustrations: a *kinikini* cloak, made from the fibre of phormium tenax, is shown, for example.[95] In describing *hinaki* (eel traps), Makereti says she was so impressed by some she had seen at Taupo that she had a small one made for her own collection.[96] She refers on occasions to items held in the Pitt Rivers Museum and the Auckland Museum. The book is illustrated by informative drawings of the tools used, meeting houses and their parts, and there are a large number of photographs of Makereti, her collections and her family.

Fragmentation and dispersal

The Old-time Maori can be seen as a process of 'writing back', of engaging with colonial texts.[97] Writing at the intellectual heart of the Empire, at Oxford University, for a degree in anthropology, Makereti nevertheless engages with colonial writers, addressing their misconceptions vigorously. The book is a counter-ethnography, an account of Maori culture that shows and explains the depth and sophistication of the actions and events that colonial writers observed and judged from positions of ignorance and misunderstanding.

Makereti 'writes back' as an *indigène*,[98] but also as a woman. Where male anthropologists tended to focus on the events connected to men and call these symptomatic of the group studied, Makereti focuses much of her work on the concerns of women. She highlights the power of the women in the tribe, for example in relation to the account of the *haka*. Where male anthropologists might have either failed to observe or omitted from their accounts these activities of women, she points them out. Where male writers might observe men and extrapolate that their customs pertain to the group as a whole, Makereti clearly distinguishes men and women, boys and girls.

In England during the 1920s, the book, the images and the objects had the potential to make up a seamless whole. The book was written around the collections, which were used as illustrations and examples. Makereti's own image and those of some of her family formed part of the narrative. The objects, images and words could have come together to create a meaningful space of signification, where each object, each image and each word was fully understood by the writer/collector and where each deepened the understanding of the other. The signified space would have been mentally and emotionally understood as part of Makereti's homeland,[99] with the writer/collector deeply embedded in both her text and her collections, which formed part of her domestic landscape, and which were used to talk about and enact her culture.

This holistic and rounded world of meaning, however, was illusionary. The complete space of signification that was desired was never fully completed; its conditions of construction were frequently adverse and effectively prevented its complete realisation. A position between clearly defined boundaries, such as those of the life-ways from which Makereti constituted her existence, is not a strong one. Although a liminal position such as this enables the creation of unique possibilities, this very uniqueness means a lack of underlying resources, no strong supporting social structures, and few people on hand to advise, to contribute, to provide a nurturing framework.

Following the end of her marriage, and her move to a smaller place, Makereti no longer had the room to house all her things[100] and began to think about selling them.[101] She had had to leave Tuhoromatakaka behind in the former marital home. Still dependent on her former husband, she had very limited funds.[102] By the end of the 1920s she was suffering from severe muscular rheumatism.[103, 104] She died from a heart-attack on 16 April 1930, a few days before she was due to present her manuscript to Oxford University. Her manuscript was incomplete, and her book was not published until 1938.[105] By then, her collections were dispersed.

Makereti had given several items to the Pitt Rivers Museum from as early as 1921.[106] In 1923 she had written to T. E. Donne of the New Zealand Tourist Department, saying that she wanted to sell all her collection together, as a collection, and that she would like the New Zealand government to have it.[107] Some cloaks were given to T. E. Donne, perhaps with the charge to take them home. He gave them to the Museum of New Zealand in 1977.[108] Her son was at a loss as to what to do with her collection after her death. At the end of May 1930, he wrote to T. E. Donne: 'With regard to my mother's Maori collection I do not know what she was going to do with it. I have the whole collection here and am prepared to part with part of it if you can arrange it.'[109] Towards the end of the year, the Pitt Rivers Museum bought, for £10, some of the smaller carvings.[110]

What became of the house Tuhoromatakaka and the other larger carvings brought to London in 1911 and used as part of the model village? The story is unclear and difficult to unravel. After the exhibition, the carvings had been moved to Oddington Grange.[111] After Makereti's death, they were moved to a neighbouring farm, Barndom, where the owner agreed to store them until Makereti's son could move them. With a change of owners, the identity and value of the carvings was lost. Some were piled in a field, some put in a loft over a barn, and one was built into the walls of a farm shed. They were recognised in 1947 by Miss Beatrice Blackwood, Assistant Curator at the Pitt Rivers, who had known Makereti. T. K. Penniman wrote to Makereti's son, William, by then living at Whakarewarewa and using his Maori name, Te Anoui; he had married Rangitiania Ratema, a well-known guide on the thermal reserve.[112] Shortly afterwards the carvings were returned to Makereti's family, and were taken into the charge of Rangi Dennan.[113] Almost certainly the ones carved by Rangi's grandfather, Tene Waitere, for Makereti's house Tuhoromatakaka, they were used on the front and inside of a new Hinemihi, built at Ngapuna in 1962.[114] On a stone by the side of the third Hinemihi reads the legend:

> A token of gratitude to the elders of Ngati Whakane for the gifted land that they gave to the survivors of the eruption of Tarawera on June 10th 1886.

Russell-Cotes and his collections

During the visit to New Zealand, Merton and Annie Russell-Cotes acquired some material for what Merton calls 'my wife's' museum. Merton mentions several stuffed kiwis, *kauri* gum specimens, stuffed parrots, and the string of shells that Annie collected.[115] He also later mentions a 'Maori marriage mat [cloak], that had belonged to King Tawphio [*sic*], the last King of the Maoris, composed of blue and white peacock's feathers'.[116] The first curator of the museum, Richard Quick, describes one or two other items that were brought back from New Zealand by Sir Merton Russell-Cotes in 1885 (he does not mention Annie). One, described in 1923, is a carved wooden figure of Te Amo, ancestor of Ngatitu Wharetoa.[117] Another, described in 1926, is 'a fine mere "Pounams" of polished jade or greenstone' which was purchased by Sir Merton in New Zealand in 1885 (again no mention of Annie).[118] Three other *mere* are described at this time, one of which, made of whalebone, is described as having belonged to Rangatira Taupopoki.[119] This was, in fact, Makereti's uncle, Mika Taupopoki, who had come to England with her for the Coronation Exhibition in 1911.

Material quickly began to be donated to the museum to join the existing Maori material. Mrs S. Beulah Burton donated four paintings by Goldie, some grass waist ornaments and a pair of decorated paddles.[120] In 1925, Mrs George W. Gray donated a small canoe model, a paddle and a drum; in 1927, Brigadier-General Crofton Atkins gave a carved wooden figure; and in 1928 Mrs H. D. Faith donated a carved wooden feather box.[121] In 1928 the Russell-Cotes *Bulletin* illustrated an unusual small free-standing carved wooden figure, castrated, with human hair attached, but it is uncertain when this object joined the collection.[122] Little seems to have been known about the figure as the article it illustrates discusses Maori culture in general, with a focus on tattooing.

The collection had been acquired by the Russell-Cotes, on their visit to New Zealand, in a piecemeal and fragmented fashion. Merton does not describe in his book any concerted or systematic effort to bring material together, or to collect material that had special meaning. It is clear from the purchase of the *mere* and the probable purchase of the carved figure Te Amo, that material that was recognisably 'Maori' was desired, but other less significant items, such as the *kauri* gum specimens and the string of shells, were also collected. From the evidence that is available, it would seem that the collecting was spasmodic and opportunistic. The resulting assemblage of material had no internal cohesion as a collection. No attempt seems to have been made to document the circumstances of collection, other than the small clues given in Merton's autobiography.

In the context of the other collections that the Russell-Cotes possessed, the Maori collection was small and insignificant. The art collection was far more important, in terms of monetary value, social significance in Britain, and of interest to museum and gallery visitors. However, although small, the New Zealand collection remained together as a collection, and acted as a magnet for the donation of other Maori objects.

Russell-Cotes' collections were displayed in the opulent mansion East Cliff Hall, built during the final years of the nineteenth century. It was built initially as a private residence, but was quickly adapted as a museum, and in 1908, seven years after the completion of the house, Annie presented it and its contents to Bournemouth to use as a museum, although she and Merton continued to live there until their deaths. Merton added an endowment to pay for a curator and the upkeep of the museum. Later, three additional galleries for art were also donated. These had been built and paid for by Annie, at a cost of £5,000, during the First World War. She also purchased the freehold of the house before handing it over to the town.[123]

The Scottish baronial architectural style of the house perhaps referred back in time to the ambitions of the young man in Glasgow, but it was built with the most innovative heating, lighting and secondary glazing systems of the period. The internal spaces were lavish and exotic. The hall was constructed as an Italian courtyard complete with a pond, palm trees and top lighting. Objects were grouped in geographic and cultural sets; the Maori canoe model sat on top of a case of birds from New Zealand. Groups of objects from other cultural areas such as Russia stood nearby. The hall was overlooked by a balcony with fine cloaks draped over the banisters; some of the Maori collections[124] were also exhibited here in a display case. The drawing room was richly decorated with patterned wallpaper, animal skin rugs, elaborate gilt furnishings and ornamented display cases. Paintings were displayed throughout the house, and formed a rich backdrop to the souvenirs and curios which presented to the visitor in one visual sweep the image of the Russell-Cotes as well-travelled discerning collectors.

Both Annie and Merton had spent time and effort in pursuing civic careers, and although some of their work had not been welcomed, they became accepted as philanthropists within the town.[125] Part of this philanthropic work was embodied in their collections and museum. Merton's picture touring scheme to municipal museums in the north of England was innovative, and although the scheme enabled him to act as philanthropist, art connoisseur and man of taste,[126] this innovation should be acknowledged. East Cliff Hall, a house-museum, was unusual among British local authority museums. Most municipal art museums were founded between the 1860s and the outbreak of the First World War; prior to this, museums with scientific, natural history or archaeological collections had been established. Opening in 1922 as a museum with mixed collections, the Russell-Cotes Art Gallery and Museum was a late addition to the many already established across the country; as a house that had been built for domestic purposes, but also for the display of art and other collections, it was highly individual. Although Bournemouth could not be regarded as a deprived part of the country, there is some evidence that the Russell-Cotes saw their museum as a morally improving space and a site for social improvement. This view would have linked them to the radical social reformers inspired by Ruskin such as Samuel and Henrietta Barnett and T. C. Horsfall.[127]

The Russell-Cotes Museum, Bournemouth opened officially in 1922 after Merton's death (Annie had died in 1921). A Resolution of Council recorded the event:

> In recognition and appreciation of their great generosity and unselfish local patriotism in conjointly presenting to the Corporation, as a free gift, their valuable residence, East Cliff Hall, together with a splendid collection of pictures, curios, bric-a-brac, sculpture and other art property therein, for use as an Art Gallery and Museum for the enjoyment of the public of Bournemouth and visitors to the town, in perpetuity, and further, to signify the Council's feeling that so public-spirited an act of liberality entitles them to the lasting good will and regard of their fellow townspeople, and also to have their names recorded high upon the scroll of those the Council and the town have been proud to honour.[128]

The private and the public, the past and the present

Writing and collecting are two forms of the production of the self. The comparison of the collections and the books of Makereti and Merton Russell-Cotes reveals sharp contrasts.

Makereti's book and her collections formed a seamless whole; she, herself, was one with her objects and her words. These together created boundaries within which was a secure, complete mental world of the self, pictured, materialised, imagined, inscribed. Makereti's collections were drawn from and formed part of the lived context of the everyday; she kept them around her and used them in her work and her studies. The collections were not, while in her possession, set aside as exotic ethnographica, but referred to experiences that had been part of her childhood. The specific objects referenced the culture lived by the child[129] that later would be reconstructed and reinvigorated by the young woman. While a mature student, Makereti would review and assess this culture, repositioning it to strike against the colonial perspectives exemplified by some of the writing of Russell-Cotes and other writers.

However, this fragile unity was achieved against a context of 'othering'; both Makereti's life and work were positioned as 'other'. As a well-educated and strong Maori woman, she was not always regarded as acceptable by the elders of the tribe; she spoke when perhaps she should have kept silent. As Maori, she was not the same as the other women in the Oxfordshire countryside; she had after all been placed on display as part of one of the 'native villages' at the Coronation Exhibition.[130] As a woman writing anthropology, her fellow writers on Maori culture were all male; women's insights have not always been recognised or welcomed by male anthropologists.[131]

Collecting is one form of producing a lasting personal memorial, especially when the collection is kept intact and made public. Makereti was not in a position to transform her possessions into a public collection, although her letters suggest that she would have liked to have done so. Merton Russell-Cotes, however, made certain that his collections were made publicly available during his lifetime; he and his wife ensured that they were accepted into the public domain and would remain there as a memorial.

East Cliff Hall was built as a public space from the start; its lavish decoration and furnishings worked best as a public spectacle, and parts of the house were used as both public display areas and private living spaces at the same time.[132] The collections, combined with the opulent public spaces, confirmed Merton Russell-Cotes, the father and husband, as a benevolent patriarch. Displaying his collections enabled Merton Russell-Cotes to claim a personal identity as a learned and tasteful connoisseur. A glamorous provenance mattered to him,[133] although this led to some rather dubious purchases.[134] By assembling what he constructed as a complete and unified whole from disparate fragments from diverse cultures, Russell-Cotes surrounded himself with a glittering *bricolage* that promoted his own sense of self-worth and personal identity. Living in the public eye, in a building destined to be used for the benefit of the town, with an endowment for its upkeep, meant that Russell-Cotes and his wife spent the final years of their lives as publicly acknowledged local benefactors. They (and especially he) took their place among the other dignitaries and worthies, and his name became embedded in local knowledge, structures of merit, and, through the structure of the museum itself, in the local urban landscape. The museum was used as a technology of memorialisation for the self as premier citizen – high on the town scroll of honour. This collection retained its unity and therefore its power to assert and consolidate the memory of Merton Russell-Cotes long after his death.

Annie's position in this story is a difficult one to unravel. Merton Russell-Cotes would not have been so successful in achieving his social ambitions had he not made an advantageous marriage. His wife was intelligent and supportive, and although at times Merton treated his children very shabbily (giving them gifts from his collections and then demanding their return for example) she seems not to have wavered in her loyalty. It was Annie's father's money that enabled the purchase of the Bath Hotel, the vast bulk of the collections, and almost certainly the building of East Cliff Hall. Annie was the more serious and systematic collector, with a keener interest in natural and social history. The museum is referred to by Merton more than once as 'my wife's museum', and may well have been her idea in the first place. Annie's diaries formed the basis for much of Merton's autobiography, but they have disappeared. Annie's contribution to the construction of the Russell-Cotes phenomenon was considerable, but shortly after the appointment of Richard Quick, the first curator, references to 'Merton Russell-Cotes and his collecting' render her invisible. Annie has remained largely invisible in the museum since then, although recent research carried out for the complete refurbishment of East Cliff Hall in 1999–2000 has partly enabled recognition of her role.

The meanings of the artefacts in the Russell-Cotes collection were ambiguous. They signified most strongly in relation to taste, style and aesthetics. They looked impressive, unusual and expensive, and were laid out as visual culture for visual consumption.[135] But in cultural terms they were poorly understood either as individual items or as linked pieces.[136] The *mere* cited as belonging to Mita Taupopoki, Makereti's uncle, was only one among a small number of similar objects. There is no evidence that it had special significance to Merton or Annie because of the association to its former owner. There is no evidence that a family link was made between the *mere* and the photograph of Makereti also in the collection. The objects had been bought because they had presented themselves as available at a time when buying was possible. For Merton Russell-Cotes, they acted to sustain a perception of the self, in that they suggested sophistication, and thereby offered social standing and prestige. The emotional or cultural investment was not in these objects alone; any other objects that acted as evidence of travel, wealth and ostensible connoisseurship would have done.

Makereti could not find the means to hold her collection together. On her death it was dispersed. Today, however, her life and her possessions are treasured as *Maori taonga*. Her mother's cloak, now belonging to Te Papa Tongarewa/National Museum of New Zealand, was included in an exhibition, 'Ngā Puna Roimata o te Arawa', which celebrated the art of three women of Te Arawa.[137] The exhibition provided the opportunity to review some of the functions of museums in New Zealand in the colonial period, when they were described as places of 'death, of bones, of plunder and relics and pillage'.[138] The exhibition was the first in the museum to show weaving and photographic portraits from a specific region exhibited within its own tribal context.[139] The curator describes how the Maori *taonga* often have limited recorded histories, but how they wait, in museums, for the reunion with their people who can bring them to life with *kōrero* and *whakapapa*.[140]

At the Russell-Cotes Museum in Bournemouth, the values of the founders are no longer taken for granted, but are instead subject to assessment and interrogation. As the Museum undergoes extensive reorganisation, a critical and reflexive stance is being adopted. The physical workings of the house and the conceptual structures and values on which the collection and its original display were based are equally being laid bare. In recent years, the collections have, as we have seen, been used to consider issues of representation, questions of the construction of identity, and to stimulate reflection about where objects come from and what should be done with them.

This case-study shows how collections of objects which may have superficial resemblances may have been brought together for widely different reasons. Objects of similar types may be understood in very different ways, depending on the position of the knowing subject. Collections may be used to construct identity, and, as this case-study shows, these identities are likely to be more firmly established and endure over a longer period of time where there is access to economic, social and cultural resources.

Objects can be placed within multiple frames of reference, some of which may become public visual statements in the form of museums. Access to resources, such as those necessary to establish a museum and to maintain collections, is affected by class, gender and ethnicity. Visual narratives, if once made public, may achieve an authority which may remain in place for long years. Those visual statements which are not made public may not be sustained for long. However, over time, and through space, frameworks for the social meanings change; the physicality of objects may resist destruction to remain open to being reinvested with new significance and incorporated into new narratives.

5

Objects and interpretive processes

Subject and object

Chapters 3 and 4 have suggested that there is no one way in which objects can be interpreted. The meanings of objects are constructed from the position from which they are viewed. The gaze of the knowing subject,[1] the individual standing in a particular place within history and culture, focuses on those aspects of the object which s/he is able to recognise and thereby grasp both visually and conceptually. The appearance of the object, how it looks and is perceived, varies according to how it is understood.[2] Meanings are plural rather than singular. A considerable amount of evidence has been presented to support these claims. But questions remain about how this works. What are the interpretive processes used to understand objects? Do they explain how it is that different subjects interpret objects in different ways? A great deal has been written about interpreting text, and some of this is relevant, but in the following discussion it will become clear how the interpretation of visual culture differs from the interpretation of texts.

This chapter analyses the processes of understanding through which objects are made meaningful. The theme has run through the earlier chapters, but in an implicit way. Here I wish to concentrate on the relationship between subject and object, between viewer and viewed. I consider, firstly, how objects are imbued with meaning-functions within everyday life and, secondly, focus on the relationship between individual interpretive processes and those of 'interpretive communities'.

My focus is on the communicative characteristics of material things, and how they are set to work to convey ideas and to motivate attention. Objects are not the same as words. Objects have material elements; they may, for example, be made of wood, and be of a certain height or colour. But I do not see 'objects' as 'brute-data' or irreducible facts.[3] It is not possible to grasp or apprehend these material elements outside an interpretive framework; equally, however, the material character of the object sets its own limits to the meanings that can be produced. Objects are sites at which discursive formation intersects with material properties.[4]

This chapter focuses on the encounter between object and viewer; these encounters are sometimes but not always in museums. The next chapter will address the conditions for interpretation within museums through analysing the encounter between museum visitors and museum displays.

What is an 'object'?

We are surrounded by objects at all times, among which we live, work and take our leisure. They indicate how we live, what we do, and who we would like to think we are. But what does the word 'object' mean? Are all things objects? Is an object something made by people as opposed to something made by nature? Is it something three-dimensional rather than flat? The terms 'object', 'artefact' and 'specimen' have all been used. Do they refer to the same kinds of things? In addition, the expressions 'material culture' and 'visual culture' have been used. How do they relate to this study? The ambiguous and overlapping meanings of all these terms indicate a terrain whose features are only just becoming clear. In addition, each of these expressions carries with it a freight of assumptions and each suggests to its users a suite of associated ideas and activities. An examination of some of these terms and their fields of analysis will clear the ground for the work of this chapter.

Chambers Dictionary gives seven definitions for the word 'object'. The first three are the most important for our purposes here. The first definition is perhaps the most obvious: an object is 'a material thing that can be seen or touched'. It is in this common-or-garden sense that the word is mainly used in this book. However, this is not as straightforward as it might at first appear, and the second and third definitions of the term indicate some of the complications. The second definition is 'an aim or purpose'; and the third, 'a person or thing to which action, feelings or thoughts are directed'.[5] An 'object', therefore, may be a thing, an intention, or a target for feelings or actions. Although the dictionary separates out these definitions, in practice, at least in relation to objects, they are intertwined – things do not exist outside interpretations of their meaning and significance. Objects are always targets for feelings and actions; their interpretation is embedded in already existing experience and knowledge. This phenomenon is a major theme of this chapter, and indeed of the book as a whole.

The use of the word 'object' by museum staff raises some interesting issues. There are major differences in its use by different categories of staff. 'Object' is a term rarely used by museum curators, who generally refer to 'the collections' as a whole, or to parts of the collection, perhaps identified by the curator whose responsibility they are – 'Pam's collections', for example, might be the decorative art objects. Specific references might also be made to collections by type and/or by date: the art collection; the sixteenth-century paintings. 'Collection' indicates a group of objects, a whole that has been assembled for some purpose. The purpose of being together implies a rationale and a guiding sensibility – 'collection' implies 'collector', and this is another way of talking about objects, with reference to the name of the collector (the Mayer collection, for example), or the name of the subject of the collection (the Irving collection).

Museum educators, or those discussing the work of museum educators, do use the word 'object'.[6] Their focus on objects (as opposed to texts) as the basis for pedagogic methods, especially for children, may be located in relation to the nineteenth-century context of object-teaching in schools.[7] Object-teaching was a major form of pedagogy in Europe and North America in the second half of the nineteenth century, at a time when the target of knowledge was the understanding, through observation, of the natural world. This was part of an attempt to establish a reliable, objective knowledge, a universal truth, that set aside all that could not be verified through observation.

The aim of object-teaching in the late nineteenth century sounds familiar to museum educators today:

> Object-teaching has for its purpose a thorough development of all the child's faculties, and their proper deployment in the acquisition of knowledge . . . Its purpose is not the attainment of facts, nor the cultivation of language as an end; but the development, to a vigorous and healthy action, of the child's powers of getting and using knowledge . . .[8]

The pedagogic methods deployed also sound familiar to today's museum educators:

> The first education should be of the perceptions, then of memory, then of the understanding, then of the judgement.[9]

> Object-teaching prepares the learner's mind by development begun through sense-perceptions, and continued by observation and reflection, to understand clearly the important facts concerning things and acts, and their relation to spoken and written language.[10]

The use of the senses, followed by observation, reflection and deduction, and finally the placing of the observations and ideas within a contextual framework, remains a standard method of object-teaching within the museum today.[11]

However, the ultimate aim of learning from objects in the late nineteenth century was the understanding of 'classification and science':

> the use of objects, the use of the child's remembered experiences, and the observations of others, which can be learned from books, are all combined for supplying the pupil with complete knowledge of the subject, thus leading to classification and science . . . Object lessons . . . should not cease with early child-hood, but should be so kept up during youth as insensibly to merge into the investigations of the naturalist and the man of science.[12]

This final statement indicates the narrow focus of nineteenth-century object-teaching, and its location within the positivist framework of a rationalist epistemology. As the modern period strove to separate itself from what was seen as an unscientific and unreliable past, so there was an attempt to cut away those aspects of knowledge that were seen as superstitious, subjective, emotive, and, ultimately, unreasonable.[13] Reason, rationality, thus became the new authority,[14] and much of the development of knowledge was carried out through the meticulous study of objects. Object-teaching, in the past, was tied closely to the task of the objectification of experience and the denial of subjectivity. The teaching of science was part of the task of the state in the making ready of the young to take their allotted places in society.

With museum-based object-teaching today, the attraction of working with 'real things' rather than with textbooks[15] can provoke a failure to acknowledge the constructed character of 'the real'. There is a sense in which the relationship between objects and textbooks, conceived as two competing pedagogic methods, is seen as an opposition between the use of primary or secondary sources, with the objects being understood as pieces of unmediated 'reality' and therefore closer to a primary world of evidence.[16] Where the character of the 'evidence' is treated uncritically, there is a danger of objects being expected to have a single unified meaning which teachers transmit to their students.

The term 'object' is complex. It is not used in this study to signify things which stand outside interpretive frameworks. However, this is sometimes the way in which it is understood in everyday use. The closeness of 'object' to 'objective' and 'objectify' reveals the tendency to regard the meanings with which objects may be imbued as emanating from their own physical existences. It is not so long since the truth of the object was taken as a given within the museum: in the museum 'it is the objects which are important: they must speak for themselves'.[17]

Where 'objects' may include natural material, the term 'artefact' has a narrower scope. An artefact is a thing made by people; something which demonstrates skill and human intervention. *Chambers Dictionary* suggests that it is especially those objects which are of architectural or historical interest that are referred to as 'artefacts'. An 'artefact' is also any thing or idea that can be shown to have been deliberately manipulated or self-consciously constructed for a specific purpose, and this can refer to more than merely material entities. The idea of the nation as an artefact was discussed in Chapter 2. 'Artefact' is sometimes also used in a derogatory way to refer to items that have been mass-produced and which are usually cheap (the example given is 'tourist artefacts'[18]).

Artefacts, as things which have been made by people, might be seen as things which are not 'specimens'. The term 'specimen' is generally limited to those things which belong to the natural world. A 'specimen' is the object of the scientific gaze of the natural historian. However, the term is also used to denote a particular type of attention. Chambers Dictionary offers 'a sample or example of something, especially one that will be studied or put in a collection', and reminds us that the root of the word is the Latin *specere*, to see.[19] From this perspective, a specimen is something that will be viewed, studied and collected; presenting anything, even an artefact, as a specimen[20] implies a certain type of attention and calls on a certain kind of legitimation.

There are two major intellectual fields that study objects in ways that may be related to the approach taken in this book. These are material culture studies and visual culture studies. They use different perspectives, and it may be helpful briefly to consider the outline character of each.

Material culture is a newly invigorated intellectual field with a focus on the study of artefacts. Embedded in the late nineteenth century, and in the birth of the human sciences, at first the study of objects as material culture attempted to deploy the approaches and techniques of the natural sciences. In Britain, the work of men such as Pitt-Rivers, Tylor, Haddon and Lubbock, and the emergence of museums of anthropology, resulted in the development of material culture as an epistemological field.[21] Later, in America as well as in Britain, shifts in the academic focus of anthropology and archaeology led to a decline in object-based epistemologies as these disciplines located themselves in the university rather than the museum.[22]

In recent decades, new approaches in material culture studies have produced an impressive and interesting body of work, much of which is in sympathy with the approach taken in this study. Models and approaches for the study of artefacts have been developed. Objects, sometimes seen as commodities, have life-histories,[23] which can be followed and analysed. In order to analyse the meanings with which objects have been imbued, and to integrate this with close study and observation of their concrete, material character, and to account for their historical circulation: 'we have to follow the things themselves, for their meanings are inscribed in their forms, their uses, their trajectories'.[24]

Material culture studies engage with the complex theoretical positions of structuralism, post-structuralism and hermeneutics.[25] This field has been developed both by anthropologists and archaeologists, especially the Cambridge School,[26] and scholars within Museum Studies;[27] it links with the new focus of Consumption Studies.[28]

Material culture largely restricts its focus to three-dimensional objects; to materials and their significance, their relationships to each other, and to the history and geography and social context of the object. Material culture studies, at their present stage of development, have only tangentially been concerned with museums, but these methodologies do offer curators and educators useful methods of researching and analysing their collections.[29] However, these studies do not offer a great deal of assistance with understanding how the analysed and research objects, placed on display, are viewed, interpreted and understood by visitors.[30] They have very little to say about the relationship between objects and museum visitors; museum pedagogy is not their main interest.

Visual culture as a new field of study largely restricts its attention to two-dimensional objects.[31] Visual culture addresses the meaning of the image in film, photography, television, advertising, or painting, and is far less concerned with the physical or material character of that image. Visual culture as an intellectual field is also concerned with display, and with vision and visuality in sites of spectacle; that is, the social frameworks for looking and seeing, the locations where looking and seeing take place, and the relationships between the viewer and the object viewed. Within this, colonialism and its visual and social legacies are important elements. In problematising the relationship between object and viewer, Jenks suggests that the field of visual culture enables the development of a considered relation between 'the analytic and the concrete; a methodic application of theory to empirical aspects of culture'.[32]

Most of the work to date within the parameters of visual culture is rooted in either art history, media studies or sociology,[33] with little work focusing directly on the museum as a scopic site. Further, although the relationships between viewer and viewed are offered as a subject for analysis, this analysis at present is largely positioned at a theoretical level, with much less attention to the empirical study of the meanings of visual culture to spectators in specific sites.

To consider objects from the perspective of visual culture is to focus on the relationship between the object and the subject – the seen and the seer. This focuses directly on processes of interpretation, and on the ways in which objects become meaningful.

Meaningful objects in everyday life

Objects, material things that can be seen and touched, are important in everyday life. Most people have some objects that have become meaningful in their homes or places of work, and apparently, approximately one-third of people in both Britain[34] and America[35] describe themselves as collectors of one sort or another. A review of some accounts of moments of contact between subject and object will reveal some of the unique interpretive characteristics of objects.

Neil Ascherson, visiting the David Livingstone exhibition at the National Portrait Gallery, London, in June 1996 describes a flat-bottomed brass bowl, which 'gleams emptily in its showcase. Once it reflected a Scottish face with a shaggy moustache, and a broad African face with narrow eyes.'[36] Ascherson uses the bowl to reflect on the relationship between Livingstone, the Christian missionary, and Sechele, chief of the Bakwena, a small group living at Kolobeng in what is now Southern Botswana. In 1851, Livingstone gave the bowl as a present to Sechele, his only convert to Christianity. Ascherson reflects on the damage that this conversion effected in this small society that shortly afterwards was destroyed by the Boers. He focuses on the different viewpoints of the two main participants in the narrative that he constructs:

> The African saw human existence as part of a whole creation. Piety meant respect for society as well as individuals, for earth, water, beasts and clouds as well as for a God. The Victorian Scot saw only the desperate need for an individual to cleave to his God, a triumph worth any sacrifice.

> Today, it is Sechele who seems enlightened and Livingstone that seems primitive . . .[37]

Objects enable reflection, and speculation. Philosophical reflection is mobilised by the artefact, and through the observation of the bowl, specific histories are recalled. Objects can bring together and give material form to elusive intangible abstract ideas such as 'home', 'nation', 'sacrifice'. In some ways, it is only through objects that these abstract ideas can be thought of at all; without the concrete material thing, the idea would remain at an abstract individual level and it would be much more difficult to share it. By using the bowl as a focus for the newspaper article, Ascherson facilitates our response to the events described.

Objects may materialise notions of the sacred. They act as powerful metaphors, material representations of complex beliefs and thoughts. The cross of Christians, the Talmud of Jews, the Koran of Muslims and the Eagle Feather of some Canadian First Nations all stand for whole systems of beliefs, rituals and ways of life.

Objects are used to construct identities, on both a personal and a national level. Objects can become invested with deeply held feelings and can symbolise powerful convictions through which life is led. They can express allegiance to specific ideologies, visions or histories. In Japan in the summer of 1999, anxiety over the future of Hinomaru, the rising sun flag, and the anthem *Kimigayo*, both symbols of nationhood, was acute. For many Japanese, the flag and the anthem are, in the words of the *Mainichi* newspaper: 'associated with Japan's emperor-worshipping militaristic past, and therefore should not be forced upon the people of this country'. The parliamentary proposal to give both symbols legal status would result in a requirement to hoist the flag and sing the anthem at school graduation ceremonies. For some years, many schools had been resisting demands to carry out these ceremonies, particularly in Hiroshima which has become a centre for peace studies since the dropping of the first atomic bomb there on 6 August 1945. However, school boards in some areas were putting pressure on head teachers to ensure that these ceremonies did occur. Rather than fly the flag, one head teacher committed suicide, and another, who failed to order the singing of the *Kimigayo*, was stabbed. A former prime minister, Morohiro Hosokawa, stressed:

> the need for reflection upon the war and reconciliation with the people in Asian countries, not the delivery of the rising sun and Kimigayo to the 21st century as though they were nothing.[38]

Personal experiences can be encoded in artefacts, so that the object represents the memory, the significance and the emotional power of those experiences. Objects can therefore be used to express a sense of self and a feeling of cultural affiliation. Sometimes it is not until the objects of everyday life are no longer part of everyday living that they become imbued with meaning. Eric Clapton, planning to sell a hundred of his guitars for charity, later decided to buy one of them back. He had not realised, he is reported as saying, what a 'wrench' he would feel at parting with the guitar: 'I've realised there is one that I just can't part with so I will be bidding in secret for it . . . It is a guitar that has been around the house for years and I've picked up in times of great stress, like a comfort blanket.'[39] The identity of the singer is reinforced with the guitar in the house, able to be seen and touched, especially at times of stress.

Identities need to be more forcibly stated when lives are lived outside of the home territory. Spaces are created that are mentally part of the original home nation.[40] Linda Waimarie Nakora describes how Maori in Hawaii and London today use objects both to remind themselves of their homelands and to signal their cultural identities and allegiances. *Taonga* are put on display in homes away from home, whereas in New Zealand they would normally be stored safely and not made public. Photographs, stone sculptures, posters from the Te Maori exhibition, paintings, *taiaha* (long staffs), *piu-piu* (flax kilts) and *patu* (clubs) all express Maoridom.[41] The size of these collections is frequently impressive, with whole rooms full of Maori objects. Makereti created a similar home from home in Oxford in the 1920s.

Men and women may use objects in different ways to signal their identities. Pearce describes how, in one family that she studied, the man collected guns, militaria and coins, while the woman collected paperweights.[42] In terms of collections, those of women focus on room ornaments, tourist material, household goods, and jewellery, while men collect sporting material, machinery, musical instruments and paintings.[43]

Artefacts have a capacity to become familiar, to represent the time when active minds can become passive, at rest, relaxed. A feeling of belonging, coming home, is invoked through recognition of familiar shapes, textures and colours. Unfamiliar objects, on the other hand, can signal difference, diversity, possibly alienation, and mobilise attention. Many of these responses involve the body and the senses, are tacit and remain unspoken.

Objects embody feelings about ourselves and about each other. They are used to construct meaningful environments. Csikszentmihalyi and Rochberg-Halton, reviewing domestic items and their use, found that those homes which were described in warm emotional terms tended to have more objects than those which were described in colder terms.[44]

Objects can produce strong reactions, and become imbued with meaning, sometimes unexpectedly. Siri Hustvedt describes her reaction on seeing a slide of Giorgione's *The Tempest* for the first time:

> I had never heard of the artist and knew little about Italian Renaissance painting, but for some reason the picture caused a physical response in me – a genuine tremor of amazement. I fell in love with it then and there, in those 40 seconds before the professor clicked to the next slide.[45]

Equally, objects can have meanings deliberately imposed upon them through the context in which they are placed, and through an anticipation of how they will be encountered. In Leicester, recently, a woman who displayed her collection of small porcelain pigs in her window was reprimanded by the police, and threatened with being charged under the Public Order Act.[46] The house was close to the main mosque in Leicester which was used by more than a thousand Muslim worshippers each week. The collector displayed her pigs next to a quotation from the Koran. The small china pigs, inoffensive to Christian viewers, became offensive when displayed in juxtaposition with the Koran, and viewed by Muslims. As Yaqub Khan, spokesman for the Leicester Federation of Muslim Organisations, said:

> The Koran is a sacred book. If that is placed in a window where pigs have been placed then that is . . . offensive. It may be a trivial matter for some sections of the community but it has to be dealt with.

This domestic window display was treated as a public exhibition by the police, who upheld the complaints from the Muslim community.

The tangibility of artefacts makes abstract notions tangible. Acting as symbols, objects link unconscious responses to real issues or relationships in society;[47] the wigwam and feather headdress that represent 'Indianness' to many people in the West render invisible the actual lived circumstances of Native Americans or Canadian First Nations. In this way, objects structure common-sense categories, some of which may be deeply destructive. Some cultures have been subjected to representative symbols chosen by outsiders unfamiliar with the beliefs and life-ways so represented. These objects serve to objectify and caricature the peoples represented through the construction of stereotypes and categories which debase or ridicule.[48] I have in my possession an object that I found in my mother-in-law's house in Wiltshire in the 1960s. She must have had it for many years. It is a mechanical money-box, made of heavy metal which has been cast in a mould. It is shaped into the head and shoulders of a black man. He holds his hand out, and on placing a coin in the hand and depressing a lever the hand is raised to the mouth and the man eats the coin. At the same time, the painted eyes roll in the head. This was still regarded as amusing by the family when I found it. This little imperial leftover shows how out deeply embedded are shocking racial stereotypes, and how long-lasting these objects and the attitudes they embody can be.

Objects are the inscribed signs of cultural memory.[49] Objects are used to materialise, concretise, represent, or symbolise ideas and memories, and through these processes objects enable abstract ideas to be grasped, facilitate the verbalisation of thought, and mobilise reflection on experience and knowledge. The patterns of thought, attitudes and beliefs that structure a society will be embodied within its artefacts. Objects construct the common-sense categories within which individuals and communities orient their lives and expectations; objects perpetuate and disseminate social values. Human experiences can be accumulated in artefacts,[50] and because of this objects can be associated with the deepest psychological needs. Objects can become imbued or charged with meaning as significance and emotion are invested in them. This can operate on personal, community and national levels. The self, in its gendered and cultured diversity, is in large part produced through objects.

Objects have the capacity to carry meanings, and these meanings can be attributed from a number of perspectives. Objects, therefore, have the capacity to be polysemic, to bear multiple meanings. The meanings of objects emerge within relationships and frameworks, and it is these elements external to the object, drawn together by a meaning-making sensibility, an active mind and body, that anchor the endless play of signification, and make provisional closure possible.

Objects are powerful within both everyday life and within pedagogy; they motivate learning and they become significant beyond their material physical selves. They enable human needs to externalise deeply felt convictions; the need to articulate tacit emotions; to visualise relationships; to picture abstract entities; to make the intangible tangible and therefore graspable.

Knowing objects in their materiality

Encounters with objects are not the same as encounters with ideas. Ideas, concepts, words, are abstract and non-material. They demand verbal and linguistic skills in their understanding. Ideas need to be placed within intellectual frameworks of intelligibility and comprehension before they 'make sense'. Cognitive processes are necessary.

The exchange between object and viewer is more than a cognitive one. The encounter between an active agent and an object has two sides to it: the interpretive framework brought to bear by the individual subject, which is both personal and social, and the physical character of the artefact. The material properties and the physical presence of the artefact demand embodied responses, which may be intuitive and immediate. Responses to objects are culturally shaped, according to previous knowledge and experience, but the initial reaction to an object may be at a tacit and sensory rather than an articulated verbal level.

In the West, it is commonly accepted that there are five senses. However, this is not the only way in which the relationship of the body and the mind to the material world has been conceptualised. Buddhism classifies the mind as a sixth sense, while the Hauser of Nigeria have two senses – sight, and everything else.[51] Diffferent cultures 'make sense' of the physical world in different ways, and different ways of knowing are constructed through these approaches to the ordering of the materiality of the physical world.

After the invention of printing, the Western world moved from a hearing-dominated culture to a sight-dominated one.[52] This transformation of the sensory order had social and intellectual effects; rational knowledge became understood as objective, linear, and analytical, premised on what could be observed and described. In the social sphere, visual objectification and the separation of people and processes resulted in individualism and depersonalisation combined with the division of labour. Sight became a dominating and conquering sense; mapping and counting, those symptoms of modernity, were used to describe and control the targets of the vision. Sight, overseeing, became co-opted as an essential attribute of masculinity, the seeing man, while the other senses, especially touching and listening, became associated with more feminine characteristics such as caring and interpreting.[53]

During the modern period, sight was to be deployed as objectively as possible; subjectivity was to be repressed so that the disembodied eye acted only as a conduit to the brain.[54] Emotions and the more intimate sensations of touch and smell were eradicated as far as possible in the search for a systematic and universally accurate scientific knowledge. In effect, attempts were made to dislocate the mind from the body and its unreliable responses.[55]

Sight is the least personal of the senses. Today in the West it is also the most powerful. The deployment of sight requires a certain focal length, a distance, from its target; otherwise things are 'out of focus'. The other senses, on the other hand, require proximity. Touching, tasting and smelling need us to be close to things, and are in that way senses which require intimacy and which enable familiarity. They involve the body more, through demanding an immediate close presence.

Embodied responses are influenced by the scale of things. Cognitive and emotional responses to objects are affected in subtle ways by their size in relation to our own body size. Very small objects may become precious or personal, something to be carried around and made special, or hidden from others. Very large objects may be experienced as imposing, or threatening. Levels of emotional comfort may relate to the relationship of the human body in the environment. Physiological and psychological comfort is promoted when the senses are kept at an optimum level of arousal; mental torpor results from too little stimulation, while too great an arousal is disturbing.[56]

Today, minds and bodies are understood to be interrelated. The behaviour of the body cannot be separated from the mind and the emotions, and, equally, mental activity (cognition) works in partnership with bodily responses. Learning is understood to involve tacit, felt knowledge in addition to knowledge that can be verbalised,[57] and styles of learning and knowing include the skills of the body, used in sports and the arts, as well as the linguistic and mathematical skills.[58]

Bodies adopt a performative relationship to objects, they enact the construction of meaning which is at once dramatic and contingent.[59] Repeated enactments stabilise the production of meaning and lead to the social estabishment of meaning. However, different forms of enactment can change the character of the meaning, and expose its contingency. For example, Maori ancestor carvings and other *taonga* are frequently treated as inert objects in museums in Europe; they are inspected and occasionally cleaned; they are measured, catalogued and documented. In museums in Aotearoa, New Zealand, in addition to normal curatorial good practice, they are treated as animate; fresh greenery is placed in front or on top of them, they are talked to and remembered within a frame-work of tribal affiliations; when appropriate, they are taken out of the care of the museum and into family or tribal ceremonies where they take their place in ceremonial rituals that affirm their histories more strongly.

The materiality, the physical quality of the object, presents itself as of a stable character; however, this materiality is subject to change and modification through time. Social relationships and dominations establish marks of their power and engrave memories on things.[60] Objects carry the scars of their life-histories. Hinemihi, for example, is now shorter in length than when she was first built[61] and the carvings on the front of the house are not the original ones. One of Merton and Annie Russell-Cotes' Maori carvings of a male figure has been castrated; it is not known by whom, but this disfigurement has resulted from a view of the requirements of the values of Christianity.

Forms of artefacts are modified, refabricated, to suit new situations. Artefactual morphologies can be major indicators of social status, of beliefs, and of fashion. An eighteenth-century woman's dress on display in the exhibition Art on Tyneside in the Laing Art Gallery, Newcastle, has clearly been modified, perhaps to fit better, or perhaps to reflect changing fashions. Paintings on canvas can also be cut to size, or taken off the stretcher and folded up, as was Branwell Brontë's portrait of himself with his sisters; additionally, the artist had changed the picture by painting out his own image. The painting was found many years later on top of a wardrobe in Ireland, having been transported there from Yorkshire. It is now in the National Portrait Gallery, London.[62]

Materiality is subject to change in other ways, too, because of fragility or lack of durability. Unfired clay, for example, can be dissolved, or fired clay may crack if it is thin; glass shatters if it falls; wood can be burnt or cut; fabric rots if placed in the ground; metals such as gold or silver can be melted down and recast into quite new objects. Although objects are seen as solid, reliable, and unchanging, materiality is unstable. It may be deliberately or accidentally changed; it may be faked or forged.

Some museum objects, treated as artefacts and displayed as such, are in fact human. Both the British Museum and the National Museum of Denmark in Copenhagen display bodies that have been discovered in peat bogs. Egyptian mummified figures are commonplace, though few museums go as far as to display a disembodied mummified head accompanied by the questions 'Who am I?', 'Do you find me funny?', as the New Walk Museum in Leicester did. Tattooed Maori heads are seldom now placed on display, though these grim commodities were once commissioned as collectors' items and were familiar in museums.[63]

It is easy to forget the humanity of these displayed pieces. Museum techniques objectify the remains, treating them as specimens in the ways in which they are catalogued, documented, and placed in glass cases as part of a narrative. These practices are changing now in some museums, with greater awareness of the significance of these relics to living people; as Ngahui Te Awekotuku has pointed out, it is now possible with DNA technology to link Maori heads to living relatives. Te Papa Tongarewa, the National Museum of New Zealand, has a ritually dedicated space for repatriated heads which is controlled by Maori scholars, and where research can be on Maori terms only.[64]

The solid 'real' character of objects is open to question. Materiality, physicality, is not constant; changes may be made many times in many ways for many reasons. To accept objects as evidence is fraught with difficulty. Questions must be raised about the materiality itself. When the physicality of the object is identified, its meaning will depend on the narrative framework into which it is placed. Narratives are constructed by interpreting subjects; the reading and the significance of the materiality of the objects is variable according to who is reading.

Understanding objects, then, is not the same as reading texts. The categories of meaning are less clear with objects than with texts. Although it could be argued that words necessarily have a material character (they may be expressed in book form, or written around a piece of pottery), the material form rarely comprises part of the meaning of the text. Textual meaning is located within the words themselves, although this is not to suggest that a single unified meaning is the result. Textual meaning remains for the most part within the realm of ideas, of discourse. It does not relate to the body or the senses. To treat an artefact as a text is to expand the concept of textual meaning too far. It is also to focus primarily on the discursive character of meaning, with the material meaning being allocated a secondary, less significant role. With the analysis of artefactual meaning, the material meaning is at least as important as the discursive meaning. With some artefacts, sensory and embodied reactions are of enormous significance.

The meanings of objects are ambiguous. Meaning is not articulated in words, and is indicated, but only partly, through context. This partial fixing remains very open: it is always possible to take an individual object and place it in a new framework or see it in a new way. The lack of definitive and final articulation of significance keeps objects endlessly mysterious – the next person to attach meaning to it may see something unseen by anyone else before.

However, the openness to re-meaning is constrained by the physical character and material identity of objects. A painting is not a Maori meeting house. But both a painting and a Maori meeting house, their specific material identity having been established, might be placed within the same cultural context, working to serve the same cultural ends. The physical character of artefacts has a material identity and a history that can be researched; but the significance that is given to this identity and this history will be determined by the frameworks of intelligibility deployed to understand the artefact. Hinemihi may be seen as either a collection of carved posts or the bosom of a loved ancestor; the *mere* of Mita Taupopoki may signify either an exotic curiosity or a precious family possession.

The power of the meaning given to objects is grounded in their material character. Specific interpretations have the quality of 'evidence' as they are supported by what can be seen. The physical character of the object naturalises the contingent meaning. To Russell-Cotes, it was self-evident that Maori carving was grotesque. Other writers had said so, and on seeing the things themselves, so they were. To Ngati Hinemihi one hundred years later, Hinemihi stood as the beautiful ancestor of the tribe as she had done for one hundred years. She affirmed the identity of the tribe, by being there 'in the flesh' as it were. The 'thinginess' of objects, the concrete 'reality', gives weight, literally, to the interpretation. It 'proves' that this is 'how it is', 'what it means'.[65]

My examples make the point in an extreme way. One of the reasons for my interest in objects that are called ethnographic is precisely because in very recent times their meanings in Western eyes have changed so radically, their histories reoriented through 180 degrees. These kinds of objects, caught in the maelstrom of colonialism and post-colonialism, illuminate the issues in particularly dramatic ways. But the point is a general one.

It is an openness to re-meaning; a capacity to carry preferred meaning; a potential for polysemia; and the material potentials and constraints, that lie at the heart of the appeal of artefacts. The dialogic relationship between what can be said and thought, and what cannot, offers opportunities for both domination *and* for empowerment.

Objects are called on to perform complex functions in everyday life. They enable abstract notions to be imagined, act as symbols for intangible ideas and can be invested with deeply felt emotions. Objects are encountered as much by the body as the mind; in fact it is not possible to split the relationship between the senses and cognitive processes. The strategies of interpretation deployed by active agents on encountering objects involve both the senses and the body (in apprehending new information from the environment), and the mind (in processing this information through relating it to existing knowledge). These interactive and dialogic processes make up acts of interpretation. It is through embodied interpretation that objects become meaningful.

Interpreting objects

The interpretive processes used in the encounter with objects can be examined using hermeneutics and learning theory.

Objects are encountered initially through the senses and the body. Much of the way they are known is tacit, felt, not brought to articulation. Tacit knowledge can be understood as all that is known by individuals, minus all that can be said. Tacit knowledge remains at an emotional, reactive level, and as it remains non-verbal, unarticulated, cannot be analysed and assessed.[66] Tacit knowledge produces powerful 'gut reactions', mobilising feelings and emotions, but in a non-examined way. Objects, known tacitly, also have this effect. Unspoken feelings influence behaviour, attitudes and values, and are perhaps especially powerful precisely because they remain unexamined.

Objects can also be read, spoken, and written about, encountered through verbal knowledge. Verbal knowledge enables an examination and evaluation of what is known, facilitates comparison with the ideas of others, enables sharing and discussion. Without verbal knowledge, it is more difficult to make changes in what is known, or to develop complex concepts. Verbal knowledge is textual knowledge – knowledge through the written, spoken or heard text.

Intertextuality refers to relationships between texts, relationships which in part shape the meaning of any one text. We might call the interrelationships between objects 'inter-artefactuality' (or, less clumsily, the 'artefactual framework') and remember that this refers to both verbal and tacit ways of knowing. Tacit ways of knowing include handling, smelling, hearing and seeing – each of these, as we saw above, has specific historical and cultural dimensions, which result in specifically inflected knowledge.

Hermeneutic theory explains that understanding is reached through the process of interpretation. 'Understanding is a process by which people match what they see and hear with pre-stored groupings of actions that they have already experienced.'[67] Interpretation aims to uncover the meaning of a work through a dialogic relationship between the detail and the whole: 'the whole of a work must be understood from the individual words and their combinations, and yet the full comprehension of the detail presupposes the understanding of the whole'.[68]

Gadamer describes it thus: 'we must understand the whole in terms of the detail and the detail in terms of the whole. This principle . . . [is applied] to the art of understanding.'[69]

Gadamer explains the processes of reading a text and viewing an art work. The process of understanding, he suggests, is a process of looking from the whole to the detail and back again. The detail contributes to the understanding of the whole. At the same time, almost without being aware of it, the object is treated as part of the whole society, both now (today) and in the past. The object is placed within existing knowledge about the present and the past. The process of making meaning moves both between the whole and the part of the object and the present and the past, simultaneously, with continual checking and rechecking, revision of ideas, the trying out of new ones and the rejection of those that don't work. The whole is a circular question and answer process.

Hermeneutics calls this circular action the hermeneutic circle, and proposes that understanding develops through the continuous dialogic movement between the whole and the parts of a work, where meaning is constantly modified as further relationships are encountered. The encounter between an individual subject and an object is influenced by prior experience and knowledge. Meaning is to be found neither wholly in the object nor wholly in the viewer. Meaning is dialogic – a dialogue between viewer and object.[70]

Gadamer suggests that experiences, objects and other materials such as texts are approached with what he calls prejudices,[71] or foreknowledge, given by our own historicity, and with a certain openness. This receptiveness to the object creates a balance or dialectic between prejudice (what is already known) and openness. This dialectic permits revision of prejudices towards a greater 'truth', but this truth is still relative, historical, and socially determined.[72]

Educational theory confirms that human beings strive after meaning,[73] and that the construction of meaning relates to pattern recognition. Things have meaning because of the frame within which they are placed: thus a brick might be used to build a wall, smash a window, warm a bed, or prevent a car from rolling away. In each case it is the same brick, but its meaning derives from its context of use. The brick as a 'fact', a material fact, gets its meaning by the way in which it fits into a pattern.[74] Understanding happens, not by being fed information or having an experience, but when new information or experience can be fitted into a pattern, when the patterned relationships between elements can be seen. These patterns are constructed by individual learners as part of the effort to mobilise meaning; experts categorise by the deep laws of the subject matter, but novice learners (of all ages) categorise by surface features.[75] The move from novice to expert in discipline-based knowledge is a move from immediate surface features to in-depth knowledge. Objects form a significant component of this move, but are also essential in the construction of self. Piaget suggested that people can only come to know themselves through acting on objects materially and mentally.[76]

Hermeneutics suggests that processes of interpretation work dialogically between 'prejudices' or foreknowledge, and an openness to new information, experiences and objects. Learning theory confirms that the brain does not simply take in new matter, it always processes it, and this processing is carried out on the basis of already existing 'schemata', or mental knowledge maps. Cognitive frames, schemata, for storing and organising everyday knowledge, are created that can be used automatically;[77] as new knowledge is encountered it is either assimilated into existing schemata, or the schemata are reorganised to accommodate the new information.[78] Perception and memory are therefore inextricably linked.[79]

Memory is organised around personal experiences and episodes rather than around abstract semantic categories;[80] memory is personalised and related to biographical experiences. Ways of knowing become increasingly more abstract as more knowledge is gained, but those concepts and beliefs that are not reviewed for ongoing relevance may remain at a very concrete and basic level. Gardner points out that research into students (as opposed to experts) suggests that children's earliest conceptions endure through the school era, and that once the young person has left the school environment these earlier views of the world may emerge more fully: 'like repressed memories of early childhood, they reassert themselves in settings where they seem to be appropriate'.[81]

As each person has their own mental maps of knowledge depending on their prior cultural and biographical experiences, each person will process new matter in ways that are specific to them as individuals.[82] Each individual will also exhibit variable preferred learning styles which can be positioned along two main axes: that of abstract or concrete apprehension of experience, and that of reflective or active processing of information and experience.[83] Any interpretation is never fully completed. 'The discovery of the true meaning of a text or a work of art is never finished: it is in fact an infinite process.'[84] As understanding grows and as new sources of knowledge emerge, so meaning is a continuing process of modification, adaption and extension. The hermeneutic circle is never fully closed, but remains open to the possibilities of change. There is always more to say, and what is said may always be changed. Meaning is never static.

The construction of meaning is partly shaped by prior knowledge and experience, and by how the past is related to the present. All interpretation is necessarily historically situated. Position in history and culture affects meaning. Meaning is constructed through and in culture. Perception, memory and interpretation are cultural constructs.[85]

The processes of interpretation[86] are complex, and are active. Constructivist learning theory insists that people make their own active interpretations of experience.[87] Individuals search for meaning, look for patterns, try to invest their experiences with significance. Across the humanities and the social sciences it has come to be acknowledged that there is no knowledge outside the knower – that knowledge is brought into being by the meaning that each individual makes of the experiences that s/he has. This is 'social constructionism' in social science;[88] 'constructivism' in learning theory;[89] 'interpretation' in literary theory[90] and archaeology[91] and largely accounts for the shift from art history to visual culture.[92] It is still hotly debated and resisted in some fields within the sciences,[93] and disputed by some of those museums which have been involved in the 'science wars'.[94] However, these museums are fighting a rearguard action defending their own positions of authority; elsewhere it is accepted that 'our relationship to reality is not a positive knowledge but a hermeneutic construct, and that all perception is already an act of interpretation'.[95]

The peculiarity of knowing objects lies in the experience of not only looking, and having a conversation, but also perhaps touching or smelling. Objects are interpreted through a 'reading' using the gaze which is combined with a broader sensory experience involving tacit knowledge and embodied responses. Both cognitive and emotive responses may result, some of which may remain unspoken.

Interpretive communities, strategies and repertoires

The previous sections have discussed how meaning is actualised, brought into being, by the negotiation of objects by the viewer.[96] These negotiations, however, are not the act of detached atomistic individuals but are the products of both individuals and communities;[97] personal interpretations are forged through social and cultural frameworks. Culture is concerned with the production and exchange of meanings; 'the giving and taking of meaning' between members of a society or a group.[98] Individual meaning-making is forged and tested in relation to communities of meaning-making, which establish frameworks of intelligibility within which individual subjects negotiate, refine and develop personal constructs. How the present and the past is understood, and how objects are interpreted, depends on personal biography, cultural background, and interpretive community.

The concept of 'interpretive communities' has been an influential one in media and communication research for the last two decades and more,[99] although very little has been written in relation to museums.[100] The way the expression has been used has varied, as has the focus of analysis.

Fish offers a definition of interpretive community which focuses on the interpretation of textual meaning:

> Interpretive communities are made up of those who share interpretive strategies for writing texts, for constituting their properties and assigning their intentions.[101]

Fish is working against the formalist assumption that there are observable facts that can be first described and then interpreted. Fish suggests that an interpreting subject, endowed with purposes and concerns, is, by virtue of this very operation, determining what counts as the facts to be observed, and that since this determining is not a neutral marking out of a valueless area, but the extension of an already existing field of interest, it *is* an interpretation.[102] If meaning develops in dynamic relationship with the expectations, conclusions, judgements, and assumptions of the interpreter, then these activities are not merely instrumental and mechanical, used to extract meaning, but are essential in the construction of meaning.[103] In the quotation above, he uses the word 'writing' to refer to the activity of reading a written text. For Fish this activity is a form of writing, as each reader constructs their own meaning and therefore 'writes' their own text. Fish goes on:

> Systems of intelligibility constrain and fashion us and furnish us with categories of understanding with which we fashion the entities to which we then point.[104]

And further: 'Readers make meanings, but meaning make readers.'[105]

The significant element of Fish's argument is that systems of intelligibility are not individual but collective. Individuals share interpretive strategies with others who share the same frames of reference, the same cultural references and the same positions within history. Learning is social.

Some interesting applications of the concept of 'interpretive communities' can be found, although again not in relation to making meaning in museums. Radway[106] studied a specific identifiable community, a small group of sixteen women romance readers clustered about a bookshop in 'Smithton'. Although not formally constituted as a reading group, she found that, as readers, the women were united by common purposes, references and interpretive procedures. In the interpretation of stories of male/female relationships (historical romances) the women operated from a transparent view of language (where words had fixed and definite meanings) that enabled the heroine of the romances to be constructed as strong, intelligent and self-reliant. Writers always initially presented their heroine as such, but the subsequent story did not confirm this presentation; however, through their interpretive strategies, the readers constructed a powerful heroine who was always perceived as converting the frequently recalcitrant hero to her feminine values. Radway identified specific textual and interpretative strategies, and also identified the uses of these strategies to the women readers. By picking up a book, the readers signalled a detaching from the everyday world of middle-class mother and wife. By reading romances, these women found temporary release from the demands of their defining social role, and psychological gratification of the needs created by that role. In that all the women in the study followed the same interpretive strategies for the same purposes, Radway was able to identify an interpretive community.

Zelizer[107] undertook a wider study which focused on American journalists to review how far the notion of 'interpretive community' might explain how journalists constituted themselves as a group which shared interpretive strategies. Looking beyond conventional analyses of journalists as a profession, and incorporating the shared journalistic discourses around key public events, she found informal networking, narrative and storytelling (about the past and present of the practice of journalism) and what she calls 'the trappings' of professionalism which all contributed to the ways in which journalists shaped meaning about themselves. These shared strategies contributed to the construction of the establishment and maintenance of the frame of mind necessary to become a journalist in America; journalists, she proposes, do constitute a definable interpretive community.

Mitra[108] studied a group of users of the World Wide Web. This group of Indian immigrants to the West was in no sense a community that met face to face, as their only common point of contact was through the Web. Mitra studied a specific website that spoke both to what he describes as an 'in-group', an interpretive community that had the interpretive history and strategies to make sense of the web pages, and an 'out-group' that visited the site by chance. The stylistics of the site, the formatting, use of language, use of images and sound, and type of textual content itself created two groups of meaning-makers – those who had the skills and predispositions to make sense out of the site and its hypertextual links, and those who did not. Such skills included language, histories of past affiliations, appreciation of the intricacies of Indian culture, and familiarity with ongoing events and changes in India. For Indians outside of India, who are frequently split up from family and community members, the Web, to those who could use it, offered a way of affirming their cultural origins. As Mitra puts it, in the relevant web pages 'the alienated and isolated immigrant can find a friendly cyber-community which acknowledges the residual cultural attributes of the diasporic individual'.[109] The use of the Web itself constituted and constructed the community.

The concept of 'interpretive community', although widely familiar in the theory of media and communication studies, is a complex and slippery concept in practice, and it has been called under-theorised.[110] As we have seen above, it has been used in a number of ways. Radway's work can be seen as a classic audience study, which describes a small group of geographically delimited women all reading very similar books. Zelizer's study is rather more unusual in that it addresses media producers – a group of journalists – rather than consumers, and the group, although meeting together at conferences and through other professional networks, is geographically dispersed. Mitra's work addresses a group that is not a group in any sense of the word except through its coming together in acts of interpretation, when common cultures and histories can be deployed. The function of these interpretive acts is to affirm the cultural frameworks of the individual meaning-makers through the collective character of the repertoires and strategies used.

Interpretive communities are located in relation to interpretive acts. It is only through the common repertoires and strategies used in interpretation that such communities can be recognised. The communities are not necessarily communities in any other sense. Radway's women did not necessarily know each other; their only concrete connection with each other was anonymous in that they all took the advice of the bookshop assistant who advised them what to buy. The Indian users of the Web might, during the course of using it, meet, but were not in communication with each other outside this activity. The journalists, although all using similar interpretive strategies and belonging to the same profession, might not meet at all throughout their professional lives. All these communities, therefore, can only be called communities because of their constitution through the media, either as media audiences or consumers (text readers), or as media producers (journalists), or in the case of the Indian Web users, both producers and consumers at the same time.[111]

121

Interpretive communities cannot be mapped onto socio-economic positions, demographic groupings or kinship structures.[112] Specific class, gender or racialised positions do not determine how meaning is made, although position in the social structure may delimit the availability of the discursive repertoires and meaning-making strategies available.[113]

Interpretive communities are fluid and unstable. Their membership changes as individuals revise their affiliations and redirect their interests. Each individual may typically belong to more than one interpretive community at any one time.

> Interpretive communities grow larger and decline and individuals move from one to another; thus while alignments are not permanent, they are always there, providing just enough stability for interpretive battles to go on, and just enough shift and slippage to ensure that they are never settled.[114]

Interpretive communities are recognised by their common frameworks of intelligibility, interpretive repertoires, knowledge and intellectual skills.[115] These will include specific uses of words and things, and particular textual and artefactual strategies. Attitudes, values and beliefs will become evident in those recurrently used systems of terms deployed to characterise and evaluate actions and events.[116]

The concept of interpretive communities is significant for several reasons. Firstly, in relation to theories of knowledge, it insists that interpretation is not based in the individual but is a shared occurrence. Although each individual actively makes sense of their own experience, the interpretive strategies and repertoires they use emerge through prior social and cultural events. Fish spells out the implications of this, by pointing out that repertoires and strategies exist prior to the encounter with the text. They:

> proceed not from [the reader] but from the interpretive community of which he is a member; they are in effect, community property, and insofar as they at once enable and limit the operations of his consciousness, he is [community property] too . . . The claims of objectivity and subjectivity can no longer be debated because the authorising agency, the centre of interpretive authority, is at once both and neither. An interpretive community is not objective because as a bundle of interests, of particular purposes and goals, its perspective is interested rather than neutral; but by the very same reasoning, the meanings and texts produced by an interpretive community are not subjective because they do not proceed from an isolated individual but from a public and conventional point of view.[117]

The concept of interpretive communities thus undermines the argument that a constructivist understanding of the character of knowledge inevitably leads to an extreme epistemological relativism. Fish subtitles his book 'The *power* of interpretive communities'; the power he has in mind is the *collective* power to produce publicly acceptable meaning. The depth or breadth of the acceptance of specific ideas will depend on the size and influence of the specific interpretive community. Thus, as Fish points out, it is possible to move beyond the subjective/objective knowledge debate to examine how knowledge and power interrelate.

Secondly, in relation to the interpretation of visual culture, the concept of interpretive community can be used to explain difference in response to specific objects. Merton Russell-Cotes, for example, can be described as belonging to a different interpretive community from that of Makereti. Different systems of intelligibility, different frames of reference and different interpretive repertoires are used to construct diverse meaning from objects that were of the same type – Maori cloaks, clubs, staffs and carvings. On one level the interpretations were personal because of the biographies of the individuals concerned, but these interpretations were also deeply rooted in the ways of thinking of the cultural and historical communities to which each belonged.

Thirdly, in relation to the significance of the concept of interpretive communities for the interpretation of visual culture in museums, it begins to suggest explanations for the difficulties some visitors have in grasping the meanings and relevance of certain displays. If exhibitions speak only to the interpretive community to which the curator belongs, then unless visitors share these interpretive frameworks, they will not feel comfortable. And fourthly, in planning exhibitions and displays, the interpretive strategies and repertoires of the interpretive communities to which intended audiences belong should be anticipated (through audience research) and enabled.

This chapter has considered a range of issues relating to the interpretive processes that characterise encounters between subjects and objects. In museums, these encounters are in part shaped in advance by the ways in which objects are selected and displayed. The museum display or exhibition sets an agenda and provides a framework within which the interpretive strategies of the visitor must be deployed. Any encounter with an object in a museum will therefore involve the articulation of the interpretive processes of museum visitors with the pedagogic provision of the museum. It is to this matter that we turn in Chapter 6.

6

Exhibitions and interpretation
Museum pedagogy and cultural change

Reformulating museum pedagogy

The discussion of the interpretation of visual culture in museums has up till now concentrated on objects and their meanings, which have been discussed through the themes of visual narrative, cultural difference, identity, and interpretive processes. One further strand remains to be brought out – the theme of museum pedagogy.

The interpretation of visual culture in museums may be considered from two points of view: that of the curator, or the museum, and that of the visitor. Curators display objects in groups along with associated images and texts, and thereby produce interpretations for visitors; meanwhile visitors deploy their own interpretive strategies and repertoires to make sense of the objects, the displays and the experience of the museum as a whole.

Museum pedagogy is structured through the narratives produced through the displays, and also through the style in which these narratives are presented. Many museums use methods other than those of display as part of their educational provision; these might, for example, include dramatic events and workshops for children and families. Frequently these methods are very creative and successful; however, for most visitors most of the time, it is the exhibitions and displays that make up the educational experience of the museum, and it is this aspect that is the focus in this chapter.

The curatorial meanings of objects in museums are produced through complex and multi-layered museological processes where museum objectives, collecting policies, classification methods, display styles, artefactual groupings and textual frameworks come together in articulation. The knowledge produced through displays has the character of inevitability, but is the result of complex decision-making processes. The meanings made by museum visitors from the visual cultures of display are a product of both individual and social interpretive processes and are complex and unpredictable.

Objects in museums are subject to curatorial procedures of registration, documentation, and classification which have, in the main, resulted in their allocation to a fixed physical and conceptual position within the collections, which in turn has tended to generate a fixed meaning. This single fixed meaning, almost always relating to an academic discipline (art history, or archaeology for example), has seemed the correct and only way in which the object should be interpreted. Recently, however, the contingent character of meaning has begun to be admitted, and new ways of thinking about how objects could be grouped, and how they might be spoken about, are emerging.

What counts as knowledge in the museum is being reconsidered, as the uses of objects are reviewed and reassessed. The ways that displays might be presented have also changed in recent years. Both the content and the style of museum pedagogy are changing, although the change in narrative content is of a lesser degree. Both these matters entail the renegotiation of the relationships between museums and their audiences.

This chapter reviews changes in museum pedagogy from a perspective based on communication and educational theory. The review is necessarily broad and in outline only. It offers a way of understanding and accounting for the major shifts in the public face of museums that occurred in the last quarter of the twentieth century. Two paradigmatic pedagogic formations are presented; pedagogy as transmission and pedagogy as culture. I locate these pedagogic formations in relation to two metaphors – the modernist museum and the post-museum.

Both of these tropes were introduced in Chapter 1. They serve as complex and multi-faceted organisational metaphors that enable the discussion of ideas about the roles played by museums in the construction of histories and cultures. In this chapter it is suggested that the pedagogic approach of the modernist museum was (and is) based on an understanding of communication as transmission; while the pedagogic approaches being developed by the post-museum can be analysed by understanding communication as an integral part of culture as a whole.

The modernist museum, which emerged during the nineteenth century and reached its apogee by the beginning of the twentieth, understood its visitors as deficient. They were those who were in search of something they did not have, who lacked information, who were in need of instruction, and who were intended to act as receivers of knowledge, empty vessels to be filled. These visitors were represented as an undifferentiated mass, as 'the general public'. Today, museum audiences are being reconceptualised. The mass is being broken down and differentiated, but new ways of thinking about visitors are themselves not yet sufficiently sophis-ticated. Marketing approaches address audiences as 'visitors' or 'non-visitors', demographic target groups which are subject to 'niche marketing'. Although these approaches can lead to a review of the 'products' of the museum in relation to the needs of each target group, this does not go far enough. An approach based on the concept of critical pedagogy, which embraces the issues of narrative, difference, identity and voice, demands a recognition both of the processes of interpretation actively used by multi-cultural audiences and of the political implications of the use of the visual culture of the museum.

Pedagogy in the modernist museum

The nineteenth-century public museum can be seen as one of the emblematic institutions of the modern period. Based on a model that was European in origin, but which would be exported world-wide, the modernist museum was tasked with the production and dissemination of authoritative knowledge. Master narratives were constructed through a range of collection-related disciplines (art, natural history, geology, archaeology, ethnography). Museums could offer opportunities for self-education and self-elevation at a time when schooling was not available for all and when there were few other opportunities for self-improvement. Although the idea of the museum as an educational institution had emerged some time before, the Victoria and Albert Museum was the first national collection in England to be explicitly founded as an agent of instruction. As the First Report of the Department of Practical Art stated: 'a Museum presents probably the only effectual means of educating the adult'.[1]

Museum pedagogy was based on the idea of the possibility of the realisation through objects of universal laws that could be taught in the same way at all times and in all places. The concept of universal law was pervasive in Victorian culture: politics, morals, history, economics, art, and education, were all governed, it was thought, by universal laws or principles true for all times and places. In 1855, in a speech given at Birmingham Town Hall, Prince Albert declared that: 'The Fine Arts . . . rest on the application of the laws of form and colour, and what may be called the science of the beautiful.'[2] Henry Cole, in the consideration of the educational role of the museum at South Kensington, also spoke about the application of laws to regulate beauty.[3] The visual culture of nineteenth-century museums illustrated those universal laws in the arts and the sciences that could be construed from arrangements of material things.

The modernist museum was intended to be encyclopaedic, to draw together a complete collection, to act as a universal archive. It was structured through deep-rooted binary divisions. Its spaces were divided between those that were private and those that were public. The private spaces were the spaces for knowledge production, irrevocably separated from the public spaces for knowledge consumption. The private spaces were spaces where specialist knowledge was deployed, where scholarly research was carried out, and where products such as exhibitions and catalogues were fashioned. The bodies occupying these spaces were professionalised, specialised and differentiated, each with its own necessary mental freight which justified its presence. The public spaces, on the other hand, were available, in theory at least, to the mass of the general public; undifferentiated bodies that assembled to partake of the specialist information laid out for them in the galleries. The galleries were spaces of consumption, of viewing and of learning. They were also spaces of controlled behaviour, guarded and surveyed by warders who would eject those who behaved in an unruly fashion.

Although critical histories of museums are still in their infancy, and histories of the pedagogic approaches developed by museums are even rarer, the historical work to date suggests that by the end of the nineteenth century specific pedagogic approaches had been developed. These pedagogic approaches operated through concepts and technologies that would remain in place until the last quarter of the twentieth century, and which would become curatorial orthodoxies, some of which remain current today. For example, many of the practices introduced into the nineteenth-century art museum are still seen as the foundation of curatorial practice.[4]

Modernist museum pedagogy was based on an understanding of objects as sites for the construction of knowledge and meaning; a view of knowledge as unified, objective, and transferable; a didactic approach of expert-to-novice transmission; and the conceptualisation of the museum and its audience as separate spheres, with, in addition, the museum as a place for learning that was held apart from the popular culture of the everyday. Although the application of these ideas varied according to specific disciplines, the basic philosophy remained constant across them. These approaches to knowledge and to the relationships between teacher and learner, which had developed by the end of the nineteenth century, were to remain largely in place until very recent years. In some places they still persist.

During the modern period, objects were viewed as sources of knowledge in themselves,[5] which through their 'proper arrangements'[6] would reveal the basic structures of natural history, history, science or art. If laid out in the correct way, both the meanings of the individual objects and a substantive body of information about particular disciplines would be explicit in the relationships between the objects. Knowledge was imagined as a classificatory table, on which all living things could find their correct position.[7] The experience of the world could be analysed in terms of order, identity, difference and measurement.[8] Analysis, comparison, enumeration, and classification were essential strategies for knowing. Finite schemes of knowledge were thought to be possible. These ideas were feasible because of a basic assumption that words and things had a single unique correspondence, and that the naming of things located them, once and for all, on the table of differences and similarities.[9]

The collection, observation, description and classification of artefacts and specimens was of major importance as this resulted in the discovery of their interrelationships, and led to knowledge about specific disciplinary or subject areas. Within the fields of botany and geology, for example, close and careful work with specimens was necessary in order to grasp the basic structures of the natural world.

The discourses of objectivity that formed the mode of enquiry for natural history were used in the description and classification of other classes of objects. In the work of authenticating the portraits at the National Portrait Gallery in London, for example, George Scharf used comparative and evidence-based methods that would have seemed familiar to geologists. The evolutionary story of national progress told through displayed portraits would also have resonated with scientists.[10]

The empirical approaches developed for the study of natural specimens were re-deployed for the study of people as part of the development of the social sciences of history, archaeology and anthropology that took place during the second half of the nineteenth century; archaeology, for example, adapted geology's strati-graphical methods.[11] In museums, these links to natural history were made explicit in the display of objects. General Pitt-Rivers in the 1850s, for example, treated artefacts as specimens in displaying boomerangs to emphasise their morphologies and the connections of form.[12] Throughout the nineteenth century, different types of objects, (including those people who were seen as objects), were subject to similar methods of systematic categorisation through objective classification. Museums, as sites for the collection and care of these objects, were understood as perfect sites for the development of knowledge. Natural history museums, for example, stood at the cutting edge of scientific understanding throughout the nineteenth century.[13]

Classification and discourses of objectivity were also used as the basis of museum displays. The guiding principle of the visual layout of displays was accuracy and clarity in the exposition of the structure of the subject concerned. At the National Gallery, London, it was thought desirable as early as 1836 that the collections should be ordered historically, geographically and biographically. Information should be given to the public by:

> fixing its name over every separate school, and, under every picture, the name, with the time of the birth and death, of the painter; the name also of the master, or the most celebrated pupil, of the artist, might in certain cases be added. This ready (though limited) information is important to those whose time is much absorbed by mental or bodily labour.[14]

The Royal Picture Gallery in Berlin and the Munich Pinakothek acted as exemplars. At the Gallery in Munich the paintings were placed so that each school of painting could be observed in its own discrete space without the distraction of others.[15] In art museums, the works of art presented the histories of art.[16]

In the natural history museum, classification automatically provided the principles of display layout.[17] In the galleries of the British Museum (Natural History) in the 1880s, for example, the specimens displayed in the Bird Galleries demon-strated their places on the classificatory epistemological table through the display design.[18] During the same period, the University Museum of Turin was organised as a 'universal Natural History . . . seen at a glance . . . as one great and well accomplished open book'.[19] Almost all provincial museums in Britain in the second half of the nineteenth century adopted the same approach to the display of geological specimens, which was systematic, geographical or temporal; the arrangements of the public displays were based on the same principles.[20]

Structures of some subjects changed over the period, and where possible museums presented to their publics the most up-to-date research through their exhibitions.[21] However, no attention was paid to the needs of individual visitors, who were in effect treated as a mass, and were all expected to learn in the same way. It was assumed that visitors would learn if the expository style of the display was such that the objects themselves were clearly visible and if the statements made by the relationships between the objects were sufficiently well articulated. The relationships between the items in the collections, rather than the objects themselves, were the priority. A walk through the museum galleries meant a walk through the structures of specific disciplines. At the National Portrait Gallery a single linear path was laid out based on chronology;[22] other museums used other organising principles to set out clear spatial directions through the museum.[23] It was assumed that, having carried out the walk, visitors would have absorbed the relationships between the objects, carefully crafted in the display itself, and would be able to understand their significance.

In order to achieve the required level of articulation of these relationships which were both concrete and abstract at the same time, and also to offer the necessary clarity of vision, the galleries themselves needed to conform to certain principles. They needed to be well lit, with the objects well positioned and spaced, with visitors able to use a measured walk, and careful and controlled looking. In the National Gallery in London, for example, the pictures were made visually accessible by being placed in a good light. In Munich, the pictures were separated from the sculptures because they responded so differently to the play of light, and the paintings were hung at specific ideal heights, with the ideal distance from which they should be viewed specified.[24]

Vision is the master sense of the modern era.[25] Modernity is inseparable from the making of the observer, who is described by Crary as one who sees within a set of rules and conventions.[26] In the museum it was these rules and conventions that constituted museum pedagogy. The ideal gaze of the visitor had certain characteristics in common with the gaze of the curator who had generated the display. It was calm and measured, as neutral as possible. It engaged the rational mind directly, but, in the same way as Descartes' disembodied eye[27] was not susceptible to emotion or to passion. Knowledge which could be spoken and thereby used in evaluation and judgement was preferred over tacit, unexpressed, emotive knowledge.[28] At the same time, other characteristics positioned the museum visitor as quite distinct from the curator. The relationship was one of expert to novice, or of teacher to taught; displays took the form of the lecture without the lecturer.[29]

Visitors were imagined as an abstract mass, unitary and ostensibly classless.[30] When numbers were very low and museum spaces were limited, as in the first few years of the National Portrait Gallery, London, it was possible to observe and comment on specific groups of visitors, but as numbers grew the individuals were reduced to ciphers, faceless numbers in the monthly museum census.[31]

The experience of a visitor to the collections was that of a quantified observation of a rationalised, visual order. Vision is the most distancing of the senses, and in museums this meant that visitors kept their distance from the displays. In art galleries paintings were hung at what was considered an optimum height and distance for viewing; in museums, the glass case performed the function of defining the appropriate viewing conditions and distance. The display cases acted as ways of dividing up both the objects and the statements made by the grouped objects – the cases acted as punctuation marks to better articulate the message of the museum.[32] The museum halls were arranged with carefully spaced and ordered identical display cases, each with its own group of objects systematically placed in their proper places, thus (it was thought) enabling the absorption of a large quantity of material. The spatial arrangements were straightforward and easy to see and comprehend and the relationship of the visitor to the knowledge offered was as far as possible direct and unmediated.

The modernist museum provides a perfect example of what Basil Bernstein has called the 'collection code'.[33] In analysing the relationships of power and control in the school curriculum, Bernstein sets out the concepts of 'classification' (the construction and maintenance of boundaries between curriculum contents), and 'frame' (the degree of control teacher and pupil possess over the selection, organisation, pacing and timing of the knowledge transmitted and received). These oddly museological metaphors enable the analysis of the grammar of the educational system, the rules of joining together and setting apart of categories of people and knowledge. In the modernist museum clear-cut, strong boundaries are observed between different classes of contents, which are so well insulated from each other that different institutions are required to house objects classified as art, history, anthropology or natural history. It is inconceivable that Impressionist paintings should be collected as part of the natural history museum, although those paintings that depict specimens would be deemed appropriate. The frame of the material to be transmitted was cold, clear and analytical; limited texts accompanied the objects, but other media were cut away to present a cool and rational display. Colour, texture, and sound were not included – the sensory regime of the museum was restricted. What was regarded as appropriate for pedagogic content was tightly controlled by curatorial and academic professionalism, the expectations of governing bodies, and the broader social and cultural networks of male clubs, groups and societies.

During the nineteenth century, museum philosophies were part of the general move towards positivism which involved cutting away all that could not be observed and measured, seen and validated. Rationality was defined as science and knowledge was understood as objective and therefore external to the knower. An epistemological realism resulted in what Jay describes as:

> a scientific world view that no longer hermeneutically read the world as a divine text, but rather saw it as situated in a mathematically regular spatio-temporal order filled with natural objects that could only be observed from without by the dispassionate eye of the neutral researcher.[34]

The idealised space of the modernist museum was positivist, objective, rational, evaluative, distanced, and set aside from the real world. The museum visitor was accorded the status of the neutral observer, walking in an ordered fashion through galleries that were in themselves ordered, well-lit, and laid out for the acquisition of knowledge – the knowledge that could be construed from objects, that, once properly arranged in the neutral space, would speak for themselves.[35]

In order to achieve this ideal space, museum pedagogy was intended to address the body as well as the mind. The space of the museum was one among a number that were developed during the nineteenth century to regulate health, cleanliness and good behaviour. In cities the provision of parks and open spaces for athletics, combined with the provision of libraries and museums, was intended to enable the development of healthy minds in healthy bodies. The opening of national museums and galleries has been described as 'the state . . . sanctifying a set of procedures that sought to regulate the urban profusion and guide its medical, moral and political order; in effect to make that order, and the sphere of culture, one'.[36] The clean, ordered spaces of the galleries, with their clean, well-disciplined works, and their unambiguous closed pedagogic codes, were intended to encourage similar efforts on the part of the audience to clean, regulate and internally discipline themselves.[37]

The founding of many museums, like that of the National Gallery, London, offered an opportunity to link culture to citizenship and to the nation itself.[38] The pedagogical intentions were generalised, abstract and more to do with creating a sense of taste, a cast of mind, an awareness of culture and a set of values than of teaching specific tightly defined parts of subject matter.

Pedagogy in the modernist museum was controlled and ordered at several levels. The first level was that of the subject matter to be learnt, which was limited to facts and information grasped through cognition. The rational mind was expected to act as a unified and focused organ of learning, limited to the reception of pre-existing information that once absorbed would add incrementally to the store of knowledge already lodged in the visitor's mind. Rationality, on the part of the museum visitor, was non-interpretive; rationality meant the recognition and acceptance of given truths.

The second level was how this information was to be gained, how it could be apprehended or learnt. The controlled body, walking at a measured pace, acted as the support for a perception that in itself acted only as a vehicle to convey sense impressions to the mind. These sense impressions, once correctly decoded by the mind, would facilitate the transfer of the authoritative factual information prepared in advance by the professional curatorial expert.

And the third level was that of the use of this information. Public museums were intended, at least in part, to convert raw humanity to civil society, to create clean and docile bodies.[39] The epistemological messages of the museum were envisioned as useful to instil better behaviour, to create model citizens, to enable self-improvement within the rigidly demarcated social structures of the Victorian age. It was not anticipated by museum founders or curators that those who learnt in museums would use the knowledge gained to seize hold of their own futures, to rewrite their own histories, or to step outside of the conventions of the age to rearrange them.

Pedagogy in the modernist museum can be summarised as based on objects which, if properly disposed, spoke for themselves. The visual arrangements on the walls, and the objects grouped in glass cases ready for inspection, carried the messages prepared in advance by the curatorial expert, sanctioned by his peers. These stories had the character of master narratives, of evolutionary progress, or of the

131

encyclopaedic mapping and classifying of the natural and material world. These authoritative master narratives were transmitted to a generalised public, whom it was assumed would benefit through a structured visual promenade through the museum galleries where their neutral gazes would be deployed in a rational manner. An abstract rhetorical educational intention was one of the primary ideals of the museum.

Pedagogy as transmission

The pedagogic approach of the modernist museum and its implications can be analysed using communication and educational theory. Although generally not linked in practice, communication and education theory are intimately connected in their underpinning assumptions about people and social process. Two paradigmatic ways of thinking about communication can be identified[40] – communication understood as a process of information transmission and communication seen much more broadly as part of culture. The first of these, an understanding of communication as transmission, offers useful concepts in the consideration of the modernist museum as a communicator.

The transmission approach has been discussed since the 1970s in the museum literature. A debate between Cameron[41] and Knez and Wright[42] about how to understand communication in museums coincided with the discussion of communication as information-processing in relation to computer technology. Miles[43] pointed out some of the problems of approaching communication in this way within museums. The concept itself has recently been reused and critiqued by Bicknell and McManus.[44]

Communication approached as a process of transmission is characteristic of mass communication, communication to a mass of people, to groups larger than crowds who are unknown to each other, and who do not necessarily occupy the same space at the same time. In Britain, mass communication began to be observed as a phenomenon towards the end of the first half of the nineteenth century,[45] and the museum can be described as one of the first institutions of the mass media.

The transmission view of communication is defined by terms such as 'imparting', 'transmitting', and 'sending'. A geographical metaphor is used – that of sending information across space, from one point to another. This is a metaphor of transportation; the sending of signals and messages over a distance for the purposes of control. The model focuses on the technological processes of communication.

American mass communication research, based on this approach to communication, was stimulated primarily by concern over the political influence of the mass press and (later) over the moral and social consequences of film and radio.[46] More general communication research was concerned with testing efficiency and effectiveness in the fields of education, propaganda, telecommunications, advertising and public relations. This research developed in the United States, a country moving rapidly during the twentieth century from social and political experiments in colonisation to a leadership position within the Western world.[47] During the 1950s in the United States a 'science of communication' began to be discussed, and in a fertile climate of conceptual model-building, a model for communication as transmission was developed.

The basics of the model are straightforward: a communicator (sender, or transmitter), sends a message through a medium to a receiver. The focus is on the technical act of transferring data from a source to a receiver, with the telephone system as an example. One of the first depictions of the model of communication as transmission was that of Lasswell, who famously once said that any act of communication could be understood as by answering the questions: Who? Says what? In which channel? To whom? With what effect?[48]

Underlying this approach to communication is a particular view of knowledge, and of learning. Knowledge is seen as factual, objective, singular and value-free, and therefore able to be transferred from those who are knowledgeable to those who are not. The 'transmission' model of communication understands communication as a linear process of information transfer from an authoritative source to an uninformed receiver. This model of communication is frequently referred to as the 'hypodermic needle', 'bull's eye' or 'magic bullet' model. The receiver of the message to be communicated is conceptualised as open to the reception of the message, which is received more or less efficiently, and in the same way by all.

This approach to communication is based upon a behaviourist explanation of education.[49] Behaviourism proposes that learning takes place through a response following a stimulus. According to this simple model of learning, effects are specific reactions to specific stimuli, so that one can both expect and predict a close correspondence between what is learnt and what is taught, or, to put it another way, between media message and audience reaction. The role of the teacher, as a knowledgeable and authoritative expert, is to structure the subject matter to be mastered so that the learners may absorb it.[50] Sometimes called the banking approach to education,[51] and very powerful in America,[52] this approach to teaching and learning separates the school from the world outside its gates. The appeal of what has been called the simple model of communication can be related to social interests in effects and effectiveness, and to the ubiquity of the stimulus–response model of learning that was fundamental to educational psychology.[53] Much of the work of communication research, both in the museum field and elsewhere, has been concerned with the question of effectiveness.[54]

The transmission model explains rather well the model used by modernist museums in the construction of displays. It was the curator as scholar, expert on the collections and knowledgeable about the relevant discipline, who led the project, chose the objects for display and decided on what to say in the text panels and labels. The audience for the exhibition was rarely defined beyond the catch-all 'general public'. A generalised mass audience was envisioned.[55]

The transmission model of communication also explains the moral imperative that underlay much of the use of culture during the nineteenth century. The somewhat secular metaphors of transmission hide the link to moral and religious practices such as philanthropy or evangelism, which were driven by similar conceptions of people, social processes and relationships. This moral component, of purportedly improving patterns of life, of making things 'better' for others by the giving of new information, underlies communication conceived as transmission. It can be found in nineteenth-century missionary work, paternalism, in gender relations, and in forms of education. As discussed in Chapter 2, as museums were established one of their most prominent functions lay in the field of education. Education was understood as a process of imparting information and, through this, values, such as to constitute the subject as an ideal citizen. The National Portrait Gallery in the 1850s and 1860s was a prime example of this.

Many of the values of the modernist museum can be explained by the transmission approach to communication. These include naturalised assumptions of separation from the quotidian, an emphasis on scholarly values which focus on collection research, the ordering of displays and exhibitions according to the structures of an academic discipline, and an abstract impressionistic view of the audiences for these displays and of the use to which the viewing of the displays might be put. These values, which became established during the later years of the nineteenth century, became the basic assumptions from which most museums operated during most of the twentieth. For many museums, these are still the values that inform everyday working methods today.

However, the understanding of the processes of communication as a process of transmission is severely limited. This approach proposes that communication is bounded by technical processes, and ignores the social and cultural aspects of these processes. It does not explain well the extremely complex relationships that structure acts of understanding between people, and it fails to take account of the active character of the interpretive strategies that are used to make meaning.

In the transmission approach, the complex, ambiguous, multidimensional and fluid processes of communication are reduced to a single, one-way, linear cognitive trajectory with the function of transporting a finite piece of information, a 'message'. Individuals within the communication process are characterised as though operating at both ends of a single axis. The selection, definition, and control of the 'message', and therefore of the meaning of the content of the communicative act, lies with the communicator, who is therefore the power-broker in the transaction. The 'receiver of the message' is considered only in so far as a judgement is made in relation to the correct reception of the message. The receiver, from this perspective, is rendered cognitively passive.

Transmission pedagogy is based on universal laws and models that can be imitated or repeated anywhere. The content to be learnt is structured according to the internal logic of the subject matter or discipline with few concessions to any relationship to the experience or knowledge of the learners. Learners are 'empty vessels to be filled', with the 'knowledge' that learners bring with them into the learning situation dismissed as irrelevant. Underlying this approach is, as we have seen, a behaviourist view of learning, with individuals conceived as atomistic. Atomism asserts that people are separate individuals constituted by their own unique states of consciousness, and by their own capacities and needs. It views the self as a monad, an impermeable integral entity radically different from all others, and, at the extreme, cut off from all others. The atomistic view of the self ignores the degree to which the self is shaped by shared meanings, inflected through experience, has the capacity to change and modify itself through learning, and may objectively consider and develop itself. In other words, people are seen as individuals without curiosity, without capacity to change, and as merely the absorbers of external stimuli.[56]

The transmission approach operates within a functionalist definition of the individual as part of a technologically driven society. Functionalism likened society to a machine, with the constituent parts each carrying out their particular function such that the smooth running of the whole is assured. A normative approach such as this does not encourage critical reflection about existing social institutions, power relations, or specific historical circumstances. Communication research that operated using this model of communication saw itself as 'a practical art in a practical context',[57] and as such consisted of unreflexive and ahistorical empirical studies.

As a communicator, the modernist museum is subject to the same criticisms that have already been identified in relation to the model itself. In the modernist museum, communication is considered as a technical process: which paintings shall be hung, which objects placed in which cases, in which arrangement, and with which attached texts. The information considered appropriate for inclusion in the labels is shorn of any everyday reference, any anecdotal story, any reference to the viewing process itself. It encodes factual information drawn from the field of study within which the object has been placed, frequently expressed in unfamiliar specialist vocabulary. There is little appreciation of the relevance of displays to visitors, and no investigation into the actual response of visitors to such displays.

The modernist period produced museums that, by the mid-twentieth century, were closed, hermetic and self-referential institutions that took for granted their right to an elite authoritative social position. Their pedagogic role, at least in Britain, was assumed through their being open to the public, and in many instances professional practices lapsed.[58] Markham, reporting on the state of museums in Britain in 1938, called them 'indescribably drab', and 'one of the most neglected and least understood of all civic services'.[59] Active provision for visitors was taken less and less seriously as collection and care of collections began to define the work of curators;[60] methods of display remained constant and became outmoded and irrelevant to many potential visitors.

Since mid-century much has changed, but in many traditionally displayed museum galleries the results of understanding communication as transmission is still evident. Specialist knowledge and a curatorial focus of interest lie behind the displays which lay out the themes and parameters of specific specialist areas of knowledge. The facts may be absorbed by visitors, if they themselves can make connections with the material provided. The language of labels is academic, and uses an aesthetic or scientific register. The collections may be enjoyed if visitors understand their context or appreciate their aesthetic qualities. Whether this is

135

done or not is unknown, as there is no audience research and therefore no information on the effectiveness of the display.

An example of a contemporary museum label that embodies the modernist approach makes the point. The National Museum of Ireland in Dublin has a nineteenth-century foundation and still produces formal displays of a rather traditional nature. The text below is from a single display-case used to show recent acquisitions (in 1998), with one item in it:

> *The Altartate Cauldron.*
> The Altartate Cauldron, found in a bog near Clones, Co. Monaghan
> during turf cutting in 1993, is made of poplar with yew handles. The find
> suggests the continuation of certain Later Bronze Age traditions into the
> Early Iron Age, although its form differs from that of later Bronze Age
> cauldrons. A band of ornament below the rim, which may be compared
> closely with that found on certain Iron Age spears, suggests that the
> cauldron may have been carved during the 2nd Century BC.

The language here suggests that the writer, and by implication the museum itself, has not seriously considered the readers at all. The vocabulary, although not difficult in itself, is that of archaeology. The cauldron is a 'find'; the Bronze Age is the technical expression for a certain specialist approach to periodisation. The level of knowledge assumed is very high. Readers are expected to be able to compare the Later Bronze Age and the Early Iron Age. They are expected to be able to compare cauldrons with other cauldrons, but also with spears of a specific date. It is assumed that the ornament can be analysed from prior collection-based knowledge. The language is not dynamic; rather it is cautious, and uses a rather pedantic academic style ('may have been carved at a certain time'; 'suggests that'). It is formal ('may be compared with'), and oblique ('certain traditions'). The style of address is that of a textbook; this is the teacher giving factual information. But the text does not have the clarity of the address of a good teacher; the tone of the text is confusing; it is uncertain, speculative even, and invites the reader to join in the discussion from the point of view of assumed knowledge and experience. In summary, the text is little more than a curatorial musing. It has little to do with any attempt at communication. This museum has not considered the relationship between the knowledge it has produced and its use by real people. If asked who this text was written for, the writer would almost certainly respond: 'For the general public'.

In the modernist museological approach the communication process is one-way. The processes of viewing, or of decoding the message, are not considered, and still less anticipated are the interpretive procedures that museum visitors might employ. In the concentration on acquiring, documenting and researching collections, and on the complex and lengthy internal processes of display development, the users of the displays are simply forgotten. For the modernist curator, the end-product of the process of display or exhibition development is the exhibition itself. Once one display is completed, the work on another begins. Typically, the developmental process is highly complex,[61] involving a range of specialists such as designers, builders, electricians, painters, lighting experts, insurers, conservators, catalogue writers and editors – in addition to the curators. Several of these agents may be contracted in from outside the museum, a number of different deadlines will be running concurrently, and the whole process may take several months or years. Timing and funding is generally very tight and it is all too easy to see the whole event as something which has internal relevance, with the visitors as optional extras.

The museum workers involved in the production of displays all have their specific expertise, but few of them are communicators. Designers were not common in museums in Britain until the 1970s, and even when designers joined the production team, their expertise lay more in the aesthetic or technical aspects of design. Design training rarely includes matters to do with interpretive processes of the users of design products. In some museums, museum educators are now a valued part of the exhibition team, but in a great many this is not the case. Exhibition plans that do not specify intended audiences, and that do not include research into the knowledge and interests these audiences have in the exhibition themes, are likely only to attract those people whose level of specialist knowledge almost matches that of the exhibition's curators. The organising principles and the display codes of these exhibitions are likely to prove problematic for visitors who are unfamiliar with the subject matter, or who do not know how to respond to exhibition techniques. Potential visitors exclude themselves where they fear they will feel inadequate.

As a visitor to French art museums put it in Bourdieu and Darbel's classic study:

> It's hard for someone who wants to take an interest. You only see paintings and dates. To be able to see the differences between things, you need a guidebook. Otherwise everything looks the same.

> I prefer to visit the museum with a guide who explains and helps ordinary mortals understand the obscure points.[62]

More recent research with first-time art museum visitors supports these findings,[63] as does recent research with teenagers in Britain. In a recent study one girl said: 'people stand there admiring it when I haven't a clue what they are looking at'.[64]

In this approach to museum communication, as the transmission model reveals, the curator, as leader of the display development team, is the power-broker. The curator will make decisions about the content of the display, the conceptual level at which verbal statements will be placed, and the perspective from which the material will be approached. Decisions will also be made about the technology to be used to transmit the information (artefact, text, image, sound, film, interactive device) and the design or style of the display (use of colour, texture, space, two- and three-dimensional exhibits). Content, perspective, technology, and stylistics may all be agreed upon with no accompanying discussion about who the display is intended for. Planning exhibitions and writing texts in the absence of an intended and researched viewer and reader at best results in displays that please those who have the same frameworks of intelligibility and strategies of interpretation as the curator.

The adequacy of a transmission approach to communication has been seriously called into question by communication theorists. In communication studies, frequently using television as the field for research, the concept of 'the active audience' has developed.[65] The transmission model of communication, based on the stimulus/response model of education, assumed the possibility of a universal effect on the targets (receivers) of the message, who were thought to be open to the persuasions of the mass media. Following a range of research studies of these assumed 'effects', mostly in relation to television,[66] it was gradually realised that people were not merely passive absorbers of the media. The media–audience relationship was found to be complex and multi-faceted, mediated by factors external to the technical process of information transfer.

In those very few museums in Britain which have carried out audience research on a consistent basis, it took until the 1990s to be able to admit that in the development of exhibitions that would communicate effectively the agenda of the audience was important. In attempting to develop a reliable technology for effective exhibitions 'the initial emphasis had been entirely on the subject matter and the efficient transmission of information, and it was only later that we began to understand and respond to the meaning of a museum visit to the visitor'.[67]

The meaning of a museum visit to the visitor is the product of complex processes of interpretation. The transmission view of communication does not adequately accommodate these processes. The second view of communication goes some way to accounting for interpretive processes, and it relates well to some of these issues that have already been discussed in previous chapters. It is to this second conceptualisation of communication as part of culture that we now turn.

Communication as culture

In social and cultural theory, the turn towards acknowledging the significance of the interpretive paradigm and the growing recognition of the generative power of culture and communication[68] leads to an insistence that representation does not reflect reality, but grants meaning and confers value;[69] in this way it is con-stitutive of reality.[70] The 'cultural turn' signals a sharper analytical focus on matters connected to the making of meaning, the diversity of interpretation, and the power that these have to shape social life.

Contemporary ways of understanding communication focus on the meaning-making activities of individuals and groups. Communication is understood as integral to the production and reproduction of culture. Carey[71] describes this broad approach to communication as a form of secular ritual, as a process of sharing, participation, fellowship and association. Carey's view of communication (and society) is overly harmonious; however, many cultural and communication theorists agree that communication is best understood as a series of processes and symbols whereby reality is produced, maintained, repaired and transformed.[72] The realities experienced by different individuals, groups and communities, are shaped by class, gender and race. Symbolic systems, such as those of art or science, shape, express and communicate our attitudes and interpretations of our experience. As beliefs and values are represented through cultural symbols (words, maps, models), so realities are constructed.

The emphasis on communication from this perspective is on its symbolic and interpretive potential. Where the concept of communication as transmission[73] focused on the most efficient way to transfer ideas across space, frequently in the context of the control of people or distance as part of society seen as a political or economic organisation,[74] the cultural view of communication addresses the methods by which what counts as 'common sense', 'art', or 'science' at any one time is brought into being. Within this view, communication is a much broader process, one which examines ideas in their historical, social and institutional matrices.[75] The significance of communication is as an integral part of culture. Culture itself arises from and is embedded within words, images, symbols, ideas and actions that in their articulation result in social effects. Naming, classifying and displaying, the basis on which museums operate, have what Hacking has called 'looping effects';[76] tacit or explicit choices made by people to adapt or resist cultural classifications that affect their lives and identities.

The view of communication as culture can be linked to some of the ideas of hermeneutics and of constructivism. Hermeneutics, as we saw in Chapter 5, concerns how understanding can be achieved and suggests that interpretation is dialogic, relational. Relational means that words and objects become meaningful within contextual and generative frameworks, but does not mean that such meaning is entirely relative. The attack on theories of meaning characterised by the expression 'anything goes' refuses to acknowledge the extremely important distinction between relational meaning, and relative meaning.

Constructivist learning theory points out that learning is both personal and social; meaning is mediated through interpretive communities. Meanings are in large part controlled by the validation accorded them by the relevant interpretive community. It is the authority of the interpretive community that enables meaning. At the same time, interpretations may differ between interpretive communities. Different systems of knowledge (art, science, history), different ontological or epistemological perspectives in relation to these systems, cultural or ethnic differences, and gendered approaches create differentiated communities whose interpretations of their experiences vary. Interpretive communities have differential access to social networks and resources, and the power to access and control these matrixes influences which meanings are heard most strongly.

In this approach to communication, the focus is on how meaning is constructed through social life by active individual agents, within social networks. Meanings are understood to be negotiated through cognitive frameworks, interpretive strategies and interpretive communities, and are plural, contingent and open to challenge. Within this second approach to communication and learning, communicators act as enablers and facilitators. The task for communicators – or, in the museum, curators, educators and exhibition developers – is to provide experiences that invite visitors to make meaning through deploying and extending their existing interpretive strategies and repertoires, using their prior knowledge

139

and their preferred learning styles,[77] and testing their hypotheses against those of others, including those of experts. The task is to produce opportunities for visitors to use what they know already to build new knowledge and new confidence in themselves as learners and as social agents.

In understanding communication as cultural through and through, and in seeking to understand what this might mean within the museum context, Giroux's concept of critical pedagogy is useful.[78] Critical pedagogy is based on the acknowledgement of culture not as monolithic and unchanging, but, as Giroux describes, as a site of multiple and heterogeneous borders where different histories, languages, experiences and voices come together amidst diverse relations of power and privilege.[79] Cultural studies[80] provides the basis for understanding pedagogy as a form of cultural production rather than as the transmission of a particular skill, body of knowledge or set of values. Critical pedagogy is proposed by Giroux as a cultural practice engaged in the production of knowledge, identities and desires.

Museums may be seen as cultural borderlands, where a range of practices are possible, a language of possibilities is a potential, and where diverse groups and sub-groups, cultures and subcultures may push against and permeate the allegedly unproblematic and homogeneous borders of dominant cultural practices. By viewing museums as a form of cultural politics, museum workers can bring together the concepts of narrative, difference, identity and interpretive strategies in such a way as to create strategies for negotiating these practices. In the post-museum, multiple subjectivities and identities can exist as part of a cultural practice that provides the potential to expand the politics of democratic community and solidarity. By being able to listen critically, museum workers can become border-crossers by making different narratives available, by bridging between disciplines, by working in the liminal spaces that modernist museum practices have produced.

Challenging the canon

Museums are one of the West's signifying systems that have been used to construct dominant canons. At the present time, the ostensibly timeless ideals of the Enlightenment (beauty, truth, knowledge) are being modifed,[81] and those structures created by the modernist state, such as the public museum, are being forced to re-examine their purposes.[82] Today, cultural maps are being re-plotted and re-territorialised. Re-plotting involves bringing to visibility nodes of significance that were formerly subsumed and rendered invisible within large Western-derived universal narratives; and re-territorialisation entails the projection and exploration of new territories formerly left off the cultural map.

Feminist critique has exposed modernist master narratives, one of which is the primacy of the male, as unsustainable;[83] post-colonial approaches have demonstrated the Eurocentric core of much of the history and culture that we take for granted in the West.[84] Knowledge is now understood as historically contingent and context-specific; the site from which knowledge is produced relates to what is accepted as rational. Knowledge is seen as situated or positioned, and as part of culture.[85] Knowledge is also seen as provisional, which enables the acknowledgement of the unstable character of meaning. The certainties of modernism have been replaced by the fluidity of post-modernism, with its indeterminacies, fragmentation, decanonisation, hybridisation and constructionism.[86]

The binary oppositions of Cartesian philosophy that imposed fixed ordering structures such as same/other, centre/margin, mind/body, black/white, are seen as redundant in a move to embrace multi-culturalism and hybridity.[87] The dualistic way of thinking that conceives questions as 'either' one option 'or' another has been called into question,[88] and is deposed in favour of a more dialectical approach where differences are not absolute or finite. Today, concepts of both/and rather than either/or seem to offer more useful explanations.

A 'vast, revisionary will in the western world, unsettling/resettling codes, canons, procedures, beliefs'[89] can be observed. As part of this, museums today are seen as sites of cultural struggle and as a result the stories that are told in museums of history, culture, science and beauty are no longer accepted as naturally authoritative. The modernist museum is being reviewed, reassessed, and reformulated to enable it to be more sensitive to competing narratives and to local circumstances; to be more useful to diverse groups; to fit current times more closely. As one critic put it: 'The museums set up to demonstrate the ideals of the Enlightenment have served their purpose . . . it is easy to see the immense contribution [these museums] have made to the Enlightenment mind. But now it is over.'[90]

The challenge to modernist museum values takes place through a number of strategies. Some of the most revealing are those used by artists. Modernist display styles, codes and narratives have been commented on by Richard Wentworth and Fred Wilson. Richard Wentworth produced a small installation at the British Museum as part of 'Collected', a multi-site exhibition curated by Neil Cummings based at the Photographers' Gallery in London. The exhibition aimed to question how and why some collections became more valued than others and how some people are able to turn their private culture, tastes and habits into public culture, to the exclusion of others.[91]

Richard Wentworth produced a display case in one of the main Egyptian galleries at the British Museum that perfectly mimicked the codes of display used throughout the museum. The material on the upper shelf was carefully selected from the collection of Egyptian Antiquities in the British Museum, spanned a period of more than 4,000 years, and originated from throughout the territory covered by ancient Egypt. All the material on the lower two shelves of this display was collected from the streets immediately surrounding the British Museum during March and April 1997, immediately prior to the exhibition. The Egyptian material was displayed as it would normally be within the museum, with texts that focused on objects' functions and the material from which the objects were made. The contemporary objects were treated in the same way:

> A. Aluminium capped, machine moulded glass bottle in generalised form of fruit with embossed surface simulating peel.

B. Polypropylene capped, machine moulded clear glass bottle with wide mouth disguised with polyvinyl chloride, shrink sleeve decorated with six-colour printing. Adapted to rubbish container by last user – contains empty crisps packet.

M. Vacuum-formed polystyrene throw-away stacking cups with rolled lip. Coloured beige to match a variety of possible contents.

Treating the familiar throw-away objects as though they were museum objects (which, of course, they became) revealed the terse, two-dimensional, essentially useless information produced by an apparently objective and scientific approach. Public culture, in this installation, was exposed as constructed through discourses, the main purpose of which is to embody privilege through empty claims to epistemological authority.

Fred Wilson exposed some of the destructive social values that museums unconsciously accept and uncritically recycle by, in one example, taking the nineteenth-century wooden sculptures of 'cigar-store Indians' that he found in the Maryland Historical Society and turning them round to face the wall. By doing this he signalled a refusal to accept the stereotype of the 'Indian' that they represented and that was endorsed by the museum in hanging them. The wall the sculptures faced was hung with photographs, that he had brought into the institution of contemporary Native Americans from Maryland; he had been told when he asked: 'There are no Indians in Maryland.'[92]

Contemporary culture is analysed as post-modern, post-colonial, and post-structural. What will be the character of culture and pedagogy in the post-museum? Some themes and ways of working which indicate some of the shape of this new museum idea are discussed in the penultimate section of this chapter.

Reorganising museum culture: provisional positions in the post-museum

The reorganisation of culture in the post-museum focuses on what counts as knowledge and how it may be known; this is one vital aspect of a renegotiation of the relationship of the museum to its audiences. One of the characteristics of the post-modern period is that cultural organisations have become much closer to their audiences[93] and have become more conscious of those to whom they are speaking. The politics of address[94] and the concept of voice have become significant. Who is being addressed, how they are spoken to, and who is speaking and how, have become major targets for analyses. These matters raise questions of identity and subjectivity. Subjectivity needs to be understood as something in process, and not as fixed and autonomous, outside history; subjectivity is always gendered, and based in class, race, ethnicity and sexual orientation.[95]

In the modernist museum, knowledge was understood to be disciplinary, or subject-based. Museums were natural history textbooks,[96] or displayed histories of art.[97] In the post-museum, specialist knowledge remains important, but it is integrated with knowledge based on the everyday human experience of visitors and non-specialists. Where the modernist museum transmitted factual information, the post-museum also tries to involve the emotions and the imaginations of visitors.

The Buried Village is a visitor attraction with a small exhibition on the site of Te Wairoa, the village at which Hinemihi was built in 1880. The exhibition tells the story of the volcanic eruption. It begins with an account of Maori life before the arrival of the missionaries, describes the consequences of that event, and moves quickly to its main subject, the eruption of Tarawera and its aftermath. In the deep display cases that are concerned with the eruption itself, the exhibition appeals directly to the feelings and imagination of visitors. Many of the exhibits, which are of domestic items (bits of broken bedstead, crockery, bottles), still remain caked in lava. The exhibition text panels use the words of the survivors to describe the experience of the earthquake, and the words of parents whose children died as the lava covered them all (see Figure 6.1). The exhibits are, of course, the results of the archaeological excavation of the site; displays at the end of the exhibition introduce archaeology as a way of investigating what happened to the houses and the people (see Figure 6.2). Geology is also presented as one way of understanding the movement of the earth and the subsequent reshaping of the landscape. Specialist knowledge is used to answer the question of how to

Figure 6.1 One of the displays at the new exhibition at The Buried Village near Rotorua. The display shows lava-covered household objects and makes them vividly significant through the reported words of Mrs Hazard as she talks to her children during the eruption. (See also Stafford, 1977: 33.)

Photo Eilean Hooper-Greenhill.

Figure 6.2 A display panel which presents the use of archaeology to understand the life of the people at Te Wairoa before the eruption and their actions on the night of 10 June 1886.

understand the dreadful things that happened here once the question has arisen through empathy with the sufferers.

In the post-museum, many voices are heard. At the exhibition 'Torres Strait Islanders'[98] at the Museum of Archaeology and Anthropology at the University of Cambridge in 1998, the introductory panel pointed out that the expedition to the Torres Straits in 1898 was part of several distinct but intersecting histories. The exhibition reviewed the expedition and its legacies, presented 'the strength and richness of Torres Strait Islander *kastom*', and highlighted different types of knowledge. It pointed out that the objects, photographs and quotations displayed carried 'rich and varied meanings through time and across cultures'.[99]

Many voices are heard in the exhibition, drawn from many different kinds of sources. The first section of the exhibition is entitled 'The Sea: Local Knowledge', and the text panel begins with a version of the legend of Gelam, abbreviated from the account told to the anthropologist A. C. Haddon by Jimmy Dei from Mer in 1898. The voice is that of an Islander; he is named and the place where he came from is named in the indigenous language (it is also known as Murray Island). The exhibition includes quotations from anthropologists such as Haddon and Rivers, missionaries and Islanders, and from Islander songs, anthropological journals, and books. Next to a case showing a turtle-shell mask is a video-clip of Ephraim Bani telling the story of the mask. The video was made on the occasion of his visit to the museum from the Torres Straits in 1995. Background research for the exhibition reopened a dialogue between the museum and Island representatives.[100]

The exhibition uses its space well: housed on a circular balcony, it is constructed so that visitors may begin either to the right, and the time of the expedition one hundred years ago, or to the left, to the very recent past and the struggle of the Islanders for self-determination within Australia. The Torres Strait Regional Authority *Annual Report 1997* makes clear the achievement of the Mabo case of 1994,[101] which is also referenced through photographs in the display case nearby.

There is a sense in the exhibition of diverse people acknowledging their connected histories and working together to both analyse it carefully and use it in the present. The exhibition acts to construct a useful past for the present, both within the exhibition and, more importantly, in the events that were entailed in its preparation that will enable a better knowledge of the past in the future.

In the post-museum, histories that have been hidden away are being brought to light, and in this, modernist master narratives are being challenged. The significance of histories which intersect, and of reciprocal historical and cultural effects, are emphasised by the exhibition at the Cambridge University Museum of Archaeology and Anthropology. At the National Portrait Gallery in London, for five months in early 1997, some of the interconnections between eighteenth-century London society and the African slave trade were being mapped out through an exhibition on Ignatius Sancho.[102]

The Sancho exhibition was set in the context of contemporary challenges to the idea of eighteenth-century culture as monolithic. The life-story of Ignatius Sancho 'enriches and diversifies' a sense of what is or is not possible. Sancho was born on a slave ship, was presented as a gift to two sisters in Greenwich, became a servant to the Montague family, a writer and musician, a friend to Laurence Sterne and David Garrick, a sitter to Thomas Gainsborough, and subsequently a grocer. The book that gave a more permanent form to the research for the exhibition was intended to contribute to the literature of Black Studies.[103]

The exhibition at the National Portrait Gallery enabled Sancho to enter the pantheon of English heroes. His former presence in a museum could be seen as less illustrious. A life-cast of his head and face was part of the collection in the museum of the Royal College of Surgeons since the eighteenth century until the museum was bombed during the Second World War.[104] It is catalogued along with casts of other body parts of African people, and also that of 'a Shetland pony, the integuments of which have been removed on one side, to expose the superficial muscles'.[105] The museum contained medical specimens such as skulls and anatomical dissections, along with paintings of people seen as exotic oddities and curiosities; these included dwarfs, albinos, early visitors from the Pacific, Native Americans and Africans. In the eighteenth century and until the middle of the twentieth, Ignatius Sancho was classified museologically as a medical specimen, a curiosity. Even in 1968, things had not changed a great deal. In a report to the Trustees of the museum Sancho's portrait by Gainsborough was illustrated next to a specimen of Pentacrinus caput-medusae.[106] These kinds of associations, though not intentionally hurtful, can be experienced as such.

For the exhibition at the National Portrait Gallery, Sancho's biography and the circumstances of his life in London were researched.[107] Objects were used to stand as witness to the events of the period. This meant refocusing their significance. A coffee cup was displayed in the exhibition. Instead of being presented as a piece of 'cream-ware', dated 1760, and seen as a piece of decorative art, it was read for its historical references and the text drew attention to the use of transfer-printed cream-ware to serve tea, coffee and chocolate. The print on the cup showed a black servant engaged in such an act.

One of the portraits familiar from the permanent display of seventeenth-century paintings was also presented in a radically different way (see Figure 6.3). The portrait of the Duchess of Portsmouth had the following label in the permanent galleries:[108]

> Louise Renee de Penancoet de Kéroualle, Duchess of Portsmouth and Aubigny 1649–1734.
>
> Mistress of Charles II; came to England in 1670 as maid of honour to Charles' sister, the Duchess of Orleans; returned to become the King's mistress in 1671, with the encouragement of the French government, who hoped she would be a diplomatic asset; created Duchess 1673; Evelyn noted her 'childish, simple and baby face'.
>
> By Pierre Mignard (1612–95)
> Oil on canvas, signed, inscribed and dated 1682
>
> In her portrait the Duchess is perhaps portrayed as the sea-nymph Thetis, mother of the hero Achilles, in allusion to her son by the King, the Duke of Richmond.

The prior information required to understand this text fully includes a good knowledge of English history, of Greek mythology and their interrelationships. The information focuses directly on the biography of the main sitter, and on the way in which she is portrayed. The black child also portrayed is ignored.

In the Sancho exhibition, part of the text placed next to the painting read:

> Ignatius Sancho was born on a slave ship crossing the Atlantic in 1729. Following the death of his mother, he was brought to England aged two and given as an exotic present to three sisters in Greenwich. Sancho was deeply unhappy in his situation as a slave-servant, where his natural abilities were discouraged. He ran away and was helped by the family of the Duke of Montagu.

Figure 6.3 Louise de Kéroualle, Duchess of Portsmouth (1649–1734) and unnamed child, by Pierre Mignard, 1682 (NPG 497).

Photo by courtesy of the National Portrait Gallery, London.

The painting is used as a historical document that stands, not for itself, but for the social relationships and cultural practices that it does in fact illustrate, but which have been formerly ignored. The black child in the portrait is not Sancho, but was treated historically like Sancho. The painting worked through analogy.

147

This is very different from the place in the continuous chronological progression of English history that the painting was used to construct in its earlier position. The exhibition was adventurous in the way it grouped and placed objects. In a prominent position stood a harpsichord. As this was contemplated, harpsichord music, composed by Sancho, could be heard. Set within the dais on which the instrument stood was a set of slave shackles, a whip and a slave collar (see Figure 6.4). The harpsichord had been borrowed from the Victoria and Albert Museum and the other items from Northampton Museum and Art Gallery. The text read:

> Instruments of restraint and torture were essential to slavery. These examples were brought from Jamaica to Northampton in 1860 by the Reverend John Turland of the Baptist Missionary Society to demonstrate the cruelty of the slave system. Despite their kindness to Sancho the Montagues, whose family home was in Northamptonshire, had in the early 18th century, owned estates and slaves in St. Lucia and Antigua.

The ways in which objects are selected, put together, and written or spoken about have political effects. These effects are not those of the objects *per se*; it is the use made of these objects and their interpretive frameworks that can open up or close down historical, social and cultural possibilities. By making marginal cultures visible, and by legitimating difference, museum pedagogy can become a critical pedagogy. By exposing the interrelationships between eighteenth-century culture and society and the slave-trade, the exhibition acknowledged a part of British history that has been ignored until recently.

The reorganisation of museum culture is premised on a new relationship between the museum and its audience, and a major part of this is a new and more dynamic approach to the encounter between the visitor and the museum narratives. Formerly austere spaces, established as sites for the use of the eye, have been reinvented as spaces with more colour, more noise, and which are more physically complex. This represents a shift in what Bennett calls 'the ratio of the senses'.[109] Museums are also using the World Wide Web to link communities, cultures and collections across the world; the Sancho exhibition, for example, had a linked website. Objects have become mobilisers of both actual and virtual conversations.

The knowledge that visitors bring with them is actively being considered in the development of approaches to exhibition content. 'Seeing Salvation', an exhibition at the National Gallery, London, in the spring of 2000, rearranged the collections to open up new possibilities. The Director set out his rationale in the introduction to the catalogue of the exhibition:

> All great collections of European painting are inevitably also collections of Christian art . . . Yet if a third of our paintings are Christian, many of our visitors now are not . . . Addressing questions of slender concern to those of other – or no – beliefs, [the paintings] seem to many irrecoverably remote . . . We have put some of the Gallery's religious

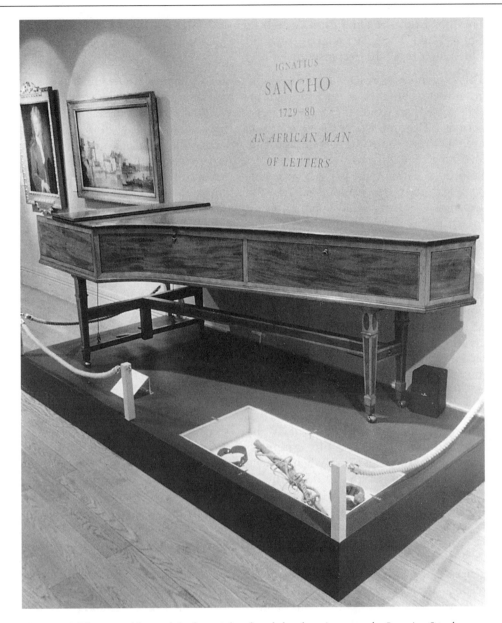

Figure 6.4 The assemblage of the harpsichord and the slave items at the Ignatius Sancho exhibition at the National Portrait Gallery, London.
Photo Eilean Hooper-Greenhill.

pictures in a new context, not – as in other exhibitions – beside works by the same artist or from the same period, but in the company of other works of art which have explored the same kinds of questions across the centuries. A new neighbour for a painting allows us to have a different dialogue with it.[110]

The themes of the exhibition, which included 'Sign and Symbol', 'The Dual Nature', and 'The True Likeness', enabled an exploration of the difficulties facing Christian artists when representing Christ.

This exhibition represents a reassessment of the relevance and meaningfulness of art museum practice to the multicultural audience of today. To structure an exhibition of art works through the categories of artists' biographies and historical periods is to group works together in a way that assumes that visitors will recognise and have some knowledge of art-historical values. This assumes a certain level of education, and also the experience of a certain form of education. Embedded within these disciplinary values are cultural values which conceal the complex interrelationships between, for example, art and religion in Western societies. Visitors may have neither the disciplinary background to make sense of the art-history based exhibition structure, nor the cultural knowledge to grasp the significance of the individual paintings. In focusing on the content of the objects in a direct way, and in grouping them in themes that arise from this content, the ideological framework for the objects is made more open and explicit.

Communication in the modernist museum was understood as a process of transmitting information; the pedagogic approach was formal, didactic, and based on disciplinary knowledge. The museum audience was treated as a unified group, and the museum given the function of both educating and elevating. Dynamic in its day, by the middle of the twentieth century, at least in Britain, the modernist museum was regarded as stultified and was no longer seen to be relevant to broad social needs.

During the twentieth century newer forms of visual media such as film, television, photography and the World Wide Web, have usurped some of the expository functions of the museum. Why is it necessary to go to a museum to see a stuffed dead animal in a glass case when a living one can be seen playing in its natural setting by turning on the TV? Why make an expensive and tiring journey to see an original painting when a high-quality reproduction can be bought on the high street? Learner-centred approaches to teaching introduced over the last thirty years have encouraged critical and questioning visitors, who are not content to be told what to think; an emphasis on consumer power has resulted in a demand for high standards of visitor facilities. At the same time, post-colonial societies generate new cultural needs which affect museum collections. Moves towards reconciliation and reparation following the destructive events of the nineteenth and twentieth centuries require museums to review their holdings and the stance they take towards them

Faced with these challenges, museums have begun to re-evaluate their social roles, and to reposition themselves in relation to their audiences. New forms of museum pedagogy are demanded. The understanding that communication is the basis on which culture is both maintained and transformed; the acceptance that culture has political effects and can be either empowering or inhibiting; the recognition of the significance of objects in relation the construction of the self, and for the development of cultural identity, all set new challenges for the interpretation of visual culture in the museum.

The rebirth of the museum

This chapter draws the themes of the book together. It summarises the character of the modernist museum and considers further the idea of the post-museum. Most of the chapter is taken up with a final case-study that enables the discussion of the interpretation of visual culture using the concepts that this study has sought to elaborate.

The modernist museum – an enduring model

The modernist museum represents a nineteenth-century European model. In contrast to earlier princely cabinets and royal collections it was conceived to play a public role as part of the nation-state, a major part of which concerned the education of large sections of society. The collection and classification of artefacts and specimens, frequently from territories under the control of the collecting nation, were drawn together to produce an encyclopaedic world-view, understood from a Western perspective. The modernist museum emerged gradually to become a fully established and very powerful institutional form by the end of the nineteenth century. It has remained the idea of what a museum is for most of the twentieth century, and is still today, at the dawn of the twenty-first, what springs to mind when the word 'museum' is used.[1]

The modernist museum collected objects and placed them on display. Visual statements, constructed through objects placed in carefully fixed relationships, presented aspects of a European world-view. The power of display as a method of communication lies in its capacity to produce visual narratives that are apparently harmonious, unified and complete. These holistic and apparently inevitable visual narratives, generally presented with anonymous authority, legitimised specific attitudes and opinions and gave them the status of truth. Display is a one-way method of mass communication – once it is completed and opened to the public it is very difficult to modify. In the modernist museum, the voice of the visitor was not heard.

The modernist museum was and is imagined as a building, which might have a classical form with columns and a pediment; might equally be the white cube of the modernist art museum; or, in recent years, might have the more unusual and dynamic appearance of museums such as the Guggenheim Museum in Bilbao. Although the form might vary, the processes of museum-making, and the museum/audience relationship, remain the same.

The post-museum – a new museum concept

Born in the nineteenth century, the modernist museum is still a force to be reckoned with. But the idea of the museum is being reborn and some of its characteristics and challenges are becoming clear. The post-museum will retain some of the characteristics of its parent, but it will re-shape them to its own ends.

The great collecting phase of museums is over. The post-museum will hold and care for objects, but will concentrate more on their use rather than on further accumulation. In addition, the post-museum will be equally interested in intangible heritage. Where the tangible material objects of a cultural group have largely been destroyed, it is the memories, songs and cultural traditions that embody that culture's past and future.

In the modernist museum display is the major form of communication. This transmission approach to pedagogy has severe limitations, as has been discussed. In the post-museum, the exhibition will become one among many other forms of communication. The exhibition will form part of a nucleus of events which will take place both before and after the display is mounted. These events might involve the establishments of community and organisational partnerships; the production of objects during educational programmes which then enter the collections; periods of time when specific community groups use the museum spaces in their own way; writers, scientists and artists in residence; or satellite displays set up in pubs and shops.[2] During these events, discussions, workshops, performances, dances, songs, and meals will be produced or enacted.

The production of events and exhibitions as conjoint dynamic processes enables the incorporation into the museum of many voices and many perspectives. Knowledge is no longer unified and monolithic; it becomes fragmented and multi-vocal. There is no necessary unified perspective – rather a cacophany of voices may be heard that present a range of views, experiences and values. The voice of the museum is one among many.

There are difficult issues to be resolved here about the continued responsibility of the museum for the production of knowledge, the care of its tangible and intangible collections, the need to balance opportunities to speak for all who wish to do so, and the question of when, whether and how to take a stand in relation to moral and ethical matters. There are no easy answers. Many museums, especially those with ethnographic collections, are already working with their various communities to negotiate their own provisional solutions to each issue as it arises. Together, the solutions will add up to new processes and ways of working.

Where the modernist museum was (and is) imagined as a building, the museum in the future may be imagined as a process or an experience. The post-museum will take, and is already beginning to take, many architectural forms. It is, however, not limited to its own walls, but moves as a set of process into the spaces, the concerns and the ambitions of communities.

The development of the post-museum will represent a feminisation of the museum. Rather than upholding the values of objectivity, rationality, order and distance, the post-museum will negotiate responsiveness, encourage mutually nurturing partnerships, and celebrate diversity. It is likely too, that much of the intellectual development of the post-museum will take place outside the major European centres which witnessed the birth of the modernist museum.

The remainder of this chapter is taken up with a final case-study which is based on the life-story (so far) of one object, a Lakota Sioux Ghost Dance Shirt. The narrative tracks the movement of one single object into a museum and out again. It shows how and why objects were collected and why they may be repatriated; it also shows how change can, on the one hand, be long and slow, but, on the other, very rapid and dramatic. The story of the Ghost Dance Shirt presents some of the dilemmas that face museums in the West today, and shows how one museum negotiated this dilemma through working together with its visitors and with other stakeholders to arrive at a provisional resolution.

I do not present this case-study to take a stand on matters to do with repatriation as a whole. These matters are complex and, today, highly politicised. Each issue must be treated on its own merits. My interest in the Ghost Dance Shirt is in terms of its meaning to a number of diverse interpretive communities. The themes of narrative, difference, identity, interpretive procedures and museum pedagogy run through the account.

The Ghost Dance Shirt: public visual culture or sacred talisman?

The life-stories of artefacts take place within a series of local circumstances, and interpretive and artefactual frameworks, which may remain stable for a long period of time, or change very rapidly. Each local circumstance will involve specific individual actors and communities, and will be linked in a range of ways to broad signifying systems. An artefact may find itself in a number of geo-graphical and institutional sites. In each site, it will be positioned within a group of related objects that together form a meaningful set. Within each local circum-stance, specific meanings will be mobilised that have provisional significance within the site concerned. These meanings may change radically as the object is moved from one site of semiosis to another. As the moves take place in time and across space, earlier meanings may be lost or recovered, overlaid by new significations, or reinterpreted by different interpreters. Meanings, as we have seen, are constructed through a range of semiotic frameworks, which include texts, artefacts, actions, events, and which involve active individuals within interactive communities. It is the issue of meaning that will form one of the main forces behind the development of the post-museum.

On 19 January 1892, Kelvingrove Museum and Art Gallery in Glasgow acquired a substantial body of Native American material.[3] The Accessions Register briefly describes each object and records what can be surmised to be comments that were made as the objects joined the collection:[4] '2a: Pair of Buckskin Leggins [*sic*], embroidered with beads worn by "Calls-the-name" Squaw Chief of the Brulé Sioux in 1976'; Waistcoat of buckskin covered with beadwork worn by "Rain-in-the-face" the Mineconjou Sioux warrior . . .' Listed along with other donated objects is 3c: '"Ghost Shirt" of cotton cloth with feather ornament, blessed by "Short Bull" the High Priest to the Messiah, and supposed to render the Wearer invulnerable. Taken from a Sioux Warrior killed at the battle of Wounded Knee, 30th Dec. 1890.' The Ghost Dance Shirt entered the museum already imbued with affiliations which were significant at the time and are so again today, although for the period of one hundred years the significance seems to have been almost lost.

The entries in the museum Register read like a roll-call of heroes: Sitting Bull, Rain-in-the-Face, Short Bull, Lone Bull, Big Foot. Four of the items are associated with Wounded Knee: the Ghost Dance Shirt, and in addition, a 'War necklace of hide fringe made from sections of deer's hoof' (92–2i); a 'Pair of Moccasins of buckskin embroidered with beadwork. Taken from "Across the room" son of Big Foot . . .' (92–3b); and a 'Sioux cradle' (92–3d).[5] During 1891–2, Buffalo Bill's Wild West Show had toured Britain. Calls The Name, Short Bull, and Lone Bull were with the Show as performers;[6] and the Show was in Glasgow at the time of the acquisition of the objects.[7] The objects may have seemed attractive to the museum as examples of an exotic way of life, and as objects that would be both educational and at the same time popular with the public, who had possibly just seen some of them used in the Wild West Show.

George Crager, who acted as translator and manager for the Native American group working for the Show, offered the objects to the museum, describing them as his 'collection'.[8] It is not known how these objects were acquired, although it is clear that Crager was at Wounded Knee shortly after the massacre; as a man who acted on many occasions as a Lakota Sioux interpreter[9] he had secured a job as special correspondent for the *New York World*.[10] It would appear that as the bodies of those killed were buried together in a trench at the site, they were stripped of any potential mementoes by some of the white soldiers in the burial party and by civilians.[11] Crager was in the area within one month of the event, and was photographed with 'Buffalo Bill and Sioux leaders at Pine Ridge Agency'.[12] It is certainly possible that the Ghost Dance Shirt could have been acquired by Crager shortly after the massacre at Wounded Knee.

The Accessions Register refers to the 'battle of "Wounded Knee"'. The events that took place have been well documented, and to refer to the event as a 'battle' is inaccurate.[13] Sitting Bull had been killed on 15 December 1890 during the process of his arrest[14] and by 28 December the members of his band, the Hunkpapa, accompanied by some of Big Foot's Miniconjou, were encamped at Wounded Knee creek, surrounded by soldiers of the 7th Regiment of the United States Army.[15] The Native American group was made up of 120 men and 250 women and children, and most of the men were disarmed. During the removal of their remaining weapons, a shot was fired and the surrounding soldiers opened fire indiscriminately; 153 people were killed at the site, and others died later from wounds: altogether close to 300 of the 370 at the camp were killed.[16]

At the camp, the men had been wearing Ghost Dance shirts, sacred and thought to be imbued with protective qualities.[17] The medicine man had protested at the removal of the weapons by dancing some Ghost Dance steps and chanting one of the holy songs, assuring the men that the soldiers' bullets could not penetrate their shirts: 'The bullets will not go toward you . . . The prairie is large and the bullets will not go toward you.'[18] The Ghost Dance religion offered hope to the Lakota tribes, who in 1890 were verging on cultural breakdown due to loss of tribal lands and the imposition by the US Government of an alien way of life.[19] A holy man, Wovoka, living in Nevada, promised a return to a traditional way of life in a land without white people, and the return of dead friends and relatives, if his faith was embraced and the Ghost Dance performed.[20] Ghost Dance shirts, worn during the Dance, were sometimes produced as a group by dancers after having been inspired by the visions.[21]

The Ghost Dance Shirt in Glasgow, prior to its acquisition by the museum, had been a sign of hope and the revival of Lakota values, of invulnerability and strength. It had possibly been worn during a performance of the Ghost Dance, a religious event, and, assuming that its provenance is correct, had been worn as a protection against betrayal and attack. It was understood as a religious object, a protective talisman with magic powers.

Crager's collection was sometimes placed on display for visitors to the Wild West Show,[22] and the latter should be examined as the background against which the objects were acquired. The Wild West Show was already in existence by the time of Wounded Knee. In 1884, William F. Cody (Buffalo Bill), in partnership with Nate Salsbury, opened the Wild West Show in St Louis, Missouri. The Show quickly became fashionable, and a performative format was evolved that would remain largely the same for the next thirty years. One of the biggest attractions were the Native Americans, the 'Indians'.[23] The formula that Cody developed presented the American West as the 'frontier', a land of heroes and glorious battles. His Show was one of what would turn out to be a large number of media events that constructed the enduring myth of the 'West'.[24]

Cody produced a master narrative of the West,[25] partly through working with real historical events and real historical figures. After Wounded Knee, a large number of Native Americans went on tour with the Wild West Show in lieu of jail.[26] Sioux who had charged Custer at Little Bighorn later charged him nightly in the Show.[27] Cody, Buffalo Bill, presented himself as having lived through the events he depicted, as indeed he had, and continued to do so as the Show developed. During the Custer Campaign and the Ghost Dance period, Cody worked intermittently for the army and each time incorporated elements of his experience into the Show.[28] Through the intermingling of history and performance he created a mythic code that presented the 'Indians' as savage attackers and the whites as vulnerable victims. The role of the 'Indians' in the Show was to attack whites. Audiences were in no doubt that this is what 'Indians' were 'actually like'.[29] Set pieces, such as the 'Capture of the Deadwood Mail Coach by Indians', were devised;[30] they presented Native Americans as aggressive killers and whites as victims who were then forced to defend themselves.[31] In this inversion of history, Buffalo Bill exploited an iconography of white victimisation that can be traced back to Puritan captivity narratives;[32] the trope transferred to the frontier was construed by audiences as 'real' through the ambiguity between history and performance.[33]

The Wild West Show and its several imitators, and dime novels (some stories were based around Cody's experiences) which presented a romanticised version of events for a mass audience, together generated an image of what Francis calls 'the Imaginary Indian'.[34] The Plains Indians represented all 'Indians' in the minds of the public. The complexity of North American native cultures, and diverse groups, was reduced to a single image – that of the mounted, war-bonneted Plains chieftain.[35] This unified and simplified stereotype had one major characteristic – its savagery. Cody, although himself sympathetic to the plight of the Native Americans, created his show in the form of an allegory: the triumph of civilised values over the barbarity of the wilderness. The more savage the wilderness, the greater the power of civilisation. The apparent reflection of history in the making underlined these values even more. Within the context of the Wild West Show, the Ghost Dance Shirt is reduced to one of the signs that sustained the stereotypical 'Imaginary Indian'. It had already attained the status of 'visual culture'.

The Ghost Dance Shirt on display

It is not known whether the Ghost Dance Shirt was placed along with the other acquisitions on display when it entered Kelvingrove Museum in January 1892, although it is possible that it has been on display continuously since that date.[36] What is sure is that it was one of the objects on display in the Ethnography Gallery at the museum, which was set out as it still is today during the late 1950s or early 1960s.[37] In a single room, objects from North America, Asia, Africa, Australia and New Zealand are gathered together. The largest groups of cases contain 'Indian' material, grouped geographically: South West Indian, North West Coast Indian, Eastern Woodland Indian (Cree, Chippewa), North West Coast Indian (Haida, Tlingit, Kwakuitl), and South American Indian (i.e. Mexico). There are two cases containing Plains Indian material, and here objects from several groups can be found, including the Brulé band of Dakota, Blood, Blackfoot, Comanche. No dates are mentioned, except in connection with the Ghost Dance Shirt. The North American section of the gallery is the most visited part, with the Plains Indian material the most popular of all.[38] One reason for this is the study of the Plains Indian at primary school level.

The Ethnography Gallery at Kelvingrove has characteristics that are recognisable as typical of galleries of this date; material drawn from wide areas of the world is grouped together, diverse and fragmented specific cultures are assembled to form a unified narrative; the narrative is timeless. The result is an exotic story – sometime in the past and somewhere in space.

One of the characters in this story, the Imaginary Indian, would already be familiar to visitors in the 1960s from children's books, John Wayne Westerns, films and Cowboy and Indian games, and the Boy Scouts.[39] The Ghost Dance Shirt might have spoken of camp-fires, wigwams, Hiawatha, beautiful Indian princesses, and bows and arrows. Little in the gallery encouraged a more critical reading – the myths were left to be recycled rather than decoded. The text: '*Neck ornament* of hide with deer's hoof fringes. Both men and women wore necklaces and ear ornaments. Taken from a warrior after the battle of Wounded Knee', echoes the Accession Register closely.

In 1992, one hundred years after the Ghost Dance Shirt had been acquired by the museum, it was loaned to 'Home of the Brave', a temporary exhibition in Glasgow. Here it was seen by John Earl, a lawyer from Atlanta, Georgia, who recognised it as other than a signifier of the 'Imaginary Indian'. He contacted the Wounded Knee Survivors Association, and set in train a series of events that resulted in the Shirt being repatriated in 1999. During the debates over whether the shirt should be 'returned home' or not, a number of interpretive strategies, some old and some new, came into play.

The Shirt itself was redisplayed twice during the period. By 1995 it had been taken out of the Ethnography Gallery and placed in the large main hall of the museum. This was clearly an attempt to respond to public interest by putting the Shirt in a more accessible position, but it was also a way of detaching it from its ethnographic significance and moving it into a new framework for making meaning. The temporary positioning had limited effectiveness – the display case dated back to about the 1930s, the Shirt was draped over a headless dressmaker's dummy, and the light was extremely poor (Figure 7.1). A large page-sized typed label was attached to the elderly wooden display case which visually obscured the object within, but did serve to highlight the moral and political dilemma. The details of the history of the Shirt, as it was known then, the nature of the claim from the Wounded Knee Survivors Association and the position of the museum (which at that stage was to retain the Shirt in Glasgow for educational reasons), were all spelt out. Comments were invited on how the dilemma should be resolved: 'Please give us your comments on whether you think the shirt should be returned.' This was the beginning of what would be an extraordinary episode in the museum's history, one that opened museum issues to public scrutiny and took a course that was actively discouraged both by prevailing professional practice and by specific professional advice from British and American curators.

Interpreting the Ghost Dance Shirt

The demands for the return of the shirt and the first visit of the Wounded Knee Survivors Association to Glasgow in 1995 generated a considerable amount of media coverage, and much of it recycled the old stereotypes. Predictably, it was the tabloids that used the most extreme language, revealing the crude and simplistic ideas of 'unschooled minds';[40] 'Indians in heap big row for shirt: a tribe of Red Indians are on the warpath . . . to claim back a sacred shirt from a Scots

Figure 7.1 The Lakota Ghost Dance Shirt redisplayed in an old showcase in the main hall of Kelvingrove Museum in Glasgow. The lengthy text on the side of the case gave extensive detail of the story of the Shirt and the dilemma facing the museum.

Photo Eilean Hooper-Greenhill.

museum';[41] 'Sioux pow-wow for the return of Ghost Shirt: In a different age they would have arrived painted for war to hurl themselves on the guns of the white men intent on killing their race.'[42] However, even more sober newspapers could barely resist the opportunity. Headlines included 'Lakota Sioux raid Glasgow to seek return of 'ghost shirt',[43] and 'Sioux on the warpath'.[44]

The *Daily Mail* gave a few clues to its readers to place the story within existing frames of reference: 'to generations of Scots bred on John Wayne Westerns', and 'the Lakota Sioux – the Indians made famous by Kevin Costner's *Dances With Wolves* blockbuster'. However, having established a visual picture the *Daily Mail* presented a human and sympathetic, if romantic, story:

> To Scots . . . it is just another dry museum piece, an artefact of a people long gone. To the Lakota Sioux . . . it is, literally, symbolic of the death of their race . . . Lawyer John Earl, a Cherokee, said . . . 'I can't describe how I felt . . .' On his return he contacted . . . Marcella Lebeau, the Lakota granddaughter of Rain-In-The-Face . . . The curator of history for Glasgow museums said: 'We are sympathetic. I wouldn't close the door on its repatriation.'[45]

Glasgow Museums had asked for comments from the public about whether the Shirt should be returned. Letters sent to the museum and published in the Press were almost unanimously of the view that the Shirt should be returned. In spite of the extreme language used by some of the newspapers, the letters were carefully and thoughtfully written. A number of interpretive strategies were used in constructing meanings for the Shirt. The debate was almost always placed within a moral framework: 'Please give it back to the rightful owners from whom it was stolen. The North American Indians have the same rights as us to have their stolen property returned to them.' Frequently Scottish complicity in the exploitation of the Sioux, and a present-day responsibility to atone for this, was mentioned: 'I may be wrong, but I am sure that I've read somewhere that the commanding officer on that dreadful day in 1890 was a Scot'; 'Prominent among our European thugs were the Spanish and British; prominent among the British were the Scots.'

Affinity between the Scots and the Sioux was a further strong theme. One writer noted 'a subtle analogy between the Sioux and the Scots . . . a clear parallel . . . between the fates of a talisman of the Sioux nation and the physical symbol of the mythical origins of the Scots, the Stone of destiny . . .' Links were made with the Highland Clearances and the loss of Sioux lands: 'We all in Scotland feel the pain when we think of the highland clearances, a pain felt in the soul . . .' Links were also made between Scottish and Sioux cultural deprivation: 'We as a nation have witnessed our own culture being ravaged and treated with disrespect and contempt . . . the Shirt should have been handed back immediately.'

The museological argument made by Glasgow Museums in initially refusing the request for repatriation on the grounds that it would create a precedent that could prove difficult for other museums at a later date (what became known as the 'floodgates' argument) was roundly dismissed: 'A precedent for what – compassion?' A parallel argument that the item should be retained on educational grounds was equally firmly rebuffed: 'Your claim . . . is repellent'; 'I can see no better demonstration of education purpose than a publicised return of this artefact.' This writer spoke to the museum on its own terms, pointing out how the situation was of relevance to 'current dialectics in the nature of the contemporary museum . . . at an international and national level'.[46]

Many of the associations and arguments made by the writers echoed points made in newspaper stories quoting the lawyers accompanying the Wounded Knee delegation to Glasgow. Mario Gonzales was reported as pointing out 'Our history is like yours; you had your massacre in a glen, ours was in a creek. You had the Highland clearances, we lost our land.' He further pointed out that the Shirt was a funerary object, 'stolen from a dead person.' Gonzales even pointed out that he himself was part Scottish on his great-great grandmother's side.[47]

The second redisplay, in time for the public hearing in 1998, moved the Shirt upstairs into its own separate gallery where three new matching display cabinets were used to show the Ghost Dance Shirt and other items with attributed Wounded Knee provenance: the necklace and moccasins, and the baby cradle. The move upstairs represented a move from a timeless ethnography to a period within living memory; a move that can be seen as from culture to history. This was reinforced by an elaborate three-screen video presentation that presented portraits of Lakota heroes past and present, and the story of Wounded Knee and the events that took place there through images, photographs and words. Images of the Shirt itself were used in the video to show the movement of the Shirt while being worn, as for example during the massacre itself, where the Shirt was lit as though by gunfire. The video positioned the Shirt clearly within its sacred, religious framework, and in relation to the struggles of the Lakota against colonial aggression. The museum here attempted to invoke the framework for the very first meanings for the shirt in order to go beyond the simplistic stereotypical interpretations that journalists and possibly others were prone to slip into. It presented the historical events as a preliminary to understanding the contemporary demands for return, which were also laid out clearly.

By 1998, changes in museum personnel,[48] support from the City Council and a uniquely open approach to the situation, had led to a public hearing where the arguments for and against the return of the shirt were fully aired. By this time, the request for repatriation was heard by Glasgow residents in a very different way. Although the result of the hearing was not a foregone conclusion, the Shirt was no longer a mere document of the past with no cultural significance apart from a reference to childhood games and macho movies. It had become part of a known history and tradition that could be used to underpin new ways of thinking and acting. In some sense, a new interpretive community had been established, able to use newly learnt interpretive strategies.

The Shirt, in conjunction with the other artefacts, the museum displays, and the public letters and debates in Glasgow, had become part of a network that generated, through interpretation, both new interpretive communities and new interpretive possibilities.[49] The events in Glasgow linked into other media events, such as the six fifty-minute programmes *History in Action: the Wild West*, screened during the autumn of 1996, where Marie-Not-Help-Him, who had become a familiar name in the Glasgow events, was seen talking about her history. One year later, in September 1997, a second event was given a high media profile; the body of Long Wolf, who had travelled with Cody and the Wild West Show, and who had died of pneumonia before returning home, was exhumed from

Brompton Cemetery in west London. The newspaper story was moving, and showed how close history is to the present. As Long Wolf lay ill, he drew a wolf and asked for it to be carved on his gravestone. It was this carving that enabled the grave to be located. Once Long Wolf's family had been found, they came to take him home. The party included his granddaughter, aged 87, who could remember her mother's story of the death of her father when she (her mother) was 12 years old, travelling with him and the Wild West Show. One newspaper report was headed by a half-page colour portrait of Long Wolf's great-grandson in full feathered war-bonnet.[50]

Eight months after the decision to repatriate the Shirt,[51] a party from Glasgow took it back to where it had come from. Prior to this, comments from visitors in a book placed close to where it stood, once again, in the main hall at Kelvingrove, described it as 'going home', which was 'the right thing to do'. On 31 July 1999, at HVJ Lakota Cultural Centre, Cheyenne River Reservation, the Ghost Dance Shirt was carried in procession by tribal elders wearing feather bonnets and speeches; singing and drumming followed. Written accounts of memories of the events at Wounded Knee were read by descendants. The next day, the Shirt was taken back to the site of the massacre at Wounded Knee and prayers and further ceremonies took place (Figure 7.2). The Shirt is now in the care of the South Dakota Historical Society, pending the building of a museum at Wounded Knee.[52]

Figure 7.2 Marie-Not-Help-Him and Sterling Hollowhorn unfold the Ghost Dance Shirt on the site of the mass grave at Wounded Knee.

Photo John Lynch.

Over the 110 years or so of the life of the Ghost Dance Shirt, its significance has been summoned to serve the causes of religion, war, entertainment, display and reconciliation. It has been used to construct narratives of heroism, massacre, sensationalism, colonial justification, scientific study, media drama, humanitarianism,[53] and historical change. It has acted as a marker and an instigator of both old and new ways of thinking. There will be more uses for the Shirt as time passes. There is no one way in which objects 'mean'. There is no essential truth of the object. Their meaning is fluid, changeable, relational and contextual. As circumstances and contexts change around them, they are seen in different ways and mean new things. Viewers in museums, and elsewhere, are social creatures, and the personal meanings they construct are influenced by their particular social contexts, by their 'interpretive communities'[54] and their 'interpretive repertoire'.[55] The meanings of the object are created through the personal and social processes of interpretation.

Towards the post-museum

The ideas on which this book has been based are not very new, and in many intellectual fields they are not very controversial; however, when they are considered in relation to the modernist museum they become both of these things. They throw up in a stark way the need for a cultural change within museums. Although there is much dynamic and exciting innovative work being done, much of this is challenged by the forces of conservatism, and in many museums the need for change is refused. The issues concern the articulation of ideologies with the prioritisation of resources. Museums are frequently large and always complex, with many key stakeholders who will have divergent views on most matters; wholesale change is rarely possible or desirable in such circumstances.

The post-museum faces considerable challenges. The character of these challenges is beginning to become clear, but the modernist values, relations and practices on which most museums are based, and which are not regarded as contentious by everyone, are deeply imbedded. Visual culture within the museum is a technology of power. This power can be used to further democratic possibilities, or it can be used to uphold exclusionary values. Once this is acknowledged, and the museum is understood as a form of cultural politics, the post-museum will develop its identity.

Notes

Preface

1 Deepwell, 1995: 7.
2 Fornas, 1995: 3.
3 Hooper-Greenhill, 1992.
4 Foucault, 1970: 132; Hooper-Greenhill, 1992: 185.
5 Visual culture denotes both a suite of artefacts, and an approach to analysis. The artefacts included within this umbrella term generally include paintings, sculpture, advertisements, film, television. I want to use the term to refer to museum collections in general. The use of the expression 'visual culture' signals an analytical approach that refuses to accept value-laden expressions such as 'Fine Art', and a more general critical and sociological approach to the study of the artefacts themselves and their social use.
6 See discussion in Fornas, 1995: 6.
7 McGuigan, 1996: 5–6.

1 Culture and meaning in the museum

1 I am using 'exhibition' and 'display' as synonymous in this study. Where I intend a distinction between permanent displays and temporary exhibitions I will make this clear.
2 Worts, 1995: 176.
3 Desai and Thomas, 1998.
4 Anim-Addo, 1998: 39.
5 Interpretive philosophy.
6 See McGuigan, 1996: 5–6.
   The number of books with the simple title *Culture* is enough to suggest this level of interest. See, for example: Williams, 1981; Jenks, 1993; Bennett, 1998a.
7 The number of books with the simple title *Culture* is enough to suggest this level of interest. See, for example: Williams, 1981; Jenks, 1993; Bennett, 1998a.
8 Williams, 1976: 76–82; quoted and discussed in Jordan and Weedon 1995: 6–8.
9 Jenks, 1993: 6.
10 Williams, 1981: 10.
11 Jordan and Weedon, 1995: 7; Hall, 1997: 2.
12 Hall, 1997: 2.
13 Bennett, 1998a.
14 McGuigan, 1996: 6.
15 Giroux, 1992: 168.
16 Ibid.: 169.
17 See Williams, 1981: 13.
18 See McGuigan, 1992 and Turner, 1990, for example.
19 Williams, 1981: 207.
20 Hall, 1997: 2.
21 Ibid.: 24.
22 O'Sullivan *et al.*, 1994: 68.
23 McCarthy, 1996: 8.
24 Hall, 1997: 3.
25 Ogbu, 1995.
26 Jordan and Weedon, 1995: 18.
27 Barrett, 1991: 123–129.
28 O'Sullivan *et al.*, 1994: 68–69.
29 Jameson, 1991: 48; Hall, 1997: 24–25; O'Sullivan *et al.*, 1994: 262.
30 Williams, 1976: 76–82.
31 Jenks, 1995: 16.
32 Ibid.: 1–25.
33 Burnett, 1995: 41.
34 Mirzoeff, 1999: 4
35 Bennett, 1998b.
36 I am using 'objects' and 'artefacts' and 'things' as the most neutral terms I can find. I include paintings and sculpture within these terms. The complex issues of terminology will be fully discussed in Chapter 5.
37 Bennett, 1995: 59–88.
38 Bryson, 1983.

39 Jenks, 1995: 1.
40 M. Merleau-Ponty, 1964, *The Primacy of Perception*, Northwestern University Press, Evanston, Ill.: 16; quoted in Jenks, 1995: 2.
41 Foucault, 1973: 9.
42 Foster, 1988: xi.
43 Jenks, 1995: 10.
44 Saumarez Smith, 1989; Davis, 1997.
45 Best and Kellner, 1991: 2.
46 Mirzoeff, 1999: 8.
47 Modernism as a concept takes its periodisation from European historical movements. These time-frames are not the same outside Europe, and in many ways the imposition of European chronologies can be seen as one of the techniques of colonisation.
48 Foucault, 1970.
49 Fornas, 1995.
50 Anderson, 1991: 163.
51 Lumley, 1988: 1.
52 King, 1996: 2.
53 Ibid.: 18.
54 Wood, 1992: 1.
55 Hackforth-Jones, 1990: 13.
56 King, 1996: 27.
57 Duclos, 1999.
58 Gadamer, 1976; Gallagher, 1992.
59 Jordan and Weedon, 1995: 563.
60 Ibid.: 13.
61 Ibid.: 556.
62 Seidman, 1994: ix–x.
63 Cultural studies have shown an interest in cultural politics, from a theoretical perspective, but much less of a willingness to engage in a politics of culture, including policy formation and analysis.
64 Hall, 1997: 10.
65 Australian Museum, n.d. [a].
66 Australian Museum, n.d. [b].
67 Kelly, 1999 (not paged).
68 Crang, 1994a, 1994b.
69 Bhabha, 1994: 22.
70 Silverman, 1995; Roberts, 1997.

2 Picturing the ancestors and imag(in)ing the nation

1 Pointon, 1993: 238.
2 Colley, 1992: 323.
3 Dodd, 1999.
4 Huyssen, 1995: 15.
5 Hutcheon, 1989: 24.
6 Quoted in ibid.: 37.
7 Hobsbawm, 1990: 3.
8 Hobsbawm, 1990; Anderson, 1991: 4.
9 Wallis, 1994: 266.
10 Minihan, 1977: 28–29.
11 Ibid.: 30, 34. See Lawson and Silver, 1973, for the introduction of the Education Act, 1870. By 1895, changes in the day school code allowed visits to museums and galleries to count as school attendances. See Hooper-Greenhill, 1991: 27.
12 Quoted in Minihan, 1977: 112.
13 Quoted in ibid.: 89.
14 Bennett, 1998a: 149.
15 Such as the Whitechapel Art Gallery (see Koven, 1994) and the South London Gallery (see Waterfield, 1991b).
16 Davidoff and Hall, 1987: 19–23.
17 Pointon, 1993: 228.
18 Colley, 1992: 174.
19 Minihan, 1977: 52.
20 Ibid.: 53. Figures for numbers of visits to museums at the time are given as: British Museum (open three days per week) in 1835 – 230,000; National Gallery in 1840 – 503,011.
21 Ibid.: 90; Taylor, 1999: 51, 100.
22 Quoted in Minihan, 1977: 32.
23 Anderson, 1991.
24 Desmond and Moore, 1991.
25 Minihan, 1977: 61.
26 Pointon, 1993; see also Taylor, 1999: 29–99.
27 *Hansard*, 4 March 1856: 1789.
28 Ibid.: 1774.
29 Bazin, 1967: 102, 134.
30 Piper, 1978: 326.
31 See, for example, Anon., 1848;
32 See, for example, Anon., 1794; Jerdan, 1830; Anon., 1833; Cooke Taylor, 1846–8.
33 Harrison, 1979.
34 Minihan, 1977: 61.
35 *Hansard* 6 June 1856: 1119.
36 Ibid.: 1120.
37 Hobsbawm, 1977: 286; Davidoff and Hall, 1987: 450.
38 Colley, 1992: 354.
39 Bennett, 1998a.
40 National Portrait Gallery, 1949: ix.
41 *First Report of the Trustees of the National Portrait Gallery*, 5 May 1858.
42 Beckett, 1986; Cannadine, 1990.
43 National Portrait Gallery, 1866.
44 Pointon, 1993: 239.
45 National Portrait Gallery, 1909.
46 Yung, 1981.
47 Hill, 1970.
48 Addington, 1st Viscount Sidmouth, NPG 5;

Orford, Robert Walpole, NPG 70; William Pitt (1759–1806), NPG 120; William Pitt (1759–1806), NPG 135a; Henry Pelham, NPG 221.

49 Charles Talbot of Hensel, NPG 42; John Scott, Earl of Eldon, NPG 181.

50 George Washington, NPG 174.

51 Elizabeth Fry, NPG 118.

52 Elizabeth Talbot, Countess of Shrewsbury, NPG 203.

53 Thought to be Nell Gwyn, later identified as Catherine, Countess of Dorchester, NPG 36; Elizabeth Hamilton, Countess of Grammont, NPG 20; Lady Anne Carleton, NPG 111.

54 Mrs Elizabeth Carter, NPG 28.

55 Elizabeth I by Nicholas Hilliard, NPG 108.

56 Princess Charlotte, NPG 206.

57 National Portrait Gallery, 1866: 2. Yung, 1981, lists two plaster casts of the effigy, apparently acquired in 1870, and an electrotype donated by John Hosack, 1870. The registry packet for NPG 307 makes it clear that at least one plaster and the electrotype were at the Gallery in 1870, but the details of the plaster listed by Scharf in 1866 are unclear.

58 *The Times*, 6 March 1856: 8.

59 National Portrait Gallery, 1866: 4.

60 NPG 200.

61 NPG 173.

62 National Portrait Gallery, 1949: xv.

63 Waterfield, 1991a: 111.

64 National Portrait Gallery, 1949: x.

65 Hall, 1992: 95.

66 Davidoff and Hall, 1987; Hall, 1992.

67 *Hansard*, 4 June 1852: 10.

68 Barlow, 1994: 518.

69 Quoted in National Portrait Gallery, 1949: xiii.

70 Barlow, 1994: 519.

71 *The Times*, 6 March 1856: 8.

72 Bennett, 1995: 47.

73 Young, 1995: 32.

74 Durkheim, 1956: 71.

75 Foucault, 1982: 141.

76 Hobsbawm, 1977: 290.

77 Davidoff and Hall, 1987.

78 *Anthropological Review*, iv (1866) quoted in Hobsbawm, 1977: 312; and see also Young, 1995.

79 Kuklick, 1993: 105, 108, 117.

80 Colley, 1992: 149.

81 NPG 26.

82 Young, 1995.

83 National Portrait Gallery, 1949: xv.

84 Hooper-Greenhill, 1989.

85 Hobsbawm, 1990: 37–38.

86 Anderson, 1991:197–199.

87 Bhabha, 1994: 23.

88 Pointon, 1993: 227–244.

89 Ibid.: 244.

90 Waterfield, 1991c: 17.

91 Pointon, 1993: 232; and see note 40, p. 261: the purchase grant for the National Portrait Gallery was £2,000 (*First Report of the Trustees*, 1858: 4), while the National Gallery's was £8,670.

92 Barlow, 1994: 520.

93 Monkhouse, 1896: 320.

94 In 1869, with 228 portraits, the Gallery moved to temporary accommodation at South Kensington. See Cust, 1901: vii.

95 Waterfield, 1991a: 111.

96 *Second Report of the Trustees of the National Portrait Gallery*, 1859: 4.

97 Scharf to William Smith, Good Friday evening, 1860, MS William Smith Correspondence, National Portrait Gallery Archive, London.

98 Pointon, 1993: 227.

99 Trustees sketch book 1, XIV.g, 1859, National Portrait Gallery Archive.

100 National Portrait Gallery, 1866.

101 *Third Report*, 1860: 3.

102 Ibid.

103 *Sixth Report*, 1963: 3.

104 NPG 1, William Shakespeare.

105 *Seventh Report*, 1864: 2.

106 *Eleventh Report*, 1868: 3.

107 *Seventh Report*, 1864: 2.

108 *Tenth Report*, 1867: 3.

109 'Snobs' are those from the lower classes.

110 Scharf to William Smith, Good Friday evening, 1860, MS William Smith Correspondence, National Portrait Gallery Archive, London; see also Pointon, 1993: 244.

111 See Perry, 2000a, for discussions of how the changing location of the National Portrait Gallery between 1858 and 1896 both signalled and enabled changing visitor constituencies, and 2000b, for suggestions of how masculine and feminine ways of looking enmeshed with notions of modernity. I am grateful to Lara Perry for letting me see these papers in advance of publication.

112 *Third Report*, 1860: 3.

113 *Thirty-fourth Report*, 1891: 20.

114 Piper, 1978: 322.

115 Edited by Malcolm Rogers.

116 Hargreaves, 1997.

117 King *et al.*, 1997, and see Chapter 6.

3 Speaking for herself? Hinemihi and her discourses

1 Wilson, 1992: 85.
2 Hodge and D'Souza, 1999.
3 Wilson, 1992: 81.
4 Foucault, 1973: ix.
5 Foucault, 1970; Hooper-Greenhill, 1992.
6 Foucault, 1973: 15.
7 Foucault, 1977b: 13.
8 Belsey, 1980.
9 Ngati Hinemihi is the tribe of Hinemihi, who are descended from Hinemihi, an important woman from the Te Arawa tribal confederation (Stafford, 1967: 66).
10 The *marae* is the area in front of the meeting house: see discussion below.
11 Within the traditional ritual structure, this ceremony was designed and organised according to the wishes of Ngati Hinemihi and Ngati Tuhourangi, incorporating their unique tribal history and genealogy, and reflecting the nature of the importance of the occasion.
12 Salmond, 1974; Walker, 1990: 73–74; Te Awekotuku, 1991: 108.
13 Very recently, and since writing this chapter, it has been suggested that perhaps this *koruru* is not, after all, representative of the ancestor herself.
14 Salmond, 1974: 195.
15 There are a range of names for meeting houses: *whare puni* (sleeping house), *whare whakairo* (carved house), *whare nui* (big house), *whare hui* (meeting house) and *whare runanga* (council house) (Salmond, 1975: 35).
16 Mead, 1984a: 21–23.
17 Salmond, 1984: 137.
18 Ibid.: 118.
19 Salmond, 1975.
20 *Surrey Advertiser*, 23 June 1995.
21 I am grateful to David Brock-Doyle for this piece of information.
22 Nietzsche, 1986: 207.
23 Ibid.: 213.
24 Gallop, 1998.
25 Ibid.: 109–110 and fig. 38, which shows Hinemihi just after the war with a flagpole erected nearby.
26 With reference to official correspondence in the New Zealand National Archives (Maori Affairs department Files, General Index 1891–2, MA-3-19), which also establishes that the house was alienated by purchase.

27 Kernot, 1975, 1976.
28 Kernot, 1975.
29 Kernot, 1976.
30 Kernot, 1975.
31 Neich, 1994: 89.
32 Ibid.: 92.
33 Mead, 1984b: 71.
34 '*Mana*' is a complex concept that is summarised by 'power', 'prestige', and 'authority', but which also has a supernatural dimension (Lewis and Forman, 1982: 47; Newton, 1994: 289).
35 Salmond, 1975: 36.
36 Ibid.: 31.
37 Ibid.: 82–84.
38 Froude, [1886] 1898: 246.
39 Ibid.: 249–251.
40 Neich, 1983: 247.
41 Kernot, 1976; Kernot, 1984: 150.
42 Gallop, 1995a.
43 Neich, 1983: 246–247.
44 Neich, 1990b: 355.
45 Neich, 1990a.
46 Savage, 1986.
47 Neich, 1983: 246.
48 Savage, 1986: 17.
49 Waaka, 1986.
50 Neich, 1983.
51 Mead, 1984b: 71; Jackson, 1972: 41.
52 Mead, 1984a.
53 Kernot, 1983; Neich, 1994: 123; Amoano *et al.*, 1984.
54 Neich, 1994: 130–131.
55 Kernot, 1983: 191–192.
56 O'Toole, 1994: 229–230.
57 Interview with Rachel Windsor, London, 9 August 1995.
58 Te Awekotuku, 1991: 110.
59 Binney, 1984: 346.
60 Neich, 1994: 123.
61 Maori tradition describes how the first people arrived in New Zealand in large canoes from Hawaiki, the mythical homeland (Walker, 1990: 37–39, 45–62).
62 Fax from John Marsh to Annalucia Wermont, New Zealand Tourism Board, 9 July 1992.
63 Neich, 1994: 123.
64 Mead, 1984b: 64; Kernot, 1983: 192.
65 Binney, 1984: 346; Kernot, 1983: 192.
66 Neich, 1994: 123.
67 Walker, 1990.
68 One of the *amo* is reproduced on each side of the old New Zealand pound note (see Gallop, 1998: 115).

69 A copy of a telegram is in existence in the New Zealand Archives from Roger Dansey, Postmaster at Rotorua, dated 23 January 1892, which says: 'I got the natives to write down the names of each carved figure with a short written statement connected with each individual represented, and numbered respectively to correspond with numbers in red paint at the back of each carving which I am translating into English; together with a short history of the whare for his Excellency's information, accompanied by a small plan shewing [*sic*] the proper position of each numbered carving should it be intended to re-erect the "whare" in England.' Unfortunately this vital document has not been traced, although the carvings are indeed numbered on the back. I am grateful to Alan Gallop for this information and for sending me a copy of the telegram.

70 Neich, 1996, personal communication.

71 Neich, 1994: 127.

72 Amoano *et al.*, 1984: 34; Jackson, 1972.

73 *Tapu* – sacred, under religious instruction. Amoano *et al.*, 1984: 34; Jackson, 1972: 51–53.

74 Te Awekotuku, 1991: 62.

75 Kernot (1976) describes the *pare* as illustrated in Hamilton's *Maori Art* (p. 149, Plate XVIII, fig. 1). He also mentions and reproduces a photograph which is held in Te Papatongarewa National Museum of New Zealand, which shows the *pare* placed over a fireplace, reputedly somewhere in England.

76 Jackson, 1972: 47.

77 Jackson, 1972.

78 See Gallop, 1998: 31, who explains the figures in a different way.

79 Stafford, 1967: 84–87.

80 Gallop suggests that this carving, a gift to the Onslows, was placed on the outside wall of the house during the period of its restoration in the First World War (Gallop, 1998: 111).

81 Gallop, 1995a.

82 Free from religious restriction, common.

83 Neich, 1994: 128.

84 Salmond, 1978; Neich, 1994: 121–160.

85 Salmond, 1978: 24.

86 Salmond, 1984: 120; Newton, 1994: 280.

87 Amoamo *et al.*, 1984.

88 Salmond, 1978.

89 Kernot, 1983: 182; Neich, 1994: 128–129.

90 Laclau and Mouffe, 1985; Butler, 1990.

91 See Salmond, 1978: 13.

92 Kernot, 1983: 196.

93 Jackson, 1972.

94 Hanson, 1989; Walker, 1990: 38.

95 Salmond, 1978; Te Awekotuku, 1991: 45.

96 Salmond, 1978: 7.

97 Foucault, 1970: xv.

98 Hall, 1992.

99 Neich, 1994: 125.

100 Amoano *et al.*, 1984: 26, 28.

101 Trollope, [1873] 1968: 473.

102 Ibid.: 470.

103 Froude, [1886] 1898: 234.

104 Savage, 1986: 17 gives a number of examples of writers who use similar language and comment on Maori culture from similar perspectives.

105 Bhabha, 1983: 209.

106 Froude, [1886] 1898: 244.

107 Walker, 1990: 9.

108 Lewis and Forman, 1982: 123.

109 Walker, 1990: 136.

110 Ibid.: 139.

111 Ibid.: 10; Walker states that by 1990, numbers had grown to over 404,185.

112 Ibid.: 147.

113 Ibid.: 116.

114 Ibid.

115 Savage, 1986: 17; Rockel, 1986: 9; Waaka, 1986: 13.

116 Blackley, 1986: 18.

117 Ibid.

118 *New Zealand Chronicle*, 1886: 1.

119 Stafford, 1977: 30.

120 *New Zealand Chronicle*, 1886: 2.

121 Gallop, 1995a; Neich, 1990a: 74.

122 Gallop, 1994: 23.

123 Letters can be found concerning the purchase negotiations in the National Archives Head Office, Wellington, file MAI/1892/2148.

124 Kernot, 1976.

125 *Surrey Advertiser*, 23 June 1995.

126 National Trust, 1994a: 10.

127 Ibid.

128 Salmond, 1984: 118; Mead, 1984a: 21–23.

129 Butler, 1990: 139–141.

130 Salmond, 1984: 137.

131 Interview with Rachel Windsor, London, 9 August 1995.

132 Salmond, 1975: 211.

133 Ibid.: 212.

134 *Surrey Advertiser*, 1992.

135 Gallop, 1992.

136 Salmond, 1975: 81.

137 Gallop, 1998: 126, 159–160.

4 Words and things

1 See p. 51.
2 See p. 74.
3 Clifford, 1988: 220.
4 Russell-Cotes Art Gallery and Museum, 1928: 40. The involvement at the White City was in the Coronation Exhibition in 1911. White City was a site for several exhibitions between 1908–14 (Greenhalgh, 1988:19).
5 Russell-Cotes Art Gallery and Museum, 1992.
6 Makereti, 1938. The 'I' who is writing is T. K. Penniman who edited the book for publication after the death of Makereti just before it would have been completed.
7 Tamarapa and Whata, 1993: 16.
8 Ibid.; Te Awekotuku, 1986: v. However, he is called 'Alfred' in Te Awekotuku, 1991: 146.
9 Dennan, 1968: 47.
10 Ibid.; Te Awekotuku, 1986: v.
11 Te Awekotuku, 1991: 146–147.
12 Ibid.: 78–79.
13 Te Awekotuku, 1986: vi.
14 Te Awekotuku, 1991: 82.
15 Dennan, 1968: 48.
16 Makereti had a child at about this time, when she was aged seventeen, named William Francis Anoui Dennan, whose father Francis Joseph Dennan she had met in 1891 (Te Awekotuku, 1986: vi).
17 Ibid.
18 She supported the establishment of the Maori court at the Auckland Museum, for example (Te Awekotuku, 1991: 148).
19 Te Awekotuku, 1986: vii. The house was carved by Tene Waitere (Neich, 1983), who had earlier been one of the junior carvers working on Hinemihi at Te Wairoa.
20 Greenhalgh, 1988: 94–95.
21 Dennan, 1968: 54.
22 Ibid.; Te Awekotuku, 1986: vii.
23 Te Awekotuku, 1986: viii.
24 The family also owned three farms, at Brashfield, Brampton and Oddington; see Tamarapa and Whata, 1993: 16. Her son later joined them and became the legal heir of Staples-Browne (Te Awekotuku, 1986: viii).
25 *Marae* – the open space in front of the meeting house, and a space for cultural meetings.
26 Te Awekotuku, 1986: viii.
27 Ibid. She was enrolled to take the degree by thesis; see Kuklick, 1993: 53, n.57.
28 Te Awekotuku, 1986: ix.
29 There is a photocopy in the Makereti Boxes (Box X) at the Pitt Rivers Museum, Oxford.
30 Tamarapa and Whata, 1993: 12.
31 Te Awekotuku, 1991: 91.
32 Savage, 1986: 18.
33 Te Awekotuku, 1991: 91.
34 'Maoris at Queen's Hall', newspaper cutting describing the concert performance (probably on 7 December 1912), at the small Queen's Hall in Langham Place, London, in Scrapbook relating to Maggie Papakura, qMS-0621, Donne, Thomas Edward, 1860–1945: papers (MS-Group-0028), Alexander Turnbull Library, New Zealand.
35 Penniman, 1938: 23; Dennan, 1968: 54.
36 Te Awekotuku, 1991: 139.
37 Several list of artefacts are held in the Pitt Rivers Museum, Makereti Box III, Bag L.
38 She lists the complete carvings of her *whare whakairo*, Tuhoromatakaka, naming each of the carved parts separately; the outside carvings of a second *whare*, Tukiterangi; a number of carvings from an old carved *pataka* (storehouse), some from a second *pataka*, and a single large carved slab. There are also 38 *whariki* (sleeping and floor mats), 51 kete (baskets); a large number of greenstones, which include adzes, weapons and more ornamental pieces (one *koropepe*, 12 *heitikis*); three whalebone weapons, including a *kotiate*; and a number of related objects – two *mako* (shark's-tooth) earrings, a chisel, and a fishhook. She lists several miscellaneous items: two funnels for feeding Tohunga (priests), partly carved; a snare, 50 *poi* balls, one bone comb. There are eight stone adzes.
39 Penniman 1938: 24. She also showed a film on Maori life at the Pitt Rivers Museum which she had been involved in making.
40 Ibid.: 23–24.
41 Te Awekotuku, 1986: viii.
42 Pratt, 1992: 7.
43 Ashcroft *et al.*, 1995: 8.
44 Olding, 1999: 7.
45 Ibid.; Waterfield, 1999: 15.
46 Olding, 1999: 8.
47 Russell-Cotes, 1921: II, 686–688; Olding, 1999: 12.
48 Russell-Cotes, 1921: 687.
49 Olding, 1999: 7.
50 Russell-Cotes, 1921: I, 469–470.
51 Annie had hurt her leg and was advised not to travel overland from San Francisco to New York, but to return home by Asia (see

52 Garner, 1992: 56), presumably because sea travel was more comfortable than by land.
52 Bills, 1999: 24.
53 Russell-Cotes, 1921: I, 397.
54 Pollock, 1994: 63.
55 Russell-Cotes was a member of the Royal Geographical Society and of the Japan Society. He presents himself on the title-page of his own book thus: 'Sir Merton Russell-Cotes, J.P., F.R.G.S., F.S.A., Author of Paper read before the Royal Geographical Society on his Exploration of Kilauea, Hawaii (the greatest active volcano in the world); Papers on the Pink and White Terraces, N.Z., "The Holy Fire", and numerous other contributions to "The World", "Truth" and to the British and American Press'. (There is, however, considerable doubt as to whether these lectures and papers were actually delivered.) He changed his name from 'Merton Russell Cotes' to 'Merton Russell-Cotes', adding a circumflex over the 'o' in Cotes towards the end of his life.
56 Colley, 1992: 173.
57 Pratt, 1992: 7.
58 For example, in the section in Volume I describing the visit to New Zealand (pp. 387–407), we hear about Annie's pocket dairy on p. 392, and it is quoted directly on pp. 392–394 and 398–399.
59 Russell-Cotes, 1921: I, 399.
60 Ibid.: I, 392. A *whare-puni* is one name for a carved house. See Chapter 3, note 15.
61 Ibid.: I, 393.
62 Ibid.: I, 394.
63 Ibid.: I, 395.
64 See the examples in Savage, 1986: 17.
65 Russell-Cotes, 1921: I, 398–399.
66 Waaka, 1986: 12.
67 Ibid.
68 Stafford, 1977: 26–27.
69 Savage, 1986: 17.
70 Russell-Cotes, 1921: I, 399.
71 Russell-Cotes uses 'Wairoa' instead of 'Te Wairoa', but it is clear that he means Te Wairoa. Earlier he describes Wairoa as 'the stopping place for Rotomahana' (Russell-Cotes, 1921: I, 396).
72 Ibid.: I, 399–401.
73 Balme, 1998: 53.
74 Te Awekotuku, 1991: 126–130. The short *poi* dances designed by Bella Papakura for the Festival of Empire Celebrations in 1911 became the established repertoire until the 1950s, when the long *poi* used today was introduced.

75 Recent research by Shaun Garner suggests that the autobiography was assembled under Merton's direction by his son, daughter and a secretary, using Annie's diaries and notes, newspaper cuttings, guidebooks and other accessible material. The only references which appear in the text are to Annie's diary.
76 Te Awekotuku, 1991: 162.
77 The manuscript was largely finished, but left incomplete at her death. It was edited by T. K. Penniman, curator at the Pitt Rivers Museum by 1937 (Blackwood, 1970: 12).
78 Penniman, 1938: 20.
79 The book is presented as an ethnography. Dealing with 'traditional' Maori life-ways, it is ambiguous as to the dates and specific location of its subject.
80 Makereti, 1938: 157.
81 Ibid.: 231.
82 Ibid.: 76.
83 Ibid.: 102, 103.
84 Ibid.: 90.
85 Sweet potato.
86 Makereti, 1938: 198–202.
87 Ibid.: 110, footnote.
88 Ibid.: 255.
89 Te Awekotuku, 1991: 148.
90 The 'tangata whenua' are the 'people of the land, original inhabitants'; here, the hosts at the wedding.
91 Makereti, 1938: 75.
92 Ibid.: 169.
93 Ibid.: 106; explanations of Maori words in the original.
94 Ibid.: 67–68.
95 Ibid.: 71, and plates IX and VIII.
96 Ibid.: 248.
97 Ashcroft *et al.*, 1995: 8.
98 Goldie, 1995; Griffiths, 1995.
99 Wassman, 1998: 9.
100 Draft letter in Scrapbook relating to Maggie Papakura, qMS-0621, Donne, Thomas Edward, 1860–1945: papers (MS-Group-0028), Alexander Turnbull Library, NLNZ.
101 Letter to T. E. Donne, 6 March 1925, in ibid.: 'I think it is now time to begin arranging the sale of my collection as you suggested a few months ago . . .'
102 Interview with her grandson Jim Dennan, Peterborough, 27 July 1995.
103 Te Awekotuku, 1991: 150–153.
104 A letter to her father dated 2 February 1929 tells him that she is moving to a cheaper house (11 Warmborough Road, Oxford) and will have to economise until she has paid off

outstanding doctors' accounts; Brown, Maggie Papakura 1872–1930; Letters Margaret Staples-Browne, MS-Papers-3880, Alexander Turnbull Library, NLNZ.

105 Her manuscripts were edited and checked before publication by T. K. Penniman who had worked closely with her in the development of the work (Makereti, 1938: 24–25).

106 The Accession registers for the museum record the acquisition of a *piupiu*-skirt of 'phormium tenax' in November 1921 (Pitt Rivers Museum Accession Register, 1921, p. 60); and in June 1923, the acquisition of seven adzes, one axe, two stone pounders and the *mako*, the shark's teeth ear-pendants (Pitt Rivers Museum Accession Register, 1923, not paged).

107 Letters to T. E. Donne, dated 12 February 1923 and 4 April 1923: Scrapbook relating to Maggie Papakura, qMS-0621, Donne, Thomas Edward, 1860–1945: papers (MS-Group-0028), Alexander Turnbull Library, NLNZ. Evidently the disposal was a reluctant one, as a year later Makereti is only just promising to have the lists of the collection ready, and a year after that, in 1925, she is still talking about beginning to think about the sale (Letters dated 30 March 1924 and 6 March 1925, in ibid.).

108 Maori collection and Information Marae files. Vol. 133, The National Museum of New Zealand/Te Papatongarewa.

109 Letter from William F. Dennan to T. E. Donne dated 31 May 1930: Scrapbook relating to Maggie Papakura, qMS-0621, Donne, Thomas Edward, 1860–1945: papers (MS-Group-0028), Alexander Turnbull Library, NLNZ.

110 Petch, 1996: 35.

111 Dennan, 1968: 58; 131.

112 Ibid.: 131.

113 Rangi was a leading guide at Whaka (having taken over as chief guide from Bella Papakura, Makereti's sister. She had married Makereti's son Te Aonui after his return to New Zealand following his mother's death. Rangi had had a second Hinemihi built in her garden at Whakarewarewa which was opened in 1928 (see Phillips, 1948: 56–57). The house was built in the style of traditional *whares*, by her grandfather Tene Waitere, and was fully carved. It was furnished with Maori cultural objects, cloaks, kete, images and carvings, and also

with *pakeha* objects such as sheepskin rugs (see also Gallop, 1998: 134).

114 This is the third Hinemihi (Dennan, 1968: 131–133). Interview at Whakarewarewa (in the second Hinemihi) on 26 April 1999 with Jim Schuster and Renee Gillies, Rangi's granddaughter and Education Officer at the Bathhouse Museum, Rotorua.

115 Russell-Cotes, 1921: I, 389–392.

116 Ibid.: II, 928–929. Tawhiao [*sic*] had led a second deputation to England (Walker, 1990: 163) to learn English and buy guns.

117 Russell-Cotes Art Gallery and Museum, 1923, p. 42 and fig. 5.

118 Russell-Cotes Art Gallery and Museum, 1926, p. 19 and fig. Maori *meres*.

119 'Rangatira' means 'chief'. Mika Taupopoki's descendant was leading tour parties round Whakarewarewa village when I last visited in 1999, and described his great-uncle with some pride. His image was displayed in the meeting house where concert parties are given for tourists.

120 Russell-Cotes Art Gallery and Museum Accession Register, 1922; Russell-Cotes Art Gallery and Museum, 1928, pp. 31–40.

121 Russell-Cotes Art Gallery and Museum Accession Registers, 1925–1928.

122 Russell-Cotes Art Gallery and Museum, 1928, p. 35. This figure first discussed contextually by Barrow, 1959: 111–120, esp. p. 114 and plate IV. I am grateful to Peter Gathercole for this reference.

123 Personal communication from Shaun Garner, 15 December 1999; see also Olding, 1999.

124 Some of the Maori collections were displayed at the Colonial Exhibition in 1886 (Shaun Garner, personal communication, 11 January 2000).

125 Olding, 1999: 10.

126 Ibid.: 12.

127 Waterfield, 1999: 20.

128 Quoted in Garner, 1992: 24.

129 For example, in the Pitt Rivers Accession Register two funnels are recorded that belonged to the uncle that brought Makereti up: '2 carved wooden funnels, used for feeding a chief who was being tattooed. Called *Ngutu ta moko*. MAORI, ROTORUA district, N. ISLAND, NEW ZEALAND. (The smaller one belonged to Maihi Te Kakauparaoa, whose grandfather, Te Aonui, had used it)' (Pitt Rivers Museum Accession Register, 1928, p. 176). Makereti gave this family name to her son.

130 Greenhalgh, 1988: 82, 94–95.
131 See Bell, 1983 and 1993 for a fascinating discussion of these matters in relation to fieldwork in Australia.
132 See Olding *et al*. 1999 for descriptions of the house.
133 Waterfield, 1999: 14.
134 He had collected, for example, an axe believed to have been used to execute Mary Queen of Scots and a piece of hem from a dress worn by Queen Elizabeth I. I am indebted to Shaun Garner for this information.
135 In the study, for example, books were laid out on coffee tables. There were no bookshelves or library of books.
136 Bills, 1999: 24.
137 Tamarapa and Whata, 1993.
138 Te Awekotuku, quoted in ibid.
139 Tamarapa and Whata, 1993: 10.
140 Ibid.:

5 Objects and interpretive processes

1 Foucault, 1973: ix.
2 Nietzsche, 1986: 207.
3 Taylor, [1971] 1976: 168.
4 Crary, 1990: 31.
5 *Chambers 21st Century Dictionary*, 1996: 943.
6 See, for example, Husbands, 1992; Durbin *et al.*, 1990; Goolnick, 1994.
7 Hooper-Greenhill, 1991: 25–27.
8 Calkins, 1880: 169.
9 Ibid.: 166.
10 Ibid.: 169.
11 See for example, Durbin *et al.*, 1990.
12 Calkins, 1880: 172.
13 Best and Kellner, 1991; Wheeler, 1997.
14 Gallagher, 1992: 87–88.
15 Hennighar Shuh, 1982.
16 West, 1985; Andreeti, 1993.
17 Wilson, 1992: 85.
18 *Chambers*, 1996: 71.
19 Ibid.: 1349.
20 Shanks and Tilley, 1987: 69.
21 Miller, 1994.
22 Conn, 1998.
23 Ibid.: 17.
24 Appadurai, 1986: 5.
25 Tilley, 1991.
26 Shanks and Tilley, 1987; Hodder, 1989; Tilley, 1993.
27 Pearce, 1994a.
28 Bocock, 1993; Miller, 1995.

29 Pearce, 1994a.
30 But see Pearce, 1994b for a helpful contribution to this theme.
31 See Mirzoeff, 1999: 129–161 for an interesting divergence from this tendency.
32 Jenks, 1995: 16.
33 Mirzoeff, 1998, 1999; Evans and Hall, 1999; Barnard, 1998; Jenks, 1995; Heywood and Sandywell, 1999. See also MacKenzie and Wajcman, 1999; and Davis, 1997.
34 Pearce, 1998.
35 Belk, 1988.
36 Ascherson, 1996.
37 Ibid.
38 Parry, 1999.
39 Watson-Smith, 1999.
40 Wassman, 1998: 9.
41 Nakora, 1998.
42 Pearce, 1998: 124.
43 Ibid.: 133–135.
44 Csikszentmihalyi and Rochberg-Halton, 1981.
45 Hustvedt, 1999.
46 Garner, 1998.
47 Bedard, 1992: 5.
48 Ibid.
49 Bhabha 1994: 7.
50 Fornas, 1995: 27.
51 Classen, 1993: 2
52 Ibid.: 5.
53 Ibid.: 9.
54 Crary, 1990: 48.
55 Butler, 1990: 129.
56 Olds, 1999.
57 Sotto, 1994.
58 Gardner, 1985, 1991.
59 Butler, 1990: 139.
60 Foucault, 1977a: 150.
61 Gallop, 1998: 111, 133.
62 NPG 1725.
63 Te Awekotuku, 1998, has described how there were at one time approximately 165 tattooed Maori heads in British Museums, about a hundred of which have now been repatriated.
64 Ibid.
65 Davey, 1999: 14.
66 Sotto, 1994.
67 Schank and Abelson, quoted in MacLachlan and Reid, 1994: 70.
68 Dilthey, 1976: 115.
69 Gadamer, 1976: 117.
70 Jensen, 1991a: 41–43.
71 'Prejudice' is not meant in the pejorative way here.

72 Wolff, 1975: 105–106.
73 Sotto, 1994: 36.
74 Ibid.: 42–3.
75 Ibid.: 44.
76 Boden, 1994: 81.
77 MacLachlan and Reid, 1994: 2.
78 Piaget, 1970.
79 MacLachlan and Reid, 1994: 69; Davey, 1999: 12.
80 Schank and Abelson, 1977, quoted in MacLachlan and Reid, 1994: 70.
81 Gardner, 1991: 29.
82 Sotto, 1994: 74–75.
83 Gunther, 1999.
84 Gadamer, 1976: 124.
85 Ogbu, 1995.
86 'Interpretation' is a very loosely defined word in the museum context. *Chambers Dictionary* suggests 'An act of interpretation or the sense given as a result' (p. 711). There is a major difference in emphasis in the way the word is used in hermeneutic philosophy and the way it is used in the museum. In the museum, interpretation is done for you, or to you. In hermeneutics, however, *you* are the interpreter for yourself. Interpretation is the process of *constructing* meaning. In the museum, 'exhibition interpretation' refers to the way the exhibition is designed to enable visitors to understand the ideas it wants to put across. 'Object interpretation' is the act of interpreting objects for others, by making the links that they might be expected to recognise. An 'Interpretation Officer' might be an education officer, a designer, or an exhibitions officer.
87 See Steffe and Gale, 1995 for a general discussion of constructivist learning theory; Roschelle, 1995, and Hein, 1998 for an exploration of this in relation to learning in the museum. Gallagher, 1992 discusses education in the context of hermeneutics.
88 Hall, 1997.
89 Steffe and Gale, 1995.
90 Fish, 1980.
91 Tilley, 1993.
92 Bryson, 1983; Burnett, 1995; Davey, 1999.
93 Hacking, 1999.
94 See Lindquist, 2000 for a number of discussions on this theme, and also MacDonald, 1998.
95 Freund, 1987, quoted in MacLachlin and Reid, 1994: 7; Bryson, 1983: xiv.
96 Fish, 1980: 2.
97 Burnett, 1995: 21.
98 Hall, 1997: 2.
99 See Schroder, 1994; Lindloff, 1988; Jensen, 1991a: 42.
100 References to interpretive communities are appearing in the museum studies literature; see for example Appadurai and Breckenridge, 1992; Perin, 1992; Hooper-Greenhill, 1999. Csikszentmihalyi and Robinson, 1990, although not undertaken from this specific perspective, does support it rather well.
101 Fish, 1980: 171.
102 Ibid.: 94.
103 Ibid.: 2
104 Ibid.: 332.
105 Ibid.: 336.
106 Radway, 1984.
107 Zelizer, 1993.
108 Mitra, 1997.
109 Ibid.: 177.
110 Radway, 1984: 8; Schroder, 1994: 337.
111 The Web users can be seen as consumers in that they used specific identifiable websites, but also producers, in that they produced web-based texts through emails and chat-rooms. In addition, they produced their own texts through their navigation of the various pages and hyperlinks. Web-based communication shows up the deficiencies of older linear models of communication, and these issues of theorising communication will be addressed in the next chapter.
112 Schroder, 1994.
113 Morley, 1992: 70.
114 Fish, 1980: 172.
115 Lindlof, 1988: 89.
116 Potter and Wetherell, 1987: 138–157.
117 Fish, 1980: 14.

6 Exhibitions and interpretation

1 Quoted in Minihan, 1977: 112.
2 Quoted in ibid.: 136, n.1.
3 Ibid.: 136.
4 Taylor, 1999: 47.
5 Conn, 1998.
6 Henry Cole, quoted in Minihan, 1977: 112, and see Chapter 2, p. 26.
7 Hooper-Greenhill, 1992: 133–166.
8 Foucault, 1970: 52.
9 Peponis and Hedin, 1982: 23.
10 Pointon, 1993: 238.
11 Kuklick, 1993: 44.
12 Chapman, 1985: 18.
13 Conn, 1998: 34.
14 Quoted in Taylor, 1999: 47.

15 Ibid.
16 Fisher, 1991: 8–9.
17 Conn, 1998: 25.
18 Peponis and Hedin, 1982: 24.
19 Findlen, 1994: 402.
20 Knell, 1996: 45.
21 Conn, 1998: 16.
22 Perry, 2000b.
23 See Peponis and Hedin, 1982, in relation to natural history, and Duncan and Wallach, 1978, for modern art museums.
24 Taylor, 1999: 47.
25 Jay, 1988: 3.
26 Crary, 1990: 5–6.
27 Ibid.: 48.
28 See Perry, 2000a, for a perceptive discussion of masculinised and feminised gazes.
29 Kirshenblatt-Gimblett, 1988: 33.
30 Taylor, 1999: 44.
31 See Table 2.2 and p. 44 for visitor numbers at the National Portrait Gallery, London. See also Greenhalgh, 1988: 21 for a discussion of those exhibitions outside museums that were aimed at the 'masses'. The real targets were those men who became newly enfranchised after the suffrage reforms of 1832 and 1867, and who needed to be educated in order to better use their votes (see Perry, 2000b).
32 Conn, 1998: 8.
33 Bernstein, 1971. See also Fyfe, 1998.
34 Jay, 1988: 9, and see also Hooper-Greenhill, 1992.
35 Conn, 1998: 4.
36 Taylor, 1999: 51.
37 Ibid.: 46–50, 64; Bennett, 1998c; Bernstein, 1971.
38 Taylor, 1999: 43.
39 Hooper-Greenhill, 1989.
40 Carey, 1989: 13–36.
41 Cameron, 1968.
42 Knez and Wright, 1970.
43 Miles, 1985.
44 Bicknell, 1995; McManus, 1991.
45 Minihan, 1977: xii.
46 McQuail and Windahl, 1993: 6.
47 Hardt, 1992: xi.
48 Morgan and Welton, 1986: 4–6.
49 McQuail and Windahl, 1993: 58–61.
50 Hein, 1998: 19–21.
51 Friere, 1972: 45–69.
52 Giroux, 1992: 155.
53 McQuail and Windahl, 1993: 7.
54 See Hein, 1998, for a thorough and critical review of museum visitor studies, the vast bulk of which have been carried out in America and very many of which have been based on this model of communication.
55 Hooper-Greenhill, 1994.
56 Fay, 1996: 30–49.
57 Hardt, 1992: 3.
58 Cf. Stocking, 1985: 9, who points out that by the 1960s 90 per cent of anthropological objects in American museums remained unresearched.
59 Markham, 1938: 11; and see Hooper-Greenhill, 1991: 42–45.
60 Hooper-Greenhill, 1991: 55.
61 Bud, 1988, describes the complex processes of exhibition development.
62 Bourdieu and Darbel, 1991: 49.
63 Walsh, 1991.
64 O'Riain, 1996.
65 See, for example, Morley, 1995.
66 Morley, 1995 and 1996 discusses the background to these points. See also Hooper-Greenhill, 1995.
67 Miles and Tout, 1994: 102.
68 Fornas, 1995.
69 Hutcheon, 1989: 8.
70 Ibid.: 18.
71 Carey, 1989.
72 Ibid.: 23. See also Hall, 1997: 25; Jordan and Weedon, 1995.
73 Carey, 1989: 22 points out that the dominant understanding of communication in American public life has been as transmission.
74 Ibid.: 15, 34.
75 Hacking, 1999: 10–11.
76 Ibid.: 34.
77 Gunther, 1999.
78 Giroux, 1992.
79 Ibid.: 169.
80 Turner, 1990; Bennett, 1998a.
81 Nicholson, 1990: 11.
82 Delanty 1997: x, 5.
83 Nicholson, 1990.
84 Williams and Chrisman, 1993; Ashcroft *et al.*, 1995.
85 McCarthy, 1996.
86 Hassan, 1986.
87 Jordan and Weedon, 1995: 484.
88 Fay, 1996: 223.
89 Hassan, quoted in Hutcheon, 1989: 18.
90 Hensher, 1999: 4.
91 Cummings, 1997. Fred Wilson was also one of the artists involved at the British Museum; see British Museum Education Service, 1997.
92 Karp and Wilson, 1996: 255–256.
93 Hutcheon, 1989: 9.
94 Ibid.: 134–135.

95 Ibid.: 39.
96 Findlen, 1994: 402.
97 Fisher, 1991: 8–9.
98 Torres Strait Islanders: an exhibition marking the centenary of the 1898 Cambridge anthropological expedition, July 1998–July 2000.
99 *Kastom* is defined as the body of customs, traditions, observances and beliefs. Herle and Philp, 1998.
100 Herle and Rouse, 1998: 22.
101 Ibid.: 61. The Murray Island Land Case (also known as the Mabo decision after one of the plaintiffs) marked the first time that the Australian government had recognised the prior ownership of land by an indigenous group.
102 'Ignatius Sancho: an African Man of Letters', January–May 1997.
103 Saumarez Smith, 1997.
104 Royal College of Surgeons, 1831: 52. Series x Models, Casts, etc., no. 735 A cast of the head and face of Ignatius Sancho, the author of 'Sancho's Letters'.
105 Ibid.: no. 737. This was a cast made by Sartini in 1791.
106 Dobson, 1968: 7.
107 King *et al.*, 1997.
108 The redisplay of these galleries opens in mid-2000.
109 Bennett, 1998c: 346.
110 MacGregor, 2000: 6.

7 The rebirth of the museum

1 The Museums and Galleries research report *Cultural Diversity: Attitudes of Ethnic Minority Populations Towards Museums and Galleries* shows how the image of the museum is common across ethnic groups in Britain. This image is the image of the modernist museum, with 'old buildings' and 'posh people' (Desai and Thomas, 1998: 1).
2 See Merriman, 1997, for a description of an exhibition that was event among many on a specific theme – 'The Peopling of London' one.
3 Maddra, 1999.
4 Accessions Register, pp. 226–228, 1892, Kelvingrove Art Gallery and Museum, Glasgow. Fourteen objects, listed 92–2a–n, were purchased for £40. The name of the seller, in accordance with the museum's practice, is not recorded. Immediately following in the Register is a further set of objects listed 3a–n, which must have been donated, as the names of donors were recorded (O'Neill, 1999: 10). The name given is George C. Crager. The Ghost Dance Shirt is listed at 3c, signifying that it must have been donated.
5 Accessions Register, 1892: 226–227; Maddra, 1996: 2244.
6 Ibid.
7 The letter offering the objects to the museum is written on notepaper headed Buffalo Bill's Wild West Co. It is dated as in 'Glasgow Dec. 19th 1891'. It reads: 'Mr. Paton, Curator, Calvin Grove Museum, Glasgow. Dear Sir, Hearing that you are empowered to purchase relics for your museum, I would respectfully inform you that I have a collection of Indian Relics (North American) which I will dispose of before we sail for America. Should you wish any of them after inspection I would be pleased to have you call at my Room at the East End Exhibition Building – Please answer when you can come. Yours Resp. Geo. C. Crager, Incharge of Indians'. Kelvingrove Art Gallery and Museum Archives.
8 Crager letter to Paton, 1891.
9 Maddra, 1995: 2.
10 Crager's Clipping Book, quoted in ibid.: n.30.
11 Maddra, 1996: 49.
12 Utley, 1963, photo 21, quoted by Maddra, 1996: 49. Crager is listed as J. C. Craiger.
13 Brown, 1991; Utley, 1963.
14 Utley, 1993.
15 Brown, 1991: 441.
16 Maddra, 1995: n.27, quotes *Nebraska History* 62 (2), 1981, and interviews concerning oral accounts of the event. Brown, 1991, cites the *US Bureau of Ethnology 14th Report, 1892–93*, Part 2, p. 885.
17 Utley, 1993: 311.
18 Brown, 1991: 442.
19 Utley, 1993: 281.
20 Ibid.: 282.
21 O'Neill, 1999: 14.
22 Personal communication from Sam Maddra, 4 January 2000.
23 Royal Armouries, 1999: 11.
24 Ibid.: 13.
25 White, 1994.
26 Francis, 1992: 92. Francis says there were thirty people, but Maddra suggests twenty-three (personal communication, 4 January 2000)

27 White, 1994:32.
28 Ibid.:32.
29 Francis, 1992: 92–93.
30 Members of the audience could ride in the stage as it was attacked (ibid.: 93).
31 White, 1994: 27.
32 Ibid.: 29.
33 Francis, 1992: 89, quotes a reporter for the Toronto Globe who on 22 August 1885, wrote: 'The Indians have been so isolated from the outside world that they are today precisely the same in manner, dress, habits and ways of thinking as they were when first taken from their reserves.'
34 Francis, 1992.
35 Ibid.: 94.
36 Interview with Antonia Lovelace, Curator of Ethnography, at Kelvingrove Museum, 28 November 95.
37 Ibid.
38 Ibid.
39 See Francis, 1992: ch. 7, for an extended discussion of this point; see also Deloria, 1999.
40 See n.81, Ch.5.
41 Bendoris, 1995.
42 McBeth, 1995a.
43 Mullin, 1995.
44 McBeth, 1995b.
45 McBeth, 1995a.
46 All excerpts are from letters held in the Ghost Dance Shirt file in the Kelvingrove Museum Archive. I am grateful to Mark O'Neill for making them available to me.
47 Donnelly, 1995.
48 During the years between the first Lakota visit in 1995 and the second in 1999, many local authority museums in Britain were subject to reorganisation. In Glasgow, museum staff were cut by one-third between 1996 and 1998.
49 Markus, 1987: 144.
50 Garner, 1997.
51 These events were watched eagerly by museums in Britain; see *Museums Journal*, 1998; Harvey, 1998, 1999.
52 O'Neill, 1999: 16–17.
53 Glasgow Council's Media Release announcing the decision to return the Shirt quoted the Arts and Council Committee convener: 'We have been impressed by the Lakota during their visit to Glasgow. They have set an example in the way they have listened to different views about the fate of the shirt, and Glasgow has lived up to its reputation as a humanitarian city' (Forbes, 1998).
54 Fish, 1980: 15.
55 Jensen, 1991a: 42.

Bibliography

Amoano, T., Tupene, T. and Neich, R. (1984)
The complementarity of history and art in
Tutamure meeting house, Omarumutu Marae,
Opotiki, *Journal of the Polynesian Society*,
93, (1), 5–37.

Anderson, B. (1991) *Imagined Communities*,
Verso, London and New York.

Andreeti, K. (1993) *Teaching History from
Primary Evidence*, David Fulton Publishers in
association with The Roehampton Institute,
London.

Andrews, P. (1986) *Tarawera and the Terraces*,
Wilson and Horton Publications, Auckland,
New Zealand.

Anim-Addo, J. (ed.) (1998) *Another Doorway:
Visible Inside the Museum*, Mango
Publishing, London.

Anon. (1794) *The Biographical Magazine
Containing Portraits and Characters of
Eminent and Ingenious Persons of Every Age
and Nation*, Printed for Harrison and Co.
London.

Anon. (1833) *The Gallery of Portraits: with
Memoirs*, Vol. 1, Under the Superintendence
of the Society for the Diffusion of Useful
Knowledge, Charles Knight, Pall-Mall East,
London.

Anon. (1848) *Catalogue of Engraved Portraits of
Nobility, Gentry, Clergymen and Others,
Born, Resident in or Connected with the
County of Warwick; Alphabetically Arranged,
with Names of the Painters and Engravers,
and the Size of Each Plate; to which are
Added Numerous Biographical Notices,
Compiled or Selected with Great Assiduity,
Research and Care*, William Pickering,
London (printed for and sold by John
Merridew, Coventry).

Appadurai, A. (ed.) (1986) *The Social Life of
Things: Commodities in Cultural Perspective*,
Cambridge University Press, Cambridge.

Appadurai, A. and Breckenridge, C. (1992)
Museums are good to think: heritage on view
in India, in Karp, I., Kreamer, C. and Lavine,
S., *Museums and Communities: the Politics of
Public Culture*, Smithsonian Institution,
Washington, DC, 34–55.

Ascherson, N. (1996) If only Livingstone had
learnt a little from his first and only convert,
The Independent on Sunday, 16 June.

Ashcroft, B., Griffiths, G. and Tiffin, H. (eds)
(1995) *The Post-colonial Studies Reader*,
Routledge, London.

Australian Museum (n.d. [a]) Indigenous
Australians: a story of survival (press release
Australian Museum, Sydney).

Australian Museum (n.d. [b]) Indigenous
Australians: a conversation with Dr. Des
Griffin, Director of the Australian Museum
(press release, Australian Museum,
Sydney).

Bal, M. (1994) Telling objects: a narrative
perspective on collecting, in Elsner, J. and
Cardinal, R., *The Cultures of Collecting*,
Reaktion Books, London, 97–115.

Balme, C. (1998) Hula and haka: performance,
metonymy and identity formation in colonial
Hawaii and New Zealand, *Humanities
Research*, 3, 41–58.

Barber, L. (1980) *The Heyday of Natural
History, 1820–1870*, Doubleday & Co. Inc
New York.

Barlow, P. (1994) The imagined hero as incarnate
sign: Thomas Carlyle and the mythology of

the 'national portrait' in Victorian Britain, *Art History*, 17 (4), 517–545.

Barnard, M. (1998) *Art, Design and Visual Culture*, St Martin's Press, New York.

Barrett, M. (1991) *The Politics of Truth*, Polity Press, Cambridge.

Barrow, T. T. (1959) Free-standing Maori images, in Freeman, J. O. and Geddes, W. R. (eds) *Anthropology in the South Seas: Essays Presented to H. D. Skinner*, Thomas Avery and Sons, New Plymouth, New Zealand, 111–120.

Bazin, G. (1967) *The Museum Age*, Desoer SA, Brussels.

Beckett, J. (1986) *The Aristocracy in England: 1660–1914*, Basil Blackwell, Oxford and New York.

Bedard, J. (1992) Foreword, in Doxtator, D., *Fluffs and Feathers: An Exhibit on the Symbols of Indianness*, Woodland Cultural Centre, Brantford, Ontario.

Bell, D. (1983) *Daughters of the Dreaming*, McPhee Gribble/Allen Unwin, Melbourne and Sydney.

Bell, D. (1993) Yes Virginia, there is a feminist ethnography: reflections from three Australian fields, in Bell, D., Caplan, P. and Karim, W. J. (eds), *Gendered Fields: Women, Men and Ethnography*, Routledge, London and New York, 28–43.

Belk, R. (1988) Collectors and collecting, *Advances in Consumer Research*, Vol. 15, Association for Consumer Research, 548–553.

Belsey, C. (1980) *Critical Practice*, Methuen, London and New York.

Bendoris, M. (1995) Indians in heap big row for shirt, *Daily Record*, 8 April.

Bennett, T. (1995) *The Birth of the Museum*, Routledge, London and New York.

Bennett, T. (1998a) *Culture: A Reformer's Science*, Sage Publications, London.

Bennett, T. (1998b) Speaking to the eyes: museums, legibility and the social order, in MacDonald, S. (ed.) *The Politics of Display – Museums, Science, Culture*, Routledge, London and New York, 25–35.

Bennett, T. (1998c) Pedagogic objects, clean eyes, and popular instruction: on sensory regimes and museum didactics, *Configurations*, 6, 345–371, The Johns Hopkins University Press and the Society for Literature and Science.

Bernstein, B. (1971) On the classification and framing of educational knowledge, in Young, M. F. D., *Knowledge and Control: New Directions for the Sociology of Education*, Collier-Macmillan London, 47–69.

Best, S. and Kellner, D. (1991) *Postmodern Theory: Critical Interrogations*, Macmillan Basingstoke and London.

Bhabha, H. (1983) Difference, discrimination and the discourse of colonialism, in Barker, F. *et al.*, (eds) *The Politics of Theory*, University of Essex, Colchester, 194–211.

Bhabha, H. (1994) *The Location of Culture*, Routledge, London and New York.

Bicknell, S. (1995) Here to help: evaluation and effectiveness, in Hooper-Greenhill, E. (ed.) *Museum, Media, Message*, Routledge, London and New York, 281–293.

Bills, M. (1999) Merton Russell-Cotes, Art and Edwin Long, in Olding, S., Waterfield, G. and Bills, M., *A Victorian Salon; Paintings from the Russell-Cotes Art Gallery and Museum*, Russell-Cotes Art Gallery and Museum, Bournemouth, Bournemouth Borough Council in association with Lund Humphries Publishers, London, 24–32.

Binney, J. (1984) Myth and explanation in the Ringatu tradition, *Journal of the Polynesian Society*, 93 (4), 345–398.

Blackley, R. (1986) At Rotomahana, *Agmanz Journal*, Winter, 18.

Blackwood, B. (1970) *The Classification of Artefacts in the Pitt Rivers Museum*, Pitt Rivers Museum, Oxford.

Block Editorial Board and Sally Stafford (1996) *The Block Reader in Visual Culture*, Routledge, London and New York.

Bocock, R. (1993) *Consumption*, Routledge, London and New York.

Boden, M. (1994) *Piaget*, Fontana Press, London.

Boswell, D. and Evans, J. (1999) *Representing the Nation: A Reader – History, Heritage and Museums*, Routledge, London and New York in association with the Open University, Milton Keynes.

Bourdieu, P. and Darbel, A. (1991) *The Love of Art*, Polity Press, Cambridge.

British Museum Education Service (1997) *A Conversation with Richard Wentworth; a Conversation with Fred Wilson*, British Museum, London.

Brown, D. (1991) *Bury my Heart at Wounded Knee: An Indian History of the American West*, Vintage, London.

Bryson, N. (1983) *Vision and Painting: The Logic of the Gaze*, Macmillan London and Basingstoke.

Bud, R. (1988) The myth and the machine: seeing science through museum eyes, in Fyfe, G. and Law, J. (eds) *Picturing Power: Visual Depiction and Social Relations*, Routledge, London and New York, 134–159.

Burnett, R. (1995) *Cultures of Vision: Images, Media and the Imaginary*, Indiana University Press, Bloomington and Indianapolis.

Butler, J. (1990) *Gender Trouble: Feminism and the Subversion of Identity*, Routledge, London and New York.

Calkins, N. A. (1880) Object-teaching: its purpose and province, *Education*, Vol. 1, Boston, Mass., 165–172.

Cameron, D. (1968) A viewpoint; the museum as a communication system and implications for museum education, *Curator*, 11 (1), 33–40.

Cannadine, D. (1990) *The Decline and Fall of the British Aristocracy*, Yale University Press, New Haven and London.

Carey, J. (1989) *Communication as Culture: Essays on Media and Society*, Unwin Hyman, Boston, Mass., 13–36.

Chambers 21st Century Dictionary: The Living Language (1996) Editor-in-chief, Mairi Robinson, Chambers, Edinburgh.

Chapman, W. R. (1985) Arranging ethnology: A.H.L.F. Pitt Rivers and the typological tradition, in Stocking, G. W. (ed.) *Objects and Others – Essays on Museums and Material Culture*, History of Anthropology, 3, University of Wisconsin Press, Wisconsin, 15–48.

Classen, C. (1993) *Worlds of Sense: Exploring the Senses in History and Across Cultures*, Routledge, London and New York.

Clifford, J. (1985) Objects and selves – an afterword, in Stocking, G. W. (ed.) *Objects and Others – Essays on Museums and Material Culture*, History of Anthropology, 3, University of Wisconsin Press, Wisconsin, 236–246.

Clifford, J., (1986) Introduction: partial truths, in Clifford, J. and Marcus, G., *Writing Culture: The Poetics and Politics of Ethnography*, University of California Press, Berkeley, Los Angeles and London, 1–26.

Clifford, J. (1988) *The Predicament of Culture: Twentieth-Century Ethnography, Literature and Art*, Harvard University Press, Cambridge, Mass. and London.

Clifford, J. (1997) *Routes: Travel And Translation in the Late Twentieth Century*, Harvard University Press, Cambridge, Mass.

Colley, L. (1992) *Britons: Forging the Nation 1707–1837*, Pimlico, London.

Compton, M. (1992) The national galleries, in Thompson, J., Bassett, D., Duggan, A., Lewis, G. and Fenton, A., *Manual of Curatorship: A Guide to Museum Practice*, 2nd edition, Butterworths, London and Boston, Mass., 86–92.

Conn, S. (1998) *Museums and American Intellectual Life, 1876–1926*, University of Chicago Press, Chicago and London.

Cooke, L. and Wollen, P. (eds) (1995) *Visual Display: Culture Beyond Appearances*, Bay Press, Seattle.

Cooke Taylor, W. (1846–8) *The National Portrait Gallery of Illustrious and Eminent Personages, Chiefly of the Nineteenth Century, with Memoirs*, Vol. 1. Peter Jackson, late Fisher, Son, and Co. The Caxton Press, London.

Crang, M. (1994a) Spacing times, telling times, and narrating the past, *Time and Society*, 3 (1), 29–45.

Crang, M. (1994b) On the heritage trail: maps of and journeys to olde Englande, *Environment and Planning D: Society and Space*, 12, 341–355.

Crary, J. (1990) *Techniques of the Observer: On Vision and Modernity in the Nineteenth Century*, MIT Press, Cambridge, Mass.

Csikszentmihalyi, M. and Robinson, R. (1990) *The Art of Seeing: An Interpretation of the Aesthetic Encounter*, J. Paul Getty Museum and the Getty Center for Education in the Arts, Malibu, Calif.

Csikszentmihalyi, M. and Rochberg-Halton, E. (1981) *The Meaning of Things: Domestic Symbols and the Self*, Cambridge University Press, Cambridge.

Cummings, N. (1997) Collected, *Great 12, The Magazine of the Photographers' Gallery*, London, 4–7.

Cust, L. (ed.) (1901) *National Portrait Gallery*, Cassell, London.

Davey, N. (1999) The hermeneutics of seeing, in Heywood, I. and Sandwell, B. (eds) *Interpreting Visual Culture: Explorations in the Hermeneutics of the Visual*, Routledge, London and New York, 3–29.

Davidoff, L. and Hall, C. (1987) *Family Fortunes: Men and Women of the English Middle Class, 1780–1850*, Hutchinson, London and Melbourne.

Davidson, B., Heald, C. L. and Hein, G. (1999) Increased exhibit accessibility through multisensory interaction, in Hooper-Greenhill, E. (ed.) *The Educational Role of Museums*, 2nd edition, Routledge, London, 223–238.

Davis, R. H. (1997) *Lives of Indian Images*, Princeton University Press, Princeton, N.J.

Deepwell, K. (ed.) (1995) *New Feminist Art Criticism*, Manchester University Press, Manchester.

Delanty, G. (1997) *Social Science: Beyond Constructivism and Realism*, Open University Press, Buckingham.

Deloria, P. (1999) *Playing Indian*, Yale University Press, New Haven.

Dennan, R. (with Annabell, R.) (1968) *Guide Rangi of Rotorua*, Whitcombe and Tombs, Ltd., Christchurch, New Zealand.

Desai, P. and Thomas, A. (1998) *Cultural Diversity: Attitudes of Ethnic Minority Populations towards Museums and Galleries*, Museums and Galleries Commission, London.

Desmond, A. and Moore, J. (1991) *Darwin*, Penguin Books, London.

Dictionary of New Zealand Biography (1990) *The People of Many Peaks: The Maori Biographies from the Dictionary of New Zealand Biography, Volume 1:1769–1869*, Bridget Williams Books and Department of Internal Affairs, Wellington.

Dilthey, W. (1976) The rise of hermeneutics, in Connerton, P. (ed.) *Critical Sociology*, Penguin Books, Harmondsworth, 104–116.

Dobson, J. (1968) *Lost Treasures*, Reprinted from Annals of the Royal College of Surgeons of England, Vol. 42, June, Royal College of Surgeons, London.

Dodd, P. (1999) Englishness and the national culture, in Boswell, D. and Evans, J., *Representing the Nation: A Reader – Histories, Heritage and Museums*, The Open University and Routledge, London and New York, 87–108.

Donnelly, J. (1995) Museum reluctant to part with sacred tribal shirt, *Scotsman*, 10 April.

Doxtator, D. (1992) *Fluffs and Feathers: An Exhibit on the Symbols of Indianness*, Woodland Cultural Centre, Brantford, Ontario.

Doy, G. (1998) *Materialising Art History*, Berg, Oxford and New York.

Duclos, R. (1999) The cartographies of collecting, in Knell, S. (ed.) *Museums and the Future of Collecting*, Ashgate, Aldershot and Brookfield, Mo., 48–62.

Duncan, C. (1995) *Civilising Rituals*, Routledge, London and New York.

Duncan, C. and Wallach, A. (1978) The museum of modern art as late capitalist ritual, *Marxist Perspectives*, Winter, 28–51.

Durbin, G., Morris, S. and Wilkinson, S. (1990) *A Teacher's Guide to Learning from Objects*, English Heritage, London.

Durkheim, E. (1956) *Education and Sociology*, The Free Press, Glencoe, Ill.

Dyer, R. (1999) White, in Evans, J. and Hall, S. (eds) *Visual Culture: The Reader*, The Open University and Sage Publications, London, 457–467.

Evans, J. and Hall, S. (eds) (1999) *Visual Culture: The Reader*, The Open University and Sage Publications, London.

Fay, B. (1996) *Contemporary Philosophy of Social Science: a Multicultural Approach*, Blackwell Publishers, Oxford.

Findlen, P. (1994) *Possessing Nature: Museums, Collecting and Scientific Culture in Early Modern Italy*, University of California Press, Berkeley, Los Angeles, London.

Fish, S. (1980) *Is There A Text in this Class? The Authority of Interpretive Communities*, Harvard University Press, Cambridge, Mass. and London.

Fisher, P. (1991) *Making and Effacing Art: Modern American Art in a Culture of Museums*, Oxford University Press, New York, Oxford.

Forbes, A. (1998) Media release: Glasgow City Council to Return Ghost Dance Shirt, Glasgow City Council, 20 November.

Fornas, J. (1995) *Cultural Theory and Late Modernity*, Sage Publications, London.

Forster, G. (1968) *A Voyage Round the World*, ed. R. L. Kahn, Berlin.

Foster, H. (ed.) (1988) *Vision and Visuality*, Bay Press, Seattle.

Foucault, M. (1970) *The Order of Things*, Tavistock Publications, London.

Foucault, M. (1973) *The Birth of the Clinic*, Tavistock Publications, London.

Foucault, M. (1977a) Nietzsche, geneaology, history, in Bouchard, D. F., *Language, Counter-Memory, Practice: Selected Essays and Interviews*, Blackwell, Oxford, 139–164.

Foucault, M. (1977b) The political function of the intellectual, *Radical Philosophy*, 17, 12–14.

Foucault, M. (1981) Questions of method: an interview with Michel Foucault, *Ideology and Consciousness*, 8, 3–14.

Foucault, M. (1982) *Discipline and Punish: The Birth of the Prison*, Penguin Books, Harmondsworth.

Francis, D. (1992) *The Imaginary Indian: The Image of the Indian in Canadian Culture*, Arsenal Pulp Press, Vancouver.

Friere, P. (1972) *Pedagogy of the Oppressed*, Penguin Books, Harmondsworth.

Friere, P. (1998) *Pedagogy of Freedom: Ethics, Democrary and Civic Courage*, Rowman and Littlefield Publishers, Inc. Lanham, Boulder, New York and Oxford.

Froude, J. A. ([1886] 1898) *Oceana, or England and Her Colonies*, Longmans, Green, and Co. London, New York and Bombay.

Fyfe, G. (1998) On the relevance of Basil Bernstein's theory of codes to the sociology of art museums, *Journal of Material Culture*, 3 (3), 325–354.

Gadamer, H.-G. (1976) The historicity of understanding, in Connerton, P. (ed.) *Critical Sociology*, Penguin Books, Harmondsworth, 117–133.

Gallagher, S. (1992) *Hermeneutics and Education*, State University of New York Press, Albany.

Gallop, A. (1992) When Maoris visited Surrey and communed with ancestral spirits from a lost village, *Surrey Advertiser*, 28 February.

Gallop, A. (1994) Surrey's secret meeting house, *Destination New Zealand*, Eastbourne, East Sussex, April, 23.

Gallop, A. (1995a) Hinemihi – the house with the golden eyes: a history, in *Te Whakatapua O Ngā Taonga Whakairo O Hinemihi Ki Ingarangi* (The Blessings of the Carvings for Hinemihi Meeting House in England), *Ngā Whakaharetanga Me Nga Whakamaramatanga* (Order of Proceedings and Explanations), New Zealand Tourism Board, Guidelines Public Relations, Middlesex and the National Trust, Southern Region, n.p.

Gallop, A. (1995b) Carving up some Maori history in Surrey, *Surrey Advertiser*, 12 May.

Gallop, A. (1998) *The House with the Golden Eyes*, Running Horse Books, Sunbury on Thames.

Gardner, H. (1985) *Frames of Mind: The Theory of Multiple Intelligences*, Paladin, London.

Gardner, H. (1991) *The Unschooled Mind: How Children Think and How Schools Should Teach*, Fontana Press, London.

Garner, S. (1992) The motives for the foundation of a museum in Bournemouth by Merton and Annie Russell-Cotes at the turn of the century, Masters dissertation, Department of Museum Studies, University of Leicester.

Garner, C. (1997) London to Wounded Knee: Custer's conqueror goes home, *The Independent*, 23 September, 1.

Garner, C. (1998) Police intervene in battle of 'offensive' china pigs, *The Independent*, 26 May, 3.

Georgel, C. (1994) The museum as metaphor in nineteenth century France, in Sherman, D. and Rogoff, I., *Museum Culture*, Routledge, London, 113–122.

Gilman, S. L. (1985) Black bodies, white bodies; towards an iconography of female sexuality in late nineteenth century art, medicine and literature, *Critical Inquiry*, 12 (1), 204–242.

Giroux, H. (1992) *Border Crossings*, Routledge, London.

Goldie, T. (1995) The representation of the indigene, in Ashcroft, B., Griffiths, G. and Tiffin, H. (eds) *The Post-colonial Studies Reader*, Routledge, London, 232–236.

Goolnik, J. (1994) *Hands On: Children's Learning from Objects in Marishal Museum*, Marishal Museum, University of Aberdeen, Aberdeen.

Greenberg, R., Ferguson, B. and Nairne, S. (1996) *Thinking About Exhibitions*, Routledge, London and New York.

Greenhalgh, P. (1988) *Ephemeral Vistas: The Expositions Universelles, Great Exhibitions and World's Fairs, 1851–1939*, Manchester University Press, Manchester.

Griffiths, G. (1995) The myth of authenticity, in Ashcroft, B., Griffiths, G. and Tiffin, H. (eds) *The Post-colonial Studies Reader*, Routledge, London, 237–241.

Gunther, C. (1999) Museum-goers: life-styles and learning characteristics, in Hooper-Greenhill, E. (ed.) *The Educational Role of Museums*, 2nd edition, Routledge, London, 118–130.

Hackforth-Jones, J. (1990) Imagining Australia and the South Pacific, in Alfrey, N. and Daniels, S., *Mapping the Landscape: Essays on Art and Cartography*, Department of Art History, University of Nottingham, Nottingham, 13–17.

Hacking, I. (1999) *The Social Construction of What?*, Harvard University Press, Cambridge, Mass. and London.

Hailstone, E. (ed.) (1869) *Portraits of Yorkshire Worthies. Selected from the Exhibition of Works of Art at Leeds, 1868. With Biographical Notices* (2 vols), Cundall and Fleming, London.

Hakiwai, A. (1990) Once again the light of day? Museums and Maori culture in New Zealand, *Museum*, 165 (1), 35–38.

Hall, C. (1992) *White, Male and Middle-class*, Polity Press, Cambridge.

Hall, S. (1993) Cultural identity and diaspora, in Williams, P. and Chrisman, L., *Colonial Discourse and Post-Colonial Theory: A Reader*, Harvester Wheatsheaf, New York, London and Singapore, 392–403.

Hall, S. (ed.) (1997) *Representation: Cultural Representations and Signifying Practices*, Sage Publications, London in association with the Open University, Milton Keynes.

Halliburton, R. (1999) Healing a wounded culture, *Independent Weekend Review*, 26 June, 8.

Hansard (1852) *Hansard's* Parliamentary debates: third series, commencing with the accession of William IV – 15th and 16th Victoriae 1852, Vol. CXXII, comprising the period from the fourth day of June to the first day of July, Cornelius Buck, London.

Hansard (1856a) *Hansard's* Parliamentary debates: third series, commencing with the accession of William IV – 19th Victoriae 1856, Vol. CXL, comprising the period from the thirty-first day of January, 1856, to the eleventh day of March 1856, first volume of the session, Cornelius Buck, London.

Hansard (1856b) *Hansard's* Parliamentary debates: third series, commencing with the accession of William IV – 19th and 20th Victoriae 1856, Vol. CXLII, comprising the period from the sixth day of May, 1856, to the twenty-seventh day of June, 1856, third volume of the session, Cornelius Buck, London.

Hanson, A. (1989) The making of the Maori: culture invention and its logic, *American Anthropologist*, 92 (4), 890–902.

Hardt, H. (1992) *Critical Communication Studies: Communication, History and Theory in America*, Routledge, London and New York.

Hargreaves, R. (1997) Developing new audiences at the National Portrait Gallery, London, in Hooper-Greenhill, E. (ed.) *Cultural Diversity: Developing Museum Audiences in Britain*, Leicester University Press and Cassell, London, 183–202.

Harrison, J. F. C. (1979) *Early Victorian Britain 1832–51*, Fontana/Collins, London.

Harvey, S. (1998) Repatriation, *Museums Journal*, 98 (12), 5.

Harvey, S. (1999) Letting go, *Museums Journal*, 98 (12), January: 34–35.

Hassan, I. (1986) Pluralism in postmodern perspective, *Critical Inquiry*, 12 (3), 503–520.

Heidegger, M. (1951) The age of the world view, *Measure*, 2, 269–284.

Hein, G. (1998) *Learning in the Museum*, Routledge, London and New York.

Hennigar Shuh, J. (1982) Teaching yourself to teach with objects, *Journal of Education*, 7 (9), Department of Education, Nova Scotia, Halifax, 8–15.

Hensher, P. (1999) I was wrong – we should hand back the Elgin Marbles, *The Independent*, 27 August, 4.

Herle, A. and Philp, J. (1998) *Torres Strait Islanders: An Exhibition Marking the centenary of the 1898 Cambridge Anthropological Expedition*, University of Cambridge, Museum of Archaeology and Anthropology, Cambridge.

Herle, A. and Rouse, S. (eds) (1998) *Cambridge and the Torres Strait: Centenary essays on the 1898 Anthropological Expedition*, Cambridge University Press, Cambridge.

Heywood, F. (1999) Museums fail diverse audience, *Museums Journal*, 99 (12), 7.

Heywood, I. and Sandywell, B. (eds) (1999) *Interpreting Visual Culture: Explorations in the Hermeneutics of the Visual*, Routledge, London and New York.

Hill, M. (ed.) (1970) *National Portrait Gallery Concise Catalogue 1856–1969*, National Portrait Gallery, London.

Hobsbawm, E. J. (1977) *The Age of Capital 1848–1875*, Abacus, Sphere Books Ltd, London.

Hobsbawm, E. J. (1990) *Nations and Nationalism Since 1780: Programme, Myth, Reality*, Cambridge University Press, Cambridge.

Hodder, I. (ed.) (1989) *The Meanings of Things: Material Culture and Symbolic Expression*, HarperCollins, London.

Hodge, R. and D'Souza, W. (1999) The museum as a communicator: a semiotic analysis of the Western Australian Museum Aboriginal Gallery, Perth, in Hooper-Greenhill, E. (ed.) *The Educational Role of Museums*, 2nd edition, Routledge, London, 53–63.

Hooper-Greenhill, E. (1980) The National Portrait Gallery; a case-study in cultural reproduction, MA thesis, Institute of Education, University of London.

Hooper-Greenhill, E. (1989) The museum in the disciplinary society, in Pearce, S. (ed.) *Museum Studies in Material Culture*, Leicester University Press, London and New York, 61–72.

Hooper-Greenhill, E. (1991) *Museum and Gallery Education*, Leicester University Press, Leicester.

Hooper-Greenhill, E. (1992) *Museums and the Shaping of Knowledge*, Routledge, London.

Hooper-Greenhill, E. (1994) Learning from learning theory in museums, *Group for Education in Museums News*, 55, 7–11.

Hooper-Greenhill, E. (1995) Museums and communication: an introductory essay, in Hooper-Greenhill, E. (ed.) *Museum, Media, Message*, Routledge, London and New York, 1–12.

Hooper-Greenhill, E. (ed.) (1997) *Cultural Diversity: Developing Museum Audiences in Britain*, Leicester University Press and Cassell, London.

Hooper-Greenhill, E. (1999) Education, communication and interpretation: towards a critical pedagogy in museums, in Hooper-Greenhill, E. (ed.) *The Educational Role of Museums*, 2nd edition, Routledge, London, 3–27.

Huggan, G. (1995) Decolonising the map, in Ashcroft, B., Griffiths, G. and Tiffin, H. (eds) *The Post-colonial Studies Reader*, Routledge, London, 407–411.

Husbands, C. (1992) Objects, evidence and learning: some thoughts on meaning and interpretation in museum education, *Journal of Education in Museums*, 13, 1–3.

Hustvedt, S. (1999) The bewildering pleasure of looking at paintings, *The Independent Weekend Review*, 10 April, 7.

Hutcheon, L. (1989) *The Politics of Postmodernism*, Routledge, London.

Huyssen, A. (1995) *Twilight Memories: Marking Time in a Culture of Amnesia*, Routledge, London.

Jackson, M. (1972) Aspects of symbolism and composition in Maori art, *Bijdagen tot de Taal-, Land- en Volkenkunde*, 128, 33–80.

Jameson, F. (1991) *Postmodernism, or, the Cultural Logic of Late Capitalism*, Verso, London and New York.

Jay, M. (1988) Scopic regimes of modernity, in Foster, H. (ed.) *Vision and Visuality*, Bay Press, Seattle, 3–23.

Jenks, C. (1993) *Culture*, Routledge, London and New York.

Jenks, C. (ed.) (1995) *Visual Culture*, Routledge, London and New York.

Jensen, K. B. (1991a) Humanistic scholarship as qualitative science: contributions to mass communication research, in Jensen, K. and Jankowski, N. (eds) *A Handbook of Qualitative Methodologies for Mass Communication Research*, Routledge, London and New York, 17–43.

Jensen, K. B. (1991b) When is meaning? Communication theory, pragmatism, and mass media reception, *Communication Yearbook*, 14, Sage Publications, Berverly Hills, Calif., 3–32.

Jerdan, W. (1830) *National Portrait Gallery of Illustrious and Eminent Personages of the Nineteenth Century; with Memoirs*, Vol. 1. Fisher, Son and Jackson, Newgate Street, London.

Jones, D. (1992) Dealing with the past, *Museums Journal*, 92 (1), 24–27.

Jordan, G. and Weedon, C. (1995) *Cultural Politics: Class, Gender, Race and the Postmodern World*, Blackwell, Oxford.

Karp, I. and Wilson, F. (1996) Constructing the spectacle of culture in museums, in Greenberg, R., Ferguson, B. and Nairne, S., *Thinking About Exhibitions*, Routledge, London and New York, 251–267.

Kelly, L. (1999) Finding evidence of visitor learning, paper presented at 'Musing on Learning' seminar, Australian Museum, Sydney, 20 April 1999.

Kernot, B. (1975) Report of the Clandon Park, Surrey, Meeting House prepared for the Maori buildings committee, Historic Places Trust, 7 June.

Kernot, B. (1976) One year later . . . Supplement to report of the Clandon Park, Surrey, Meeting House, June 1975.

Kernot, B. (1983) The meeting house in contemporary New Zealand, in Mead, S. M. and Kernot, B. (eds) *Art and Artists of Oceania*, The Dunmore Press, Palmerston North, New Zealand, 181–197.

Kernot, B. (1984) Ngā tohunga whakairo o mua (Maori artists of the time before), in Mead, S. M. (ed.) *Te Maori: Maori Art from New Zealand Collections*, Harry N. Abrams, Inc., New York, in association with The American Federation of Arts, 138–155.

Keys, D. (1993) House saved villagers from volcano, *The Independent*, 30 November, 28.

King, G. (1996) *Mapping Reality: An Exploration of Cultural Cartographies*, Macmillan Press, Basingstoke and London.

King, R., Sandhu, S., Walvin, J. and Girdham, J. (1997) *Ignatius Sancho: An African Man of Letters*, National Portrait Gallery, London.

Kirshenblatt-Gimblett, B. (1998) *Destination Culture: Tourism, Museums and Heritage*, University of California Press, Los Angeles and London.

Knell, S. (1996) The roller-coaster of museum geology, in Pearce, S. (ed.) *Exploring Science in Museums*, New Research in Museum Studies 6 – an International Series, The Athlone Press, London, 29–56.

Knez, E. and Wright, G. (1970) The museums as a communication system: an assessment of Cameron's viewpoint, *Curator*, 13 (93), 204–212.

Koven, S. (1994) The Whitechapel Picture Exhibition and the politics of seeing, in Sherman, D. J. and Rogoff, I. (eds) *Museum Culture: Histories, Discourses, Spectacles*, Routledge, London, 22–48.

Kuklick, H. (1993) *The Savage Within: The Social History of British Anthropology, 1885–1945*, Cambridge University Press, Cambridge.

Kuper, A. (1982) *The Invention of Primitive Society: Transformations of an Illusion*, Routledge, London.

Laclau, E. (1989) Politics and the limits of modernity, in Ross, A., *Universal Abandon: The Politics of Postmodernism*, Edinburgh University Press, Edinburgh, 63–82.

Laclau, E. and Mouffe, C. (1985) *Hegemony and Socialist Strategy: Towards a Radical Democratic Politics*, Verso, London.

Laclau, E. and Mouffe, C. (1987) Post-Marxism without apologies, *New Left Review*, 166, November/December, 79–106.

Lawson, J. and Silver, H. (1973) *A Social History of Education in England*, Methuen and Co. Ltd, London.

Lewis, D. and Forman, W. (1982) *The Maori – Heirs of Tane*, Orbis, London.

Lindlof, T. (1988) Media audiences as interpretive communities, *Communication Yearbook*, 11, Sage Publications, Berverly Hills, Calif., 81–107.

Lindquist, S. (ed.) (2000) *Museums of Modern Science*, Science History Publications, Watson Publishing International, Nantucket, Mass.

Lorimer, D. (1978) *Colour, Class and the Victorians*, Leicester University Press, Leicester, and Holmes and Meier Publishers, Inc., New York.

Lumley, R. (1988) *The Museum Time-machine*, Comedia for Routledge, London and New York.

Lyon, D. (1999) *Postmodernity*, 2nd edition, Open University Press, Buckingham.

MacDonald, S. (ed.) (1998) *The Politics of Display: Museums, Science, Culture*, Routledge, London and New York.

MacKenzie, D. and Wajcman, J. (eds) (1999) *The Social Shaping of Technology*, Open University Press, Buckingham.

MacLachan, G. and Reid, I. (1994) *Framing and Interpretation*, Melbourne University Press, Victoria, Australia.

Maddra, S. (1995) The Wounded Knee Ghost Dance Shirt, unpublished paper for Glasgow Museums.

Maddra, S. (1996) The Wounded Knee Ghost Dance Shirt, *Journal of Museum Ethnography*, 8, 41–58.

Maddra, S. (1999) *Glasgow's Ghost Dance Shirt*, Glasgow Museums, Glasgow.

Makereti (Maggie Papakura) (1938) *The Old-time Maori*, Victor Gollancz, Ltd, London.

Makereti (Maggie Papakura) (1986) *The Old-time Maori*, New Women's Press, Ltd, Auckland.

Markham, S. F. (1938) *A Report on the Museums and Art Galleries of the British Isles*, Carnegie United Kingdom Trust, Dunfermline.

Markus, G. (1987) Diogenes Laertius contra Gadamer: universal or historical hermeneutics?, in Fekete, J., *Life after Post-modernism: Essays on Value and Culture*, New World Perspectives, Montreal, Canada.

McBeth, J. (1995a) Sioux pow-wow for the return of Ghost Shirt, *Daily Mail*, 10 April, 3.

McBeth, J. (1995b) Sioux on the warpath, *The Scotsman*, 8 April.

McCarthy, E. D. (1996) *Knowledge as Culture: The New Sociology of Knowledge*, Routledge, London and New York.

McGregor, N. (2000) Introduction, in Finaldi, G. (ed.) *The Image of Christ: The Catalogue of the Exhibition Seeing Salvation*, National Gallery, London, 6–7.

McGuigan, J. (1992) *Cultural Populism*, Routledge, London.

McGuigan, J. (1996) *Culture and the Public Sphere*, Routledge, London.

McManus, P. (1991) Making sense of exhibits, in Kavanagh, G. (ed.) *Museum Languages: Objects and Texts*, Leicester University Press, Leicester, 33–46.

McQuail, D. and Windahl, S. (1993) *Communication Models for the Study of Mass Communication*, Longman, London and New York.

Mead, S. M. (1984a) Ngā timunga me ngā paringa o te mana Maori (The ebb and flow of *mana* Maori and the changing context of Maori art), in Mead, S. M. (ed.) *Te Maori: Maori Art from New Zealand Collections*, Harry N. Abrams, Inc., New York, in association with The American Federation of Arts, 20–36.

Mead, S. M. (1984b) Ka tupu te toi whakairo ki Aotearoa (Becoming Maori art), in Mead, S. M. (ed.) *Te Maori: Maori Art from New Zealand Collections*, Harry N. Abrams, Inc., New York, in association with The American Federation of Arts, 63–75.

Mead, S. M. and Kernot, B. (eds) (1983) *Art and Artists of Oceania*, The Dunmore Press, Palmerston North, New Zealand.

Merriman, N. (1997) The 'Peopling of London' project, in Hooper-Greenhill, E. (ed.)

Cultural Diversity: Developing Museum Audiences in Britain, Leicester University Press, London and Washington, 119–148.

Miles, R. (1985) Exhibitions: management, for a change, in Cossons, N. (ed.) *The Management of Change in Museums*, National Maritime Museum, London, 31–33.

Miles, R. S. and Tout, A. F. (1994) Impact of research on the approach to the visiting public at the Natural History Museum, London, in Hooper-Greenhill, E. (ed.) *The Educational Role of the Museum*, 1st edition, Routledge, London, 101–106.

Miller, D. (1994) Things ain't what they used to be, in Pearce, S. (ed.) *Interpreting Objects and Collections*, Leicester Readers in Museum Studies, Routledge, London and New York, 13–18.

Miller, D. (ed.) (1995) *Acknowledging Consumption: A Review of New Studies*, Routledge, London and New York.

Miller, H. (1966) *Race Conflict in New Zealand 1814–1865*, Greenwood Press, Westport, Conn.

Minihan, J. (1977) *The Nationalisation of Culture: The Development of State Subsidies for the Arts in Great Britain*, Hamish Hamilton, London.

Mirzoeff, N. (1998) *The Visual Culture Reader*, Routledge, London and New York.

Mirzoeff, N. (1999) *An Introduction to Visual Culture*, Routledge, London and New York.

Mitra, A. (1997) Diasporic web sites: ingroup and outgroup discourse, *Critical Studies in Mass Communication*, 14, 158–181.

Monkhouse, C. (1896) The National Portrait Gallery, *Scribners' Magazine*, September, 317–334.

Morgan, J. and Welton, P. (1986) *See What I Mean: An Introduction to Visual Communication*, Edward Arnold, London and New York.

Morley, D. (1992) *Television, Audiences and Cultural Studies*, Routledge, London and New York.

Morley, D. (1995) Theories of consumption in media studies, in Miller, D. (ed.) *Acknowledging Consumption: A Review of New Studies*, Routledge, London, 296–328.

Morley, D. (1996) Populism, revisionism and the 'new' audience research, in Curran, J., Morley, D. and Walkerdine, V. (eds) *Cultural Studies and Communications*, Arnold, London and New York, 279–293.

Morris, N. (1979) Mana – the story of two carvings, *Te Marae*, Vol. 1 (2), 3, 7.

Mouffe, C., (1989) Radical democracy: modern or postmodern?, in Ross, A., *Universal Abandon: The Politics of Postmodernism*, Edinburgh University Press, Edinburgh, 31–45.

Mullin, J. (1995) Lakota Sioux raid Glasgow to seek return of 'ghost shirt', *The Guardian*, 11 April.

Museums Journal (1998) Democracy rules, *Museums Journal*, 98 (10), 5.

Nakora, L. W. (1998) Maori traditional and contemporary identities, paper at the conference, 'Claiming the Stones: Naming the Bones: Cultural Property and the Negotiation of National and Ethnic Identity in the American and British Experience', St John's College, Oxford, 19–21 April.

National Portrait Gallery (1866) *List of Portraits and Busts in the National Portrait Gallery, 29, Great George Street, Westminster, Christmas, 1866*, National Portrait Gallery, London.

National Portrait Gallery (1909) *Consecutive List Of Portraits Acquired from March 1856 to April 1909, with Dates and Registration Numbers*, printed for the exclusive use of the Trustees, HMSO, London.

National Portrait Gallery (1949) *Catalogue of the National Portrait Gallery 1856–1947: with an Index of Artists*, National Portrait Gallery, London.

National Portrait Gallery Trustees Reports: 1st Report, 1858; 2nd Report, 1859; 3rd Report, 1860; 6th Report, 1863; 7th Report, 1864; 9th Report, 1866; 10th Report, 1867; 11th Report, 1868; 34th Report, 1891.

National Trust (1994a) *Clandon Park, Surrey* (guidebook), The National Trust, London.

National Trust (1994b) *Clandon Park, Surrey* (leaflet), The National Trust, London.

Neich, R. (1983) The veil of orthodoxy: Rotorua Ngati Tarawhai woodcarving in a changing context, in Mead, S. and Kernot, B. (eds) *Art and Artists of Oceania*, The Dunmore Press, Palmerston North, 245–265.

Neich, R. (1990a) The Maori carving art of Tene Waitere, traditionalist and innovator, *Art New Zealand*, 57 (1990/91), 73–79.

Neich, R. (1990b) Wero Taroi, Dictionary of New Zealand Biography, *The People of Many Peaks: The Maori Biographies from the Dictionary of New Zealand Biography, Volume 1: 1769–1869*, Bridget Williams Books, Department of Internal Affairs, Wellington, 354–355.

Neich, R. (1994) *Painted Histories: Early Maori Figurative Painting*, Auckland University Press, Auckland.

New Zealand Chronicle (1886) Collectors' Edition No. 1 (second printing), June facsimile.

New Zealand Tourism Board (1992) 'Hinemihi' – The Maori Meeting House at Clandon Park – A Centenary Exhibition, New Zealand Tourism Board, London (exhibition leaflet).

New Zealand Tourism Board, Guidelines Public Relations, and the National Trust, Southern Region (1995) *Te Whakatapua O Ngā Taonga Whakairo O Hinemihi Ki Ingarangi* (The Blessings of the Carvings for Hinemihi Meeting House in England), *Ngā Whakaharetanga Me Ngā Whakamaramatanga* (Order of Proceedings and Explanations).

Newton, D. (1994) Old wine in new bottles, and the reverse, in Kaplan, F. (ed.) *Museums and the Making of 'Ourselves': The Role of Objects in National Identity*, Leicester University Press, London and New York, 269–290.

Nicholson, L. (1990) *Feminism/postmodernism*, Routledge, London.

Nietzsche, F. (1986) The will to power, in Taylor, M. (ed.) *Deconstruction in Context: Literature and Philosophy*, University of Chicago Press, Chicago and London, 191–215.

O'Biso, C. (1987) *First Light*, Heinemann, Auckland.

Ogbu, J. U. (1995) The influence of culture on learning and behaviour, in Falk, J. and Dierking, L. (eds) *Public Institutions for Personal Learning: Establishing a Research Agenda*, American Association of Museums, Washington, 79–95.

Olds, A. (1999) Sending them home alive, in Hooper-Greenhill (ed.) *The Educational Role of the Museum*, Routledge, London, 332–336.

Olding, S. (1999) A Victorian salon: an introduction, in Olding, S., Waterfield, G. and Bills, M., *A Victorian Salon; Paintings from the Russell-Cotes Art Gallery and Museum*, Russell-Cotes Art Gallery and Museum, Bournemouth, Bournemouth Borough Council in association with Lund Humphries Publishers, London, 7–13.

Olding, S., Waterfield, G. and Bills, M. (1999) *A Victorian Salon; Paintings from the Russell-Cotes Art Gallery and Museum*, Russell-Cotes Art Gallery and Museum, Bournemouth, Bournemouth Borough Council in association with Lund Humphries Publishers, London.

O'Neill, M. (1999) The Glasgow Ghost Dance Shirt: a case study in repatriation, unpublished working paper, Glasgow Museums.

O'Riain, H. (1996) *'Old Objects in Glass Cases', Girl, (14): A Report on the Attitudes of 775 Secondary Pupils from a Survey Conducted in Two Comprehensive Schools in South London*, Autumn 1996, Harwood, O'Riain and Associates, London.

O'Sullivan, T., Hartley, J., Saunders, D., Montgomery, M. and Fiske, J. (1994) *Key Concepts in Communication and Cultural Studies*, 2nd edition, Routledge, London and New York.

O'Toole, M. (1994) *The Language of Displayed Art*, Leicester University Press, London.

Parry, R. L. (1999) Anthem and flag battle splits Japan, *The Independent*, 6 August, 11.

Pearce, S. (ed.) (1994a) *Interpreting Objects and Collections*, Leicester Readers in Museum Studies, Routledge, London and New York.

Pearce, S. (1994b) Objects as meaning; or narrating the past, in Pearce, S. (ed.) *Interpreting Objects and Collections*, Leicester Readers in Museum Studies, Routledge, London and New York.

Pearce, S. (1998) *Collecting in Contemporary Practice*, Sage Publications, London and New Delhi.

Penniman, T. K. (1938) 'Makereti', in Makereti (Maggie Papakura) *The Old-time Maori*, Victor Gollancz, Ltd, London, 19–29.

Peponis, J. and Hedin, J. (1982) The layout of theories in the Natural History Museum, *9H* (3), 21–25.

Perin, C. (1992) The communicative circle: museums as communities, in Karp, I., Kreamer, C. and Lavine, S. (eds) *Museums and Communities*, Smithsonian Institution Press, Washington, DC and London, 182–220.

Perry, L. (2000a) Looking like a woman: gender and modernity in the nineteenth century National Portrait Gallery, in Corbett, D. P. and Perry, L. (eds) *English Art 1860–1914*, Manchester University Press, Manchester.

Perry, L. (2000b) The National Portrait Gallery and its constituencies, 1858–1896, in Barlow, P. and Trodd, C., *Governing Cultures: Institutions of Art in Victorian England*, Ashgate Press, Basingstoke.

Petch, A. (ed.) (1996) *Collectors: Collecting for the Pitt Rivers Museum*, Pitt Rivers Museum, Oxford.

Phillips, W. J. (1948) Carved houses of Te Arawa, *Dominion Museum Records in Ethnology*, 1 (2), August, Wellington.

Piaget, J. (1970) Extracts from Piaget's theory, in Mussen, P.H. (ed.) *Manual of Child Psychology*, Wiley, London, pp. 703–732, reprinted in *Cognitive Development to Adolescence*, eds Richardson, K. and Sheldon, S. (1988) The Open University, Lawrence Erlbaum Associates Ltd, East Sussex, 3–18.

Piper, D. (1978) *The English Face*, National Portrait Gallery, London.

Pointon, M. (1993) *Hanging the Head: Portraiture and Social Formation in Eighteenth Century England*, Yale University Press, New Haven and London.

Pollock, G. (1994) Territories of desire: reconsiderations of an African childhood, in Robertson, G., Mash, M., Tickner, L., Bird, J., Curtis, B. and Putnam, T., *Travellers' Tales: Narratives of Home and Displacement*, Routledge, London, 63–89.

Potter, J. and Wetherell, M. (1987) *Discourse and Social Psychology: Beyond Attitudes and Behaviour*, Sage Publications, London.

Pratt, M. L. (1992) *Imperial Eyes: Travel Writing and Transculturation*, Routledge, London.

Radway, J. (1984) Interpretive communities and variable literacies: the functions of romance reading, *Daedalus*, 113 (3), 49–73.

Roberts, L. (1997) *From Knowledge to Narrative: Educators and the Changing Museum*, Smithsonian Institution Press, Washington, DC and London.

Robertson, G., Mash, M., Tickner, L., Bird, J., Curtis, B. and Putnam, T. (1994) *Travellers' Tales: Narratives of Home and Displacement*, Routledge, London.

Rockel, I. (1986) Introduction, in Rotorua Museum and Rotorua Art Gallery, *Tarawera Eruption Centennial Exhibition 1886–1986*, catalogue to the exhibition, Rotorua District Council, Rotorua, New Zealand, 8–10.

Roschelle, J. (1995) Learning in interactive environments: prior knowledge and new experience, in Falk, J. and Dierking, L., *Public Institutions for Personal Learning: Establishing A Research Agenda*, American Association of Museums, Washington, DC, 37–52.

Rotorua Museum and Rotorua Art Gallery (1986) *Tarawera Eruption Centennial Exhibition 1886–1986*, Catalogue to the exhibition, Rotorua District Council, Rotorua, New Zealand.

Royal Armouries (1999) *Buffalo Bill's Wild West*, Royal Armouries, Leeds.

Royal College of Surgeons (1831) *Catalogue of the Contents of the Museum of the Royal College of Surgeons in London; Part VI Comprehending the Vascular and Miscellaneous Preparations in a Dried State*, London.

Russell-Cotes, M. (1921) *Home and Abroad – An Autobiography of an Octogenarian*, Vols I and II, published by Herbert Russell-Cotes, Bournemouth, for private circulation only.

Russell-Cotes Art Gallery and Museum (1923) *Bulletin of the Russell-Cotes Art Gallery and Museum*, Bournemouth, Vol. II (4), December.

Russell-Cotes Art Gallery and Museum (1926) *Bulletin of the Russell-Cotes Art Gallery and Museum*, Bournemouth, Vol. V (2), June.

Russell-Cotes Art Gallery and Museum (1928) *Bulletin of the Russell-Cotes Art Gallery and Museum*, Bournemouth, Vol. VII (3), September.

Russell-Cotes Art Gallery and Museum (1992) *Images of People: Teachers' Activities and Resources for Use with the Exhibition*, Russell-Cotes Art Gallery and Museum, Bournemouth.

Said, E. (1993) *Culture and Imperialism*, Vintage Books, London.

Salmond, A. (1974) Rituals of encounter among the Maori: a sociolinguistic study of a scene, in Bauman, R. and Sherzer, J., *Explorations in the Ethnography of Speaking*, Cambridge University Press, Cambridge, 192–212.

Salmond, A. (1975) *Hui*, A. H. and A. W. Reed Ltd, Wellington, New Zealand.

Salmond, A. (1978) Te Ao Tawhito – a semantic approach to the ancient Maori cosmos, *Journal of the Polynesian Society*, 87 (1), 5–28.

Salmond, A. (1983) The study of traditional Maori society: the state of the art, *Journal of the Polynesian Society*, 92 (3), 309–332.

Salmond, A. (1984) Ngā huarahi o te ao Maori (Pathways in the Maori world), in Mead, S. M. (ed.) *Te Maori: Maori Art from New Zealand Collections*, Harry N. Abrams, Inc., New York, in association with The American Federation of Arts, 109–137.

Saumarez Smith, C. (1989) Museums, artifacts and meanings, in Vergo, P. (ed.) *The New Museology*, Reaktion Books, London, 6–21.

Saumarez Smith, C. (1997) Director's foreword, in King, R. *et al.*, *Ignatius Sancho: An African Man of Letters*, National Portrait Gallery, London, 7–8.

Savage, J. (1807) *Some Account of New Zealand; Particularly the Bay of Islands, and Surrounding Country; with a Description of the Religion and Government, Language, Arts, Manufactures, Manners, and Customs of the Natives, &c. &c.*, Murray and Constable, London.

Savage, P. (1986) In the shadow of the mountain, in Rotorua Museum and Rotorua Art Gallery, *Tarawera Eruption Centennial Exhibition 1886–1986*, Catalogue to the exhibition, Rotorua District Council, Rotorua, New Zealand, 14–20.

Scharf, G. (1888) *Historical and Descriptive Catalogue of the Pictures, Busts &c in the National Portrait Gallery, on Loan at the Bethnal Green Museum*, new and enlarged edition, Eyre and Spottiswoode, London.

Schroder, K. (1994) Audience semiotics, interpretive communities and the 'ethnographic turn' in media research, *Media, Culture and Society*, 16, 337–347.

Seidman, S. (1994) *Contested Knowledge: Social Theory in the Postmodern Era*, Blackwell, Oxford.

Shanks, M. and Tilley, C. (1987) *Re-constructing Archaeology: Theory and Practice*, 2nd edition, Routledge, London and New York.

Silverman, L. (1995) Visitor meaning-making in museums for a new age, *Curator*, 38 (3), 161–170.

Sotto, E. (1994) *When Teaching Becomes Learning: A Theory and Practice of Teaching*, Cassell, London.

Stafford, D. (1967) *Te Arawa: A History of the Arawa People*, A. H. and A. W. Reed, Wellington, Auckland and Sydney.

Stafford, D. (1977) *The Romantic Past of Rotorua*, A. H. and A. W. Reed, Wellington, Sydney and London.

Steffe, L. and Gale, G. (1995) *Constructivism in Education*, Lawrence Erlbaum Associates, Hillsdale, N.J.

Stephen, A. (1993) Familiarising the South Pacific, in Stephen, A. (ed.) *Pirating the Pacific: Images of Travel, Trade and Tourism*, Powerhouse Publishing, Sydney, Australia, 62–77.

Stocking, G. W. (ed.) (1985) *Objects and Others – Essays on Museums and Material Culture*, History of Anthropology, Vol. 3, University of Wisconsin Press, Wisconsin.

Sullivan, A. (1984) Ngā paiaka o te Maoritanga (The roots of Maori culture), in Mead, S. M. (ed.) *Te Maori: Maori Art from New Zealand Collections*, Harry N. Abrams, Inc., New York, in association with The American Federation of Arts, 37–62.

Surrey Advertiser (1992) Koha and karanga in meeting house centenary ceremony, *Surrey Advertiser*, 31 July.

Surrey Advertiser (1995) Ceremony at dawn sees traditions carved out, *Surrey Advertiser*, 23 June.

Tamarapa, A. and Whata, S. (1993) *Ngā puna roimata o Te Arawa*, Te Papa Tongarewa, Museum of New Zealand, Wellington.

Taylor, B. (1999) *Art for the Nation*, Manchester University Press, Manchester.

Taylor, C. ([1971] 1976) Hermeneutics and politics, in Connerton, P. (ed.) *Critical Sociology*, Penguin Books, Harmondsworth, 153–193.

Te Awekotuku, N. (1986) Introduction – Makereti: Guide Maggie Papakura in Makereti, *The Old-time Maori*, New Women's Press, Auckland, New Zealand, v–xi.

Te Awekotuku, N. (1991) *Mana Wahine Maori: Selected Writings on Maori Women's Art, Culture and Politics*, New Women's Press, Auckland, New Zealand.

Te Awekotuku, N. (1998) To moko: more than skin deep: issues of appropriation and identity in Maori tattoo, paper at the conference 'Claiming the Stones: Naming the Bones: Cultural Property and the Negotiation of National and Ethnic Identity in the American and British Experience', St John's College, Oxford, 19–21 April.

The Times (1956) National Portrait Gallery Press cuttings 1848–1866, 6 March, 8.

Thomas, N. (1991) *Entangled Objects; Exchange, Material Culture and Colonisation in the Pacific*, Harvard University Press, Cambridge, Mass.

Thomas, N. (1993) The beautiful and the damned, in Stephen, A. (ed.) *Pirating the Pacific: Images of Travel, Trade and Tourism*, Powerhouse Publishing, Sydney, Australia, 44–61.

Tilley, C. (1991) *Material Culture and Text: the Art of Ambiguity*, Routledge, London and New York.

Tilley, C. (1993) Interpretation and a poetics of the past, in Tilley, C. (ed.) *Interpretative Archaeology*, Berg, Providence, R. I. and Oxford, 1–27.

Trollope, A. ([1873] 1968) *Australia and New Zealand*, Volume II, Dawsons of Pall Mall, London.

Turner, G. (1990) *British Cultural Studies: an Introduction*, Unwin Hyman, Boston, Mass.

Utley, R. (1963) *Last Days of the Sioux Nation*, Yale University Press, New Haven, Conn.

Utley, R. (1993) *The Lance and the Shield: The Life and Times of Sitting Bull*, Ballantine Books, New York.

Waaka, P. (1986) Tarawera – 100 years before the eruption, in Rotorua Museum and Rotorua Art Gallery, *Tarawera Eruption Centennial Exhibition 1886–1986*, catalogue to the exhibition, Rotorua District Council, Rotorua, New Zealand, 11–13.

Walker, R. (1990) *Ka whawhai tonu matou: Struggle Without End*, Penguin Books, Auckland and London.

Wallis, B. (1994) Selling nations: international exhibitions and cultural diplomacy, in Sherman, D. and Rogoff, I. (eds) *Museum Culture: Histories, Discourses, Spectacles*, Routledge, London, 265–281.

Walsh, A. (ed.) (1991) *Insights: Museums, Visitors, Attitudes, Expectations – A Focus Group Experiment*, Getty Center for Education and the Arts, Los Angeles and the J. Paul Getty Museum, Malibu, Calif.

Wassmann, J. (ed.) (1998) *Pacific Answers to Western Hegemony: Cultural Practices of Identity Construction*, Berg, Oxford and New York.

Waterfield, G. (1991a) National art museums, in Waterfield, G. (ed.) *Palaces of Art: Art Galleries in Britain 1790–1990*, Dulwich Picture Gallery, London, 99–120.

Waterfield, G. (1991b) Public and philanthropic galleries, in Waterfield, G. (ed.) *Palaces of Art: Art Galleries in Britain 1790–1990*, Dulwich Picture Gallery, London, 83–98.

Waterfield, G. (1991c) Palaces of art, in Waterfield, G. (ed.) *Palaces of Art: Art Galleries in Britain 1790–1990*, Dulwich Picture Gallery, London, 17–28.

Waterfield, G. (1999) A home of luxury and a temple of art, in Olding, S., Waterfield, G. and Bills, M., *A Victorian Salon; Paintings from the Russell-Cotes Art Gallery and Museum*, Russell-Cotes Art Gallery and Museum, Bournemouth, Bournemouth Borough Council in association with Lund Humphries Publishers, London, 14–23.

Watson-Smith, K. (1999) Clapton to bid for his own guitar at auction, *The Independent*, 2 June, 9.

West, J. (1985) The evidence in hand, *Journal of Education in Museums*, 6, 41–44.

Wheeler, W. (1997) *The Enlightenment Effect*, a Signs of the Times discussion paper, London (Signs of the Times, PO Box 10684, London N15 6XA).

White, R. (1994) Frederick Jackson Turner and Buffalo Bill, in Grossman, J. (ed.) *The Frontier in American Culture*, University of California Press, Berkeley, Los Angeles and London, 7–65.

Wickham, G. (1986) Power and analysis: beyond Foucault, in Gane, M. (ed.) *Towards a Critique of Foucault*, Routledge and Kegan Paul, London, 149–179.

Williams, J. (1840) *A Narrative of Missionary Enterprises in the South Sea Islands; with Remarks upon the Natural History of the Islands, Origin, Languages, Traditions, and Usages of the Inhabitants*, John Snow, London.

Williams, P. and Chrisman, L. (1993) *Colonial Discourse and Postcolonial Theory: A Reader*, Harvester Wheatsheaf, New York, London and Singapore.

Williams, R. (1976) *Keywords: A Vocabulary of Culture and Society*, Fontana/Croom Helm, Glasgow.

Williams, R. (1981) *Culture*, Fontana Paperbacks, Glasgow.

Wilson, D. (1992) National museums, in Thompson, J., Bassett, D., Duggan, A., Lewis, G. and Fenton, A. (eds) *Manual of Curatorship: A Guide to Museum Practice*, 2nd edition, Butterworths, London and Boston, Mass., 81–85.

Wolff, J. (1975) *Hermeneutic Philosophy and the Sociology of Art: An Approach to Some of the Epistemological Problems of the Sociology of Knowledge and the Sociology of Art*, Routledge and Kegan Paul, London and Boston, Mass.

Wood, D. (1992) *The Power of Maps*, The Guilford Press, New York and London.

Wood, J. G. (1870) *The Natural History of Man, Being an Account of the Manners and Customs of the Uncivilised Races of Men – Australia, New Zealand, Polynesia, America, Asia, and Ancient Europe*, George Routledge and Sons, London.

Worts, D. (1995) Extending the frame: forging a new partnership with the public, in Pearce, S. (ed.) *Art in Museums*, Athlone Press, London and Atlantic Highlands, N.J., 164–191.

Young, R. (1995) *Colonial Desire: Hybridity in Theory, Culture and Race*, Routledge, London.

Yung, K. K. (1981) *National Portrait Gallery Complete Illustrated Catalogue 1856–1979*, National Portrait Gallery, London.

Zelizer, B. (1993) Journalists as interpretive communities, *Critical Studies in Mass Communication*, 10, 219–237.

Index

action 19, 50
active audience 138
administrative system 32–3
Albert, Prince 126
Albertina, Vienna 27
Altartate Cauldron 136
amo 60, 61, 166
ancestor figures 60
ancestors: Maori culture 59, 60, 65;
    nation's and National Portrait
    Gallery 43–8
anti-slavery movement 31
Aonui, Te (William Dennan) 96,
    168, 170
Aporo, Mika 70–1
Aporo Te Wharekaniwha, Chief 56,
    57, 58
aristocracy 37, 38; family portraits
    28, 30
artefacts 106, 107; modification of
    113–14; *see also* objects
artists 39–40
arts, the 25–6; culture and 10, 11;
    portraits of people concerned
    with 36, 38, 40
Ascherson, Neil 108
Atkins, Brigadier-General Crofton
    97
atomism 134–5
Australian Museum, Sydney 19–20
Austria 27
authenticity 25; portraits 38–40
autoethnography 86

Bani, Ephraim 145
Barlow, P. 38
Barndom farm 96
Barthes, R. 24
Bath Hotel, Bournemouth 87
behaviourism 133
Bennett, T. 148
Bernstein, Basil 130

'best of what a society produces' 10,
    11
Bicknell, S. 132
Blackwood, Beatrice 96
blessings ceremony (at Hinemihi)
    51–3
body: and mind 113; museum
    pedagogy and 130–1
body of works 11
Bourdieu, P. 137
bourgeois 41
Britain 26–7
British Empire 24, 42; *see also*
    colonialism
British Museum 27, 114, 128,
    141–2
Brontë, Bramwell 114
Buffalo Bill's Wild West Show 154,
    155–6
Buried Village 143–4; *see also* Te
    Wairoa
Burton, Mrs S. Beulah 97
Butler, J. 73

Cambridge University Museum of
    Archaeology and Anthropology
    144–5
Cameron, D. 132
canoes, war 57
canons 21; challenging 140–2
Carey, J. 138
Carlyle, Thomas 37, 38–9
Carpenter, William Hookham 37
carved meeting houses 55, 57; *see
    also* Hinemihi, meeting houses
Cecil, Lord Robert 38
celebrated individuals 29–30, 32–3,
    35–6, 37
census 17
children, stolen 20
Christian art 148–50
Christianity 58, 63

churchmen, portraits of 36, 38, 40
'cigar-store Indians' 142
citizenship 131
Clandon Park 51, 54, 60, 71, 72–3
Clapton, Eric 109
Clarendon collection 30
class structure 42; *see also* middle
    class
classification 105, 127–8, 130
Clontarf model village 81
Cobden, Richard 37
Cody, William F. (Buffalo Bill) 154,
    155–6
Cole, Henry 26, 126
'Collected' 141–2
collecting 87, 99–101
collection code 130
collections 104; Makereti 81, 85–6,
    96–7, 99–100; maps, museums
    and 18; meaning and 3;
    Russell-Cotes 87, 97–9, 100–1;
    see also National Portrait Gallery
Colley, Linda 31, 88
colonial gaze 84–5
colonialism 7, 33, 42, 53, 68–9
communication 132–40; as culture
    125, 138–40; as transmission
    5–6, 125, 132–8
community: imagined 28;
    interpretive communities 119–23
constitutive nature of culture 13
constructivist learning theory 6,
    118–19, 139
content, pedagogic 5–8
control: of image 82–4; social and
    moral control 32–3
Cook, Captain James 42, 94
cosmologies 58–67
Crager, George 154, 155
Crary, J. 129
critical pedagogy 140
Csikszentmihalyi, M. 110

cultivation of food 94
culture 1–22, 131; challenging the
canon 140–2; communication as
125, 138–40; cultural politics in
the museum 19–22; Maori
culture *see* Maori culture;
museum in modern culture 24–5;
objects and cultural memory
111; reorganising museum
culture 142–50; understanding
10–14; utility of 25–8; visual
14–16, 107–8; writing the
culture of the self 92–5
Cummings, Neil 141
Cunningham, Allan 26
curator 124; power-broker 137;
relationship to visitor 129

Daily Mail 159
Dansey, Roger 70
Darbel, A. 137
Dei, Jimmy 145
Dennan, Rangi 96, 170
Dennan, William (Te Anoui) 96,
168, 170
designers 137
'disciplinary' society 41
disciplines/subject areas 127–9
discourse: culture and 13; discourses
of objectivity 127–8; family
discourse 76
display cases 129–30
donations 37
Donne, T.E. 96
doorway of a meeting house 61–3
Durkheim, E. 41

Earl, John 157, 159
East Cliff Hall, Bournemouth 98–9,
100; *see also* Russell-Cotes
Museum
Eastlake, Sir Charles 29, 37
education 1–2, 134; National
Portrait Gallery and 31–2, 41;
purpose of the arts 25–6; *see also*
pedagogy
effectiveness 133
elite culture 11
Ellesmere, Earl of 33, 37
Enlightenment 16, 17, 140
ethnography of occasions 74
European humanism 72
European traders 94
exhibitions/displays: and
interpretation 10, 124–50; lively
6–7; and meaning 3–4

Faith, Mrs H.D. 97
familiarity 110
family discourse 76
family portrait collections 28, 30
female figures, carved 62–3

Fish, S. 119–20, 122–3
food 93, 94
foreknowledge 117–18
Foucault, M. 41, 49–50, 67
fragility 114
frame 130
France 26, 27
Francis, D. 156
Froude, James 56–7, 68
Fry, Elizabeth 36
functionalism 135
fundamental patriarchal system
32–3

Gadamer, H.-G. 117
Gainsborough, Thomas 145
galleries 129–30
Gardner, H. 118
Garrick, David 145
gaze 49
gender 42, 110
genealogies 58, 59, 65–6
geography, power structures and 42
Ghost Dance Shirt 10, 153–62; on
display 156–7, 158, 160;
interpretation 157–62; public
visual culture or sacred talisman
153–6
Giorgione, *The Tempest* 110
Giroux, H. 12, 140
Gladstone, W.E. 27
Glasgow 157–8, 159–60, 161
Gonzales, Mario 160
'good conduct' 31–2, 46
Gray, Mrs George W. 97
Great George Street 44
Griffin, Des 20
Gwyn, Nell 36

Hacking, I. 139
Haddon, A.C. 145
haka (dance) 88, 90–2, 94–5
Hall, S. 13
harpsichord 148, 149
Hawaiki 60
Hayles, John 44, 45
herehere (prisoners of war) 93–4
hermeneutics 116–19, 139, 172
hidden curriculum 5
hierarchies of value 24–5
high culture 11
Hillier, William (4th Earl of
Onslow) 54, 70, 73
Hinemihi 9, 49–75, 76, 113, 115;
blessings ceremony 51–3;
building Hinemihi at Te Wairoa
55–8; disruption, displacement
and new frameworks for
meaning 69–75; eruption of
Tarawera 69–70; interpreting
cosmologies and histories 58–67;
haka dance 90–2; new versions

54, 96–7, 170; politics of
tourism in the 1880s 67–9; taken
to Clandon Park 53–4, 70–2
Hinemoa 64–5
Hinomaru (rising sun flag) 109
history 8; interpretation of Hinemihi
58–67; structures of power 42–3
History in Action: the Wild West
160
Hobson, Captain William 68
Hohaia, Inia 57
Hollowhorn, Sterling 161
*Home and Abroad – An
Autobiography of an
Octogenarian* (Russell-Cotes)
88–92
'Home of the Brave' 157
Horniman Museum, South London
7
Hosokawa, Morohiro 109
Hot Lakes 67, 88
human museum objects 114
humanism, European 72
Hustvedt, Siri 110
Hyde, Edward (Lord Clarendon) 30

identities: Maori culture and 73–5,
109–10; national identity 25,
109; *see also* self
images 82–6
'Images of People' 77–9, 80
'Imaginary Indian' 156
imagined community 28
imagining 16–19
Indian immigrant Web users 121
'Indigenous Australians' 19–20
interpretation 8, 10, 103–23, 172;
exhibitions and 10, 124–50;
Ghost Dance Shirt 157–62;
interpretive communities,
strategies and repertoires
119–23; of objects 116–19;
visual culture 15
Isles, George 84
Italy 27

Japan 109
Jay, M. 130
Jenks, C. 107
Johnston, H. Dunbar 69–70
'joss-house' 68
journalists 120, 121

Kataore 65, 67
Kelvingrove Museum and Art
Gallery, Glasgow 153–4, 156–7,
158, 160, 161
Kernot, Bernie 54, 58, 66
Kéroualle, Louise de (Duchess of
Portsmouth) 146, 147
Khan, Yaqub 110
Kimigayo anthem 109

Knez, E. 132
knowledge 19, 140–1, 142–3;
  objects as sources of 5, 127; and
  power 49–50, 76–7; seeing and
  knowing 49–51; tacit 116; verbal
  116
Koran 110

Lakota Cultural Centre 161
Lakota Ghost Dance Shirt *see* Ghost
  Dance Shirt
Lakota tribes 155
Lasswell, H. 133
leaders, public 35–6, 38, 40
learning 2, 6, 20; constructivist
  learning theory 6, 118–19, 139;
  see also pedagogy
learning theory 116–19
Lebeau, Marcella 159
Leoni, Giacomo 72
life-long learning 2
lintel, door 62–3
lively display styles 6–7
Livingstone, David 108
London Maori Club (Ngati Ranana)
  51, 73
Long Wolf 160–1
looping effects 139
Louvre, Paris 26, 27

Macaulay, Lord 37
Mair, Captain Gilbert 67
Makereti 9, 77–86, 92–7, 99–101,
  110, 123; constructing the self
  through images, objects and
  words 82–6; dispersal of
  collection 96–7; story of 80–2;
  writing the culture of the self
  92–5
male bourgeois 41
Malfroy, Jean Camille 70
mana 55, 57, 166
Maori art 57–8; ancestral art 85,
  113
Maori culture: blessings ceremony at
  Hinemihi 51–3; British
  colonialism and destruction of
  68–9; cosmologies and histories
  58–67; identity 73–5, 109–10;
  Makereti 81, 82, 83, 93–5;
  taonga (treasures) 52–3, 73, 101,
  109–10, 113
Maori Pioneer Battalion 54
Maori Room 81, 86
mapping 16–19
marae 55, 59, 60, 66
Marie-Not-Help-Him 160, 161
Markham, S.F. 135
Marsh, John 54, 59, 74
Maryland Historical Society 142
mass communication 132
mass culture 11

master narratives 24–5, 28–30
material culture 95, 107
materialising 16–19
materiality 112–16
McManus, P. 132
meaning 103, 153; communication
  as culture 139–40; culture and
  12–13; and Hinemihi 72–5;
  issues of meaning-making 1–5;
  meaningful objects in everyday
  life 108–11; openness to
  re-meaning 115; seeing and
  knowing 49–51; textual 114–15,
  119–20; visual culture and 15;
  see also interpretation
meeting houses 53, 55, 57, 75,
  89–90; interpretation 58–67; *see
  also* Hinemihi
memory 118
men, portraits of 35–6, 38
mental exertion 31–2
mental knowledge maps 118
middle class 26, 28–9, 31, 37, 38
Mignard, Pierre 146, 147
Mines Royal, Mineral and Battery
  Societies 37
Mitra, A. 121
modernism 16–17
modernist museum 8, 17–18, 21,
  125; challenges to 140–2;
  communication as culture
  138–40; enduring model 151–2;
  pedagogy in 126–42;
  transmission 132–8
modification of artefacts 113–14
moral control 32–3
Munich Pinakothek 128, 129
municipal museums 98
museum educators 137
Museum of Manufactures 27
museum pedagogy *see* pedagogy
Museum of Popular Arts and
  Traditions, Paris 4
museums: cultural politics in 19–22;
  issues of meaning-making 1–5;
  maps as metaphor 17–18; in
  modern culture 24–5; in mid-
  nineteenth-century Britain 25–8
Museums Act 1845 27
Museums Bill 27
Muslims 110–11
myths 59

Nakora, Linda Waimarie 109–10
names 17
narratives, master 24–5, 28–30
nation(-state) 24, 25, 131; pedagogic
  lessons of the imag(in)ed nation
  40–3; promoting the power of
  37, 40; viewing the nation's
  ancestors 43–8
National Gallery, London 27, 128,

129, 131; 'Seeing Salvation'
  148–50
national identity 25, 109
National Museum of Denmark 114
National Museum of Ireland, Dublin
  136
National Museum of New Zealand
  (Te Papa Tongarewa) 101, 114
National Portrait Gallery, London
  8–9, 23–48, 127, 129, 134; new
  master narrative 28–30;
  pedagogic lessons of the
  imag(in)ed nation 40–3; portraits
  of the first ten years 33–40;
  Sancho exhibition 48, 145–8,
  149; social functions 31–3;
  viewing the nation's ancestors
  43–8
National Trust 51, 54, 72
Native Americans 142, 155–6; *see
  also* Ghost Dance Shirt
natural history 127–8
Neich, R. 59, 67
Netherlands 26
New Zealand 55, 60, 75, 96; and
  Hinemihi 54; National Museum
  101, 114; Russell-Cotes account
  88–92
New Zealand Company 68
New Zealand Room 81, 86
Ngati Hinemihi 51, 54–5, 59, 75,
  115, 166
Ngati Ranana (London Maori Club)
  51, 73
Ngati Tarawhai 57–8
Ngati Tuhourangi 57, 68, 69, 70,
  80–1, 90–2
Ngati Wahiao 80
Ngatokowaru II 58–9
Ngatoroirangi, Priest of the Te
  Arawa canoe 59
Nietzsche, F. 53
noa 65, 66–7
noble actions 31–2
'non-original' portraits 39–40

object-teaching 105–6
objectivity, discourses of 127–8
objects 10, 103–23; classification of
  127–8; constructing the self
  through images, objects and
  words 82–6; interpreting
  116–19; interpretive
  communities, strategies and
  repertoires 119–23; knowing
  objects in their materiality
  112–16; and meaning 3, 9, 10,
  49–51, 76–7; meaningful objects
  in everyday life 108–11;
  modification of artefacts 113–14;
  multiple meanings 76–7;
  provenance of 15–16, 25; 'real'

14–15, 18–19; sources of knowledge 5, 127; subject and object 103–4; visual culture and 14–16; what is an object 104–8
occasions, ethnography of 74
Oddington Grange, Oxfordshire 81, 85, 96
Ohinemutu 67–8, 89–90
Old-time Maori, The (Makereti) 80, 86, 92–5, 96
Onslow, Fourth Earl 54, 70, 73
Onslow, Lord 51, 53
Onslow family 72–3
Onslow Room 72–3
openness 117–18
oppositions 66–7
oral tradition 59
'original' portraits 39–40
'othering' 99
ownership 72–3
Oxford Unversity School of Anthropology 81–2, 86, 95, 96

Palgrave, Sir Francis 37
Palmerston, Lord 31
Papa 59
Papakura, Maggie *see* Makereti
pare (carved lintel) 62–3
Parr, Dr 34
patriarchal system, fundamental 32–3
Pearce, S. 110
pedagogy 3, 10, 124–50; challenging the canon 140–2; communication as culture 125, 138–40; in the modernist museum 126–32; National Portrait Gallery 40–3; object-teaching 105–6; post-museum 142–50; reformulating museum pedagogy 124–5; structure of museum pedagogy 5–8; as transmission 5–6, 125, 132–8
Penniman, T.K. 85, 93, 96
Pepys, Samuel 44, 45
perception 15, 118–19
personal cultivation 11
personal identity 109
personal meaning 4–5
philanthropy 98–9, 100
Piaget, J. 117
pigs, display of 110–11
Pikiao 60
Pink and White Terraces 56–7, 69–70, 88, 90
Pitt-Rivers, General 128
Pitt Rivers Museum, Oxford 85, 86, 96
Plains Indians 156
Pointon, M. 29
politics, cultural 19–22
porch of a meeting house 61–4

portraits *see* National Portrait Gallery
positivism 130
postcards 84–5
post-museum 8, 22, 125, 162; new museum concept 152–3; reorganising museum culture 142–50
power: cultural politics in the museum 19–22; knowledge and 49–50, 76–7; National Portrait Gallery and structures of power 42–3; promoting the power of the nation-state 37, 40; structures of local and national power 32–3
Prado, Madrid 26–7
Pratt, Mary Louise 86, 88
prejudices 117–18
prestige, tribal (*mana*) 55, 57, 166
print collections 30
private, and public 99–102
private spaces 126
production of portraits 39–40
provenance 15–16, 25
pseudo-speciation 68
public, and private 99–102
public leaders, portraits of 35–6, 38, 40
public order 27
public spaces 126

Quick, Richard 97, 100

race 42, 47
Radway, J. 120, 121
Raleigh, Sir Walter 35
Rangi 59
rationality 130
'real' objects 14–15, 18–19
realized signifying system 12–13
reflection 13, 108
repertoires, interpretive 119–23
re-plotting 140
re-territorialisation 140
ridgepole 63–4
Rihi, Pia Ngarotu Te 80
Rijksmuseum, Amsterdam 26
rising sun flag (Hinomaru) 109
Rochberg-Halton, E. 110
romance readers 120, 121
Rotorua 80
Royal Academy 27, 43
Royal College of Surgeons 145–6
Royal Ontario Museum, Toronto 4
Royal Picture Gallery, Berlin 128
royalty, portraits of 36, 40
Russell-Cotes, Annie (née Nelson Clark) 79, 87, 88, 89, 97, 98, 99; role in the Russell-Cotes collection 100
Russell-Cotes, Merton 9, 79, 93,

99–101, 115, 123; and his collections 97–9; seeing man 87–92
Russell-Cotes Art Gallery and Museum, Bournemouth 77, 79, 98–9, 100, 101

sacred, the 109
Sala, George Augustus 69
Salmond, A. 66, 66–7, 74
Salsbury, Nate 155
Sancho, Ignatius, exhibition 48, 145–8, 149
Scharf, George 33, 34, 44, 46, 47, 127
schemata 118
Schuster, Cathy 54–5
Schuster, Jim 53, 54–5
science 105–6; portraits of people concerned with 36, 38, 40
Scotland 159–60
Sechele, chief of the Bakwena 108
seeing, and knowing 49–51
'seeing man' 88
'Seeing Salvation' 148–50
Select Committee on Arts and Manufactures 27
self 9; constructing through images, objects and words 82–6; meaningful objects of evveryday life 109; writing and collecting and production of the self 99–101; writing the culture of the self 92–5
senses 112–13
sexuality, exotic 68
Shakespeare, William 33
shared experiences 12
signification 12–13
Sioux Indians 159; *see also* Ghost Dance Shirt
Sitting Bull 154
size of objects 113
slave trade 145–8
social control 32–3
social management, systems of 32–3
social relationships 50
socialisation 41
South Dakota Historical Society 161
South Kensington museums complex 27, 43
South Seas maiden postcards 84–5
space, organisation of 65, 128–31
Spain 26–7
specimens 106
Spencer, Reverend Seymour 90
Stanhope, Earl 29, 37, 38
Staples-Brown, Margaret *see* Makereti
Staples-Browne, Richard Charles 81
state 25; *see also* nation(-state)

stereotypes 111
Sterne, Laurence 145
stolen children 20
strategies, interpretive 119–23
structuralist analysis 66–7
style, pedagogic 5–8
subject areas/disciplines 127–9
subject and object 103–4
subjectivity 142
Sweden 26
symbols 111

tacit knowledge 116
Talbot, Elizabeth ('Bess of
    Hardwick') 36
taonga (Maori treasures) 52–3, 73,
    101, 109–10, 113
tapu 65, 66–7
Taranaki Herald 68
Tarawera, Mount 54, 69–70, 80,
    143–4
Tarawhai people (Ngati Tarawhai)
    57–8
Taroi, Wero 57, 58
Taupopoki, Mita 81, 97, 101
Te Amo 97
Te Arawa tribe 57, 68
Te Awekotuku, Ngahui 85, 114
Te Papa Tongarewa (National
    Museum of New Zealand) 101,
    114
Te Uoro 80, 81
Te Wairoa 53; building Hinemihi
    55–8; Buried Village exhibition
    143–4; destroyed by eruption
    of Tarawera 69–70, 80,
    143–4; tourism 68, 69, 88,
    90, 92

Tempest, The (Giorgione) 110
textual meaning 114–15, 119–20
Thom, Margaret *see* Makereti
Thom, William Arthur 80
Tierney, George 37
tiki 80, 85
Times, The 39
'Torres Strait Islanders' 144–5
tourism 56–7, 80–1; politics of in
    the 1880s 67–9; Russell-Cotes
    87–92
transmission 5–6, 125, 132–8
tribal prestige (*mana*) 55, 57, 166
Trollope, Anthony 57, 67
Tuhoromatakaka 81, 82, 85, 96–7,
    168
Tuhourangi people (Ngati
    Tuhourangi) 57, 68, 69, 70,
    80–1, 90–2
Turland, Reverend John 148
Tutanekai 64–5, 67

Uffizi, Florence 27
understanding 116–17
United States 132–3
universal laws 126
University Museum of Turin 128

values 134
verbal knowledge 116
Victoria and Albert Museum 27,
    126
vision 112, 129–30; seeing and
    knowing 49–51
visitors: meanings from displays
    4–5, 124; modernist museum
    and 128–30; to National
    Portrait Gallery 44–7;

post-museum and 148–50;
    transmission and 137–8
visual culture 14–16, 107–8

Wahiao people (Ngati Wahiao) 80
Waiana, Katene 57
Waikingi, Hare 51–2, 75
Waitere, Tene 57, 70, 81, 96
Walker Art Gallery, Liverpool 87
war canoes 57
Wemyss, Earl of 37
Wentworth, Richard 141–2
Whakarewarewa 80–1, 93
White and Pink Terraces 56–7,
    69–70, 88, 90
Wilberforce, William 34
Wild West Show 154, 155–6
Williams, R. 11–12
Wilson, Fred 141, 142
women: Maori culture 66–7;
    portraits of 36, 38
words 82–6
works of art 76
World Wide Web 121
Wounded Knee, battle of 154–5,
    160, 161
Wounded Knee Survivors
    Association 157, 160
Wovoka (holy man) 155
Wright, G. 132
Wright, Joseph 34
writing 99–101; the culture of the
    self 92–5

Young, Robert 41

Zelizer, B. 120, 121
zones of culture 12